Will Davies is a film-maker ... lives in Sydney.

Private Edward Patrick Fran... served in France with the Aus... 1919. He died in 19... a soldier on the We... ... in ... school ... s that were subsequent... edited ... Will Davies ... ...ed posthumously as the acclaimed *Somm...*

Acclaim for *Somme Mud*:

'As haunting and graphic a description of trench warfare as any I have read . . . this is a warrior's tale . . . a great read and a moving eye-witness account of a living hell from which few emerged unscathed' *Daily Express*

'Such is the force of Lynch's direct, compelling account of war . . . we grow to care about him and his companions, and to see what they see' *Guardian*

'In its honesty and earthiness it has quite justifiably been compared to *All Quiet on the Western Front*' *Good Book Guide*

'The voice of an ordinary, but highly literate, private soldier who simply endured the horrors that surrounded him and got on with his job . . . it truly is "a time capsule"' *Birmingham Post*

'This gripping memoir . . . will have the hairs standing up on the back of your neck . . . [an] excellent book' *BBC who do you think you are?*

'Here is the stink and stench of war . . . horrifying, scarifying and very humbling as well' *Herald Sun*

'Brilliantly evokes the terror, horror, elation, friendship, gore and depression that made a combat infantryman's life so dangerous, so traumatic and, if he survived, so memorable' *Courier Mail*

*Also by Will Davies*

SOMME MUD

*and published by Bantam Books*

# IN THE
# FOOTSTEPS OF
# PRIVATE LYNCH

## WILL DAVIES

**BANTAM BOOKS**

LONDON • TORONTO • SYDNEY • AUCKLAND • JOHANNESBURG

TRANSWORLD PUBLISHERS
61–63 Uxbridge Road, London W5 5SA
A Random House Group Company
www.rbooks.co.uk

**IN THE FOOTSTEPS OF PRIVATE LYNCH**
**A BANTAM BOOK: 9780553824155**

First published in Australia in 2008 by Vintage,
an imprint of Random House Australia

This edition first published in Great Britain
in 2009 by Doubleday
an imprint of Transworld Publishers
Bantam edition published 2010

This book is a work of non-fiction based on the life of Edward Francis Lynch, and his
book *Somme Mud*. The author has stated to the publishers that the details both of the
life of Private Lynch and the facts as contained in the book are accurate, based on
extensive research and with the assistance of the Lynch family. It can also be
stated that the contents of this book are true.

A CIP catalogue record for this book
is available from the British Library.

Addresses for Random House Group Ltd companies outside the UK
can be found at: www.randomhouse.co.uk
The Random House Group Ltd Reg. No. 954009

The Random House Group Limited supports The Forest Stewardship Council
(FSC), the leading international forest certification organisation. All our titles
that are printed on Greenpeace approved FSC certified paper carry the FSC
logo. Our paper procurement policy can be found at
www.rbooks.co.uk/environment

Typeset in 11.5/15.5 Garamond by
Falcon Oast Graphic Art Ltd.
Printed in the UK by CPI Cox & Wyman, Reading RG1 8EX.

2 4 6 8 10 9 7 5 3 1

**Mixed Sources**
Product group from well-managed
forests and other controlled sources
www.fsc.org Cert no. TT-COC-2139
© 1996 Forest Stewardship Council
FSC

*This book is dedicated to Edward Lynch and the men of the First AIF, many of whom returned to Australia wounded, shell-shocked, diseased and sick, limbless, blind and disabled, burnt and blistered by gas, mentally changed and traumatised, disfigured, impotent and forever altered. May we remember their suffering and torment.*

# CONTENTS

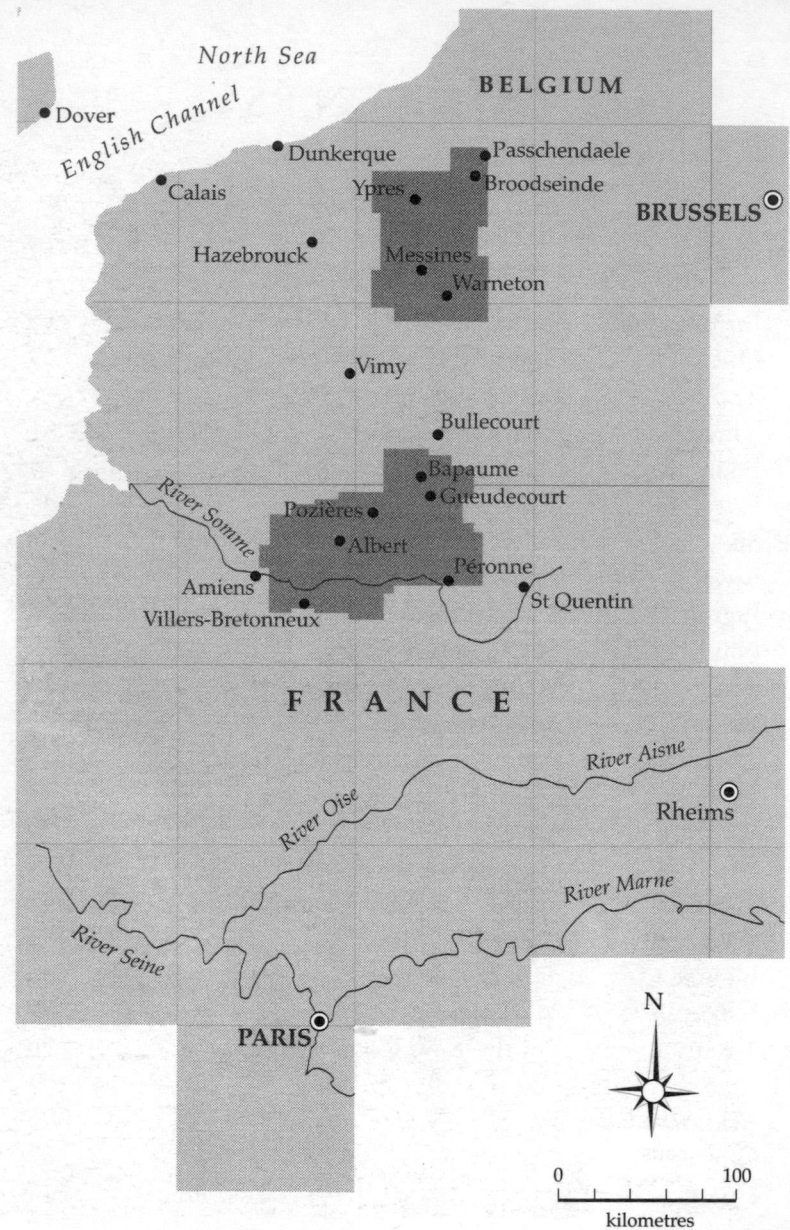

Overview of the Western Front

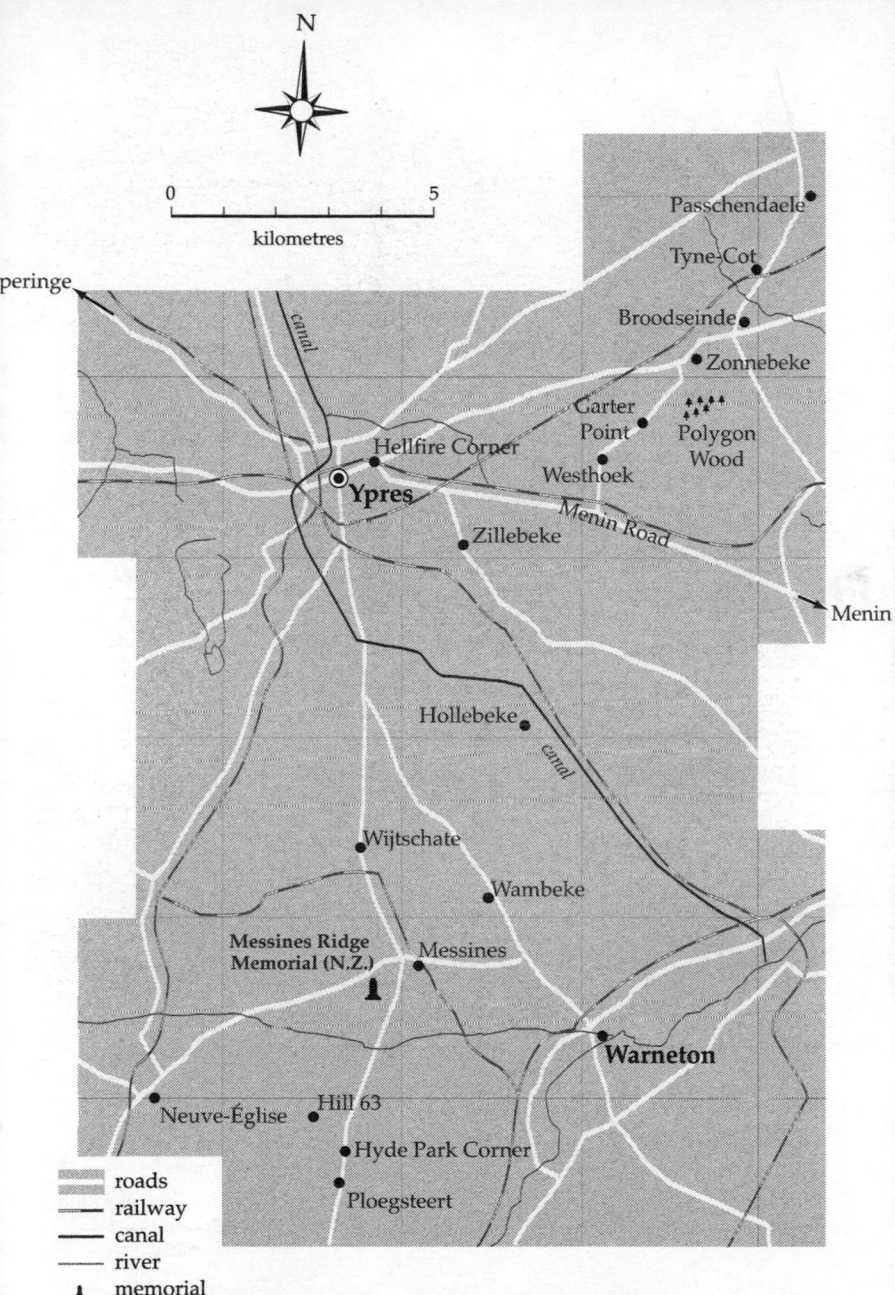

Overview of the main battlefields of Belgium in *Somme Mud*

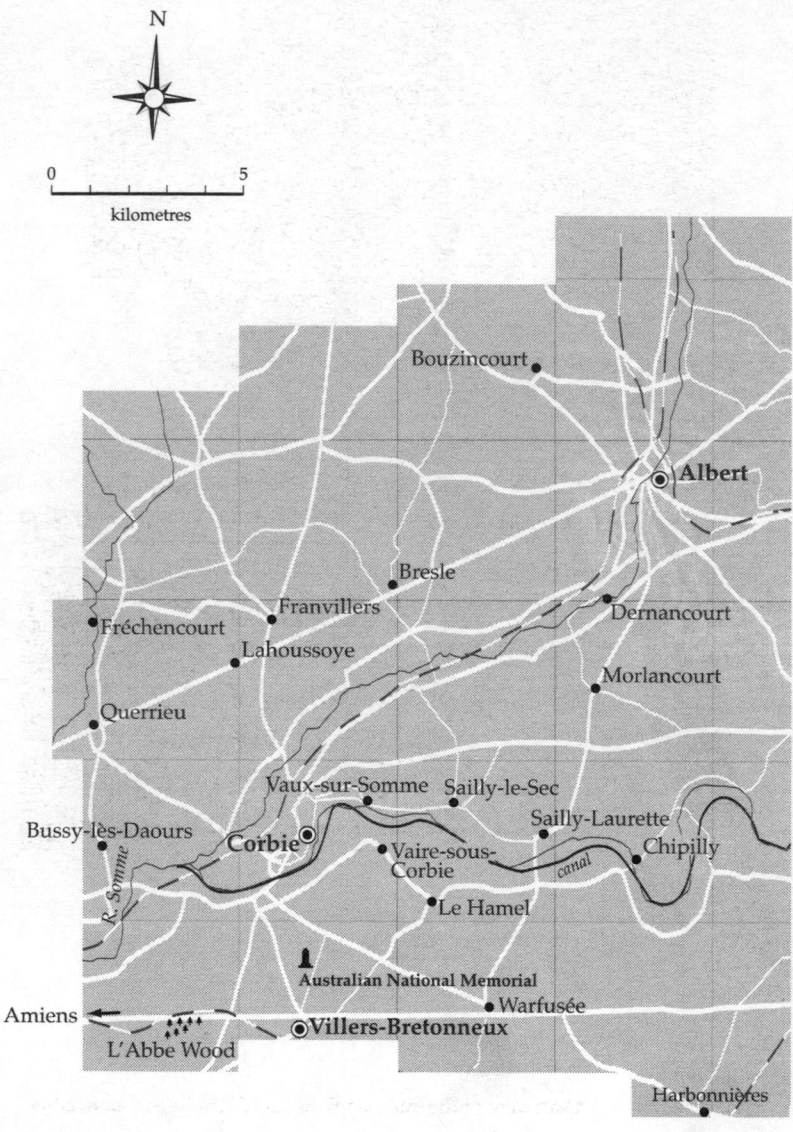

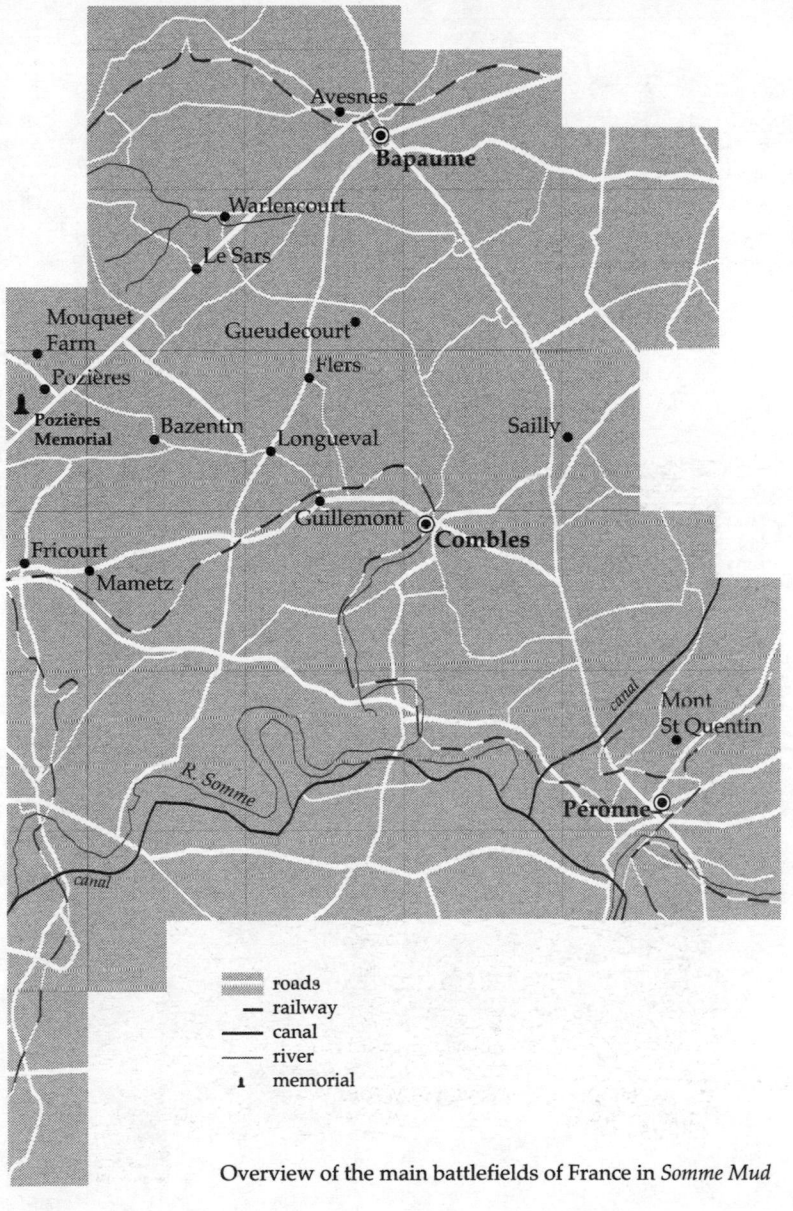

roads
— railway
— canal
— river
⚓ memorial

Overview of the main battlefields of France in *Somme Mud*

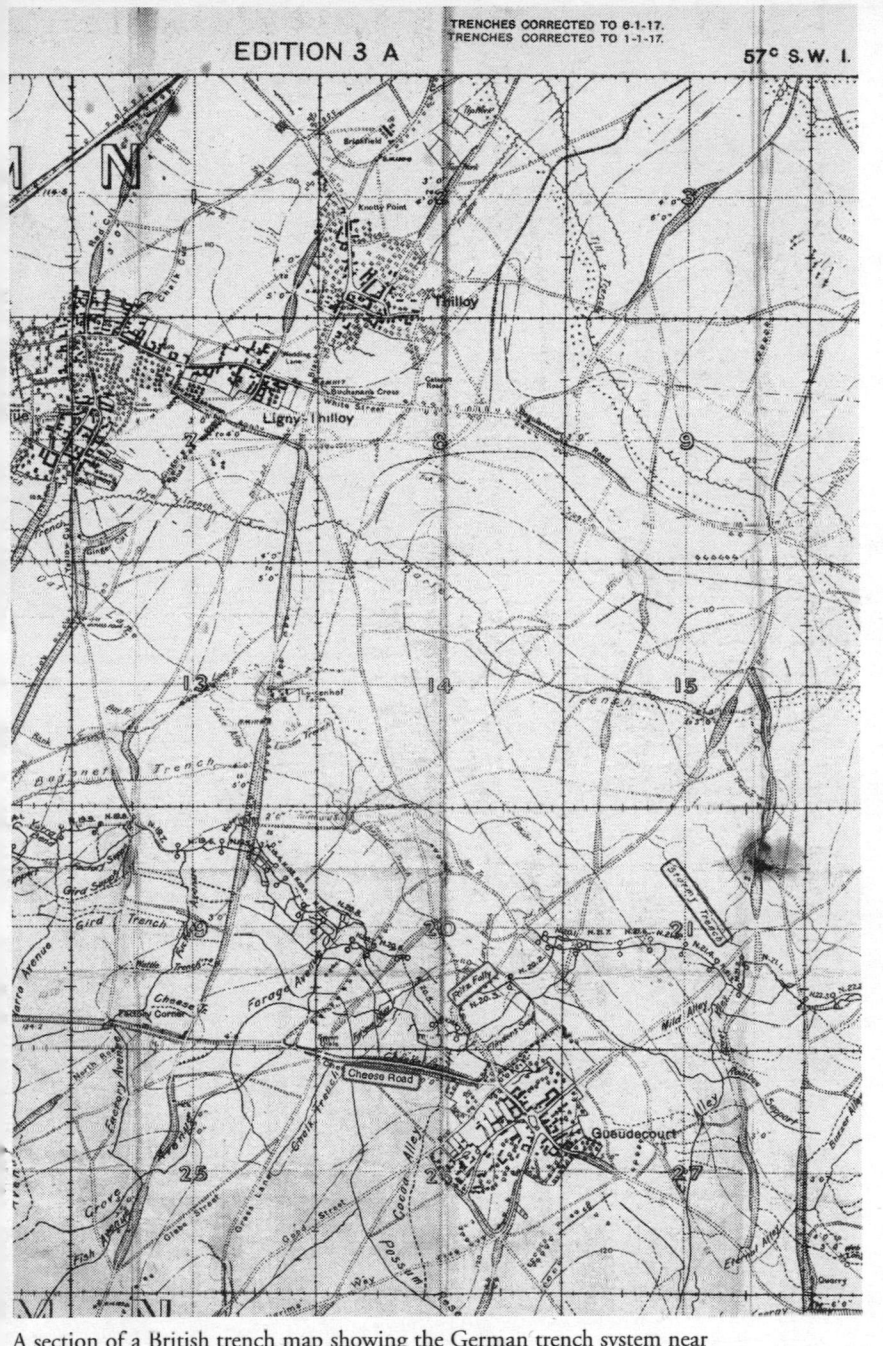

A section of a British trench map showing the German trench system near
Gueudecourt in 1916

# INTRODUCTION

Imagine this. You are a country boy and just 18. The war has been raging for two years and, because of your age, you have not been eligible for enlistment. Your mates, older by a few months, have joined up and disappeared to the great adventure across the world, in Europe. You hear the constant talk of the need for reinforcements, for men like you to join up and support the Empire, Australia and your mates in the line.

It is time to go.

Such was the case for Edward Patrick Francis Lynch, a typical country boy from Perthville, near Bathurst, in New South Wales. When war was declared in early August 1914, he was only 16 and still at school, but, like a generation of young males in Australia, he felt there was something to prove.

In 1901, when Edward Lynch was only four years old, Federation in Australia had brought together six disparate colonies into a new nation, the Commonwealth of Australia. With Federation came a desire to forge a national identity and separate Australia from Mother England. There were two ways of permanently cutting the apron strings and demonstrating true independence: sport and war. Australia displayed its strength on the field by continually beating England for a decade at cricket and rugby, the two dominant international sports of the time. But in war it was not so accomplished. While Australia showed itself useful in the Boer War of 1899–1902, this involvement was still limited and did not highlight Australia's full capability. What it needed was a real war and, in August 1914, the nation had its chance.

When war was declared, Australia greeted it enthusiastically, keen to show England its loyalty and strength, and the world its deserving status as a new nation. The Australian government was aware of the growing strength and military technology of the Asian giants to the north, and had already embarked on a programme of military training. From as early as the 1880s, it established school cadet corps to impart the basics of military-style instruction. Children were also taught to sing patriotic songs, recite nationalistic verse and salute the flag, their monarch and their country.

Lynch, at Perthville Primary School, would have shared these experiences and, along with his schoolmates, recited 'I love God and my country, I honour the flag, I will serve the King and cheerfully obey my parents, teachers and the law,' before giving three cheers to the King and saluting the flag. At 18, like other men his age, he joined the 41st Infantry. The militia was a citizens' army and service in it was compulsory for men aged 18 to 26.

So, when the bugle call came from Mother England to gather her distant sons, Private Lynch was ready. But despite the government's best efforts to prepare the nation, when he proudly marched down George Street, Sydney, in August 1916 to set off for a distant European war, he had little idea of the slaughter and carnage that awaited him.

Although I was a graduate historian, the First World War never held a great or abiding interest for me. I knew very little of the battles fought by the Australian Imperial Force, nor anything about the then fledgling Royal Australian Navy – except perhaps for the sinking of the German raider *Emden* – or the even newer Australian Flying Corps. My knowledge was limited to what I'd read in Bill Gammage's *The Broken Years* and Patsy Adam-Smith's *The Anzacs*.

In November 1993 something happened that changed that: the re-interment of the Unknown Soldier at the Australian War Memorial in Canberra. In 1920, the body of an unknown soldier killed on the Western Front had been entombed in Westminster Abbey in London to represent all the men of the British Empire who had lost their lives in the First World War. France and other Allied nations also entombed unknown soldiers around the same time, but it was not until 1993, on the 75th anniversary of the end of the war, that an unknown Australian soldier was laid to rest in a ceremony at the Hall of Memory at the Australian War Memorial. As I read about the funeral service, I felt a deep sadness for this poor unknown Aussie boy who had been killed during the fighting at Villers-Bretonneux in April 1918 and who was buried 'Known unto God' in the Adelaide Cemetery just outside that village. I suddenly needed to know more and somehow pay my respects to this man and his mates who had fought in that long-distant war and been forgotten. But where would I start?

On a visit to London, I decided to visit the battlefields, so I took the Friday night train to Dover and the ferry across the grey, choppy Channel – much like Private Lynch did – to the port of Calais. I found myself a cheap hotel by the docks, had an early night and was up before dawn the next day to pick up a rental car and head for Ypres, in southern Belgium, near the French border.

Armed with a copy of John Laffin's book, *Guide to Australian Battlefields of the Western Front 1916–1918*, and two maps, I visited Polygon Wood, Zonnebeke, Broodseinde, Passchendaele, Hellfire Corner, the Menin Road and Messines. As the sun set, I found myself at the imposing Lochnagar Crater near the village of La Boisselle in the Somme. It was raining – a sleety rain – but even in the low light I was awestruck by the enormous size of the crater, 200 metres across and 30 metres deep. It was formed by one of ten massive underground explosions that shattered the German frontline on the first day of the infamous Battle of the Somme on 1 July 1916.

There was evidence of other craters – blown by 27 tonnes of the explosive ammonal placed in tunnels under the German lines – that had long been filled in, the enormous patches of white chalk still clearly visible. Standing there so many decades later, looking out across the calm, undulating fields, it was hard to imagine the chaos and devastation the explosions must have wrought on the enemy.

Reaching for Laffin's book, I found there was somewhere to stay in nearby Pozières village, an inn at which I was to stress that I was Australian. I parked outside, pushed through the old wooden door and found myself in a cosy room with a bar on one side and walls covered with memorabilia from the First World War: slouch hats and rising sun badges, an Australian flag and a gaudy mannequin in an Australian battledress, complete with colour patches and rifle. I asked in my broken French for a room for the night but was shooed out by the dear old madame, who waved her arms at me as if she were driving pigs. So much for the welcome to Australians!

By chance, there were two Englishmen drinking at the bar, the only people in the place. Hearing my accent, they asked if I was Australian. 'Yes,' I said proudly.

'Then come and join us for a drink. *Madame, une bière, s'il vous plaît.*'

They were part of a group of four collectors who regularly travelled from England to dig the battlefields and swap relics. Not long after I sank my first beer, the others arrived and excitedly called on us to follow them outside to their large Bedford van. They flung open the back doors to reveal a mangled, rusty Vickers gun that lay in the back. This was the standard-issue British machine-gun, a heavy, tripod-mounted weapon that fired 650 rounds per minute. This one, they explained, was dug up by workers digging a trench for new telephone lines just outside the village. Along with other pieces of rusty detritus, it had made for an exciting day for them.

After dinner, and after a terse word to the madame, resulting in a room for me, they invited me to join them on a visit to a local collector in the village. The old chap and his wife welcomed us all into their small, typically French home and offered coffee and cake, and soon all kinds of relics and military pieces were being handed about, discussed and swapped. One of the Englishmen had an interest in grenades, another in metal tunic badges, while another collected bullets and spent cartridge cases. All I had found in my scavenging that day was a small brass ring at Messines, which one of the Englishmen quickly identified as a part from a German gas respirator – it would have held one of the glass eyepieces in place. The old Frenchman invited me to take something from part of his collection, and to this day I still have the rusty German helmet, eggshell thin, displayed on a bookshelf.

After an early breakfast the next day, I was keen to get on the road and I headed for the Pozières heights. I still remember that cold dawn very well: the sun was low and shrouded in mist and the grass was brittle with frost. I could just make out the open land dropping away below me as I looked out from the top of the ridge where the Pozières windmill had once stood. A small mound was all that remained of the objective of so many Australian attacks up that slight, muddy slope. Behind me, traffic hummed on the straight Roman road that ran from Albert to Bapaume, oblivious to the memorial – a neat patch of lawn bordered by a low hedge, with a chiselled block of stone on a low plinth a few metres from my feet. With tears streaming down my face, I read the simple yet poignant inscription by Australian journalist and official war historian Charles Bean:

> The ruin of the Pozières windmill which lies here was the centre of the struggle in this part of the Somme battlefield in July and August 1916. It was captured on August 4th by Australian troops who fell more thickly on this ridge than on any other battlefield of the war.

As I wiped away those cold tears and stared at Charles Bean's sad understatement, I realised that I had to understand and appreciate those forgotten Australians, but looking out across the former battlefield I simply did not know what I was looking at. None of the moonscape and destruction, stark and monochrome, that I remembered from old photographs was there. Instead, benign fields, which lay green and lost in the gentle, blowing mist, added to my sense of bewilderment and disorientation.

When I returned home to Australia, I began to read and learn all that I could about that brutal and bloody war, and found myself engrossed in the minutiae of Bean's *Official History of Australia in the War of 1914–18*. As I pored over the six-volume work that Bean had compiled, I found that the names of the tiny French towns and his detailed descriptions of the battles that raged among them now meant so much more to me.

I again had the opportunity to visit the battlefields and develop a much deeper understanding of them in 1998, the 80th anniversary of the end of the Great War. The Department of Veterans Affairs asked me to write a guide titled *Villers-Bretonneux to Le Hamel: A Battlefield Driving Tour* and this gave me my first experience of walking the ground and piecing together the events I had read about in the history books – the attacks, the counter-attacks, the advances and the sites where the AIF under General Monash made such a name for themselves. The driving tour has since become a popular side trip for Australians paying their respects at the more oft-visited battlefields of Villers-Bretonneux, Le Hamel and along the Somme, where the Anzacs saw most of their action in the last two years of the war.

But it was not until 2002 that something unexpected happened that gave me a new understanding and appreciation for the young Australian men who gave their lives in the Great War. It came not via a history book, nor through talking with experts, nor by painstakingly reconstructing battles in my mind while walking the battlefields of France and Belgium. It came through the writings of a young soldier who had fought on those fields: Private Edward Patrick Francis Lynch.

A colleague of mine, Mike Lynch, had lent me the manuscript of his grandfather's unpublished book, a weighty foolscap tome with the words *Somme Mud* embossed down the spine. It was awkward to lift and read but, within a few pages, I knew this story was something very special.

The images were vivid and real and I was quickly swept along to become one of the young men marching through the streets of Sydney, being cheered on by waving crowds, my mates beside me, as we headed to the wharves to embark on the great adventure. As I followed Lynch's down-to-earth narrator, Nulla, and his mates on their journey from enthusiastic, naive young recruits to battle-hardened soldiers, I was struck by his unerring eye for detail, the realism of his writing, his wry humour, his effective use of understatement, his almost filmic imagery and his unique insight into the spirit and attitudes of Australian soldiers. All of these, in my eyes, made *Somme Mud* an undiscovered Australian classic.

So I sent it to an old mate, Bill Gammage, an academic and historian at the Australian National University in Canberra, who has written a number of books about Australians in the First World War and was the historian on Peter Weir's film *Gallipoli*. I remember his initial comment clearly: 'Mate, I read one of these a month and *this* is Australia's *All Quiet on the Western Front.*' He was referring to the unflinching novel written by Erich Maria Remarque, a German soldier during the First World War.

I knew I had to get this wonderful manuscript published, to share this unique account and give people, not only in Australia but around the world, an insight into the bloody and messy war that was fought out in the Somme mud. The publishing team at Random House quickly realised the special nature of this lost manuscript and was as enthusiastic as me, but asked that I edit the book to 120,000 words.

As difficult as it was, the editing process was a labour of love. As I read of Nulla's movements, I meticulously tracked his travels on maps and compared them to the history books – his long route marches to flea-ridden billets; to the frontline at such places as Messines, Dernancourt, Stormy Trench and Villers-Bretonneux; to rest areas behind the lines; and, finally, on the great push to the final victory after August 1918.

I had images of the battlefields in my head, from the stark black-and-white photographs of official war photographers Frank Hurley and Hubert Wilkins and others; and I knew the towns because I had walked them, retraced the attacks and dug the clinging mud from my boots as I sought out the trench-lines. I had collected the detritus of war: rusty pieces of shrapnel, clips of bullets, brass shell heads and screw pickets. I had even stupidly picked up old grenades, Stokes mortars and large-calibre shells that still litter these areas today. But it was part of what I needed to do to get a greater understanding. Now, Lynch's manuscript was giving me an insight that I'd never had before into the battles and an intimacy with the infantrymen.

The pages screamed a graphic, brutal yet unexpectedly humorous Australian story to me. The book was a lost treasure: a soldier's story that only one who had been through the trenches – seen the mud and misery and smelt the gas and the stench of death – could write. In places I found it nearly too frightening to read, too horrendous and graphic – then, just as quickly, it would become a tale of larrikinism and mateship, inspirational bravery and typical Australian humour.

From the moment you take up the story of Nulla and his mates as they prepare to embark for Europe, you are thrust into the adventure, into their larrikin pranks and juvenile behaviour – and then, when they reach the frontline, into their fear and their sadness and the horror of their war. There is no letting up and you are often forced to put the book down, take a deep breath and consider the moment, even pinch yourself to end what seems like a bad dream but is, in fact, historically accurate.

For the next 30 months, the violence of the trenches swirls about Nulla and his diminishing band of mates. He tells of the carnage and death, the mud and the suffering, as the 'butcher's picnic' grinds his unit into the slime and mud of war.

Nulla's war continues until the armistice, in November 1918. He is wounded a number of times and sees his mates cut from the ranks, but is rarely away from the dangers of the front. He spends much of his time in the perilous role of a runner, his duty to find the very frontlines in the black of night, under shellfire or during enemy raids, to deliver messages or lead new troops in for their stint in the line.

Private Lynch returned to Australia in 1919, trained to become a teacher and worked in remote country schools in southern New South Wales. He married in 1922 and, in the late 1920s and into the 1930s, as the worst of the Depression bit, he wrote *Somme Mud*, hoping that he could have it published to boost his income.

There is no evidence Lynch kept a diary during the war and no one in the family recalls him referring to one when he was writing the manuscript. But he almost certainly would have had a copy of the battalion history at hand during his writing in order to get the precise details he might not have known or to jog his memory on dates, places and casualties. Each battalion was required to keep an official war diary during active service. Entries were made daily at battalion headquarters, noting the unit's location, the events of the day, casualties, intelligence summaries, orders, reports and messages; and these were often accompanied by photographs, sketches and maps. After the war, these diaries were used to compile the official battalion history, which was then sold to the men as a reminder of their war service. The history of Lynch's 45th Battalion (*The Chronicle of the 45th Battalion AIF*) was written by Major Lee and published first in late 1924. It would have been beside Lynch when writing the first draft of his book.

Though Lynch claimed that the narrator, Nulla, was based on a friend of his, it is easy to imagine that *Somme Mud* could be a memoir, or at least close to it. I have spent a considerable amount of time comparing the events in *Somme Mud* with the battalion history and the army's personal records of Private Lynch, and from there comparing Edward Lynch's life with that of Nulla's. There is very little to tell them apart.

As the battalion diaries focused on a unit's overall operations, they rarely mentioned individual soldiers by name and a soldier's personal records did not include day-to-day activities, so it is impossible to know for sure how closely Nulla's experiences follow Lynch's own. Yet I have found a few places in the book where it is clear that Lynch chose a divergent path for his character Nulla, perhaps to try to convince himself and the reader he was not in fact Nulla or perhaps to include in his story, battles and incidents that he knew about but was not involved in. These mostly had to do with the type and timing of wounds sustained in battle. When it came to recounting his battalion's military operations and movements, though, he stuck faithfully to historical fact.

He completed the chapters in pencil in 20 school exercise books, hoping to get the manuscript published, but the public did not want to be reminded of the Great War and he could not find a publisher. While some excerpts were printed in the RSL's magazine, *Reveille*, the book would not be published in his lifetime.

When Lynch's account of the war finally made its way onto bookshelves after nearly 70 years, it became an instant success, telling as it does the very personal story of the men of the First AIF in France and Belgium. Many readers craved to know more of the background to Nulla's story and his small place in a complex war, so I embarked on this contextual history for the lay reader to explain the battles, the ebb and flow of the war. In the process, I have tried to join the dots and explain what was going on: the campaigns and offensives, the weapons and equipment, the food, the diseases and the minutiae of war.

For all of us, the First World War is today represented in stark black and white photos, so I thought it would be interesting for the reader to see these same places as they are today – and in colour. My travels took me to many of the places Private Lynch would have been: to battlefields and trench lines, to rest areas and camps, to the roads he trod and the sights he may well have seen. For the battlefield visitor today, these are an interesting diversion.

In writing this book, I have tried to pay my respects to that Unknown Soldier who pricked my conscience all those years ago and inspired me to find out about the Australian men who sacrificed their youth to the First World War. Little did I know then that my journey would lead me to Private Edward Lynch and one of this country's great and historically significant books. That I played a part in giving Lynch a voice so many years after his death is one of the proudest achievements of my career.

I am just sorry I never had the chance to shake his hand.

# ONE

# Good-bye, Sydney Town, Good-bye

On 5 April 1916, Edward Lynch presented himself to the Recruiting Officer at the Depot Camp, Bathurst, New South Wales. Because he was under 21, he needed a parent's permission to join up, so he came bearing an Application to Enlist signed by his father.

Lynch was born in 1897 at Bourke, a remote town in far northwestern New South Wales, but at the time of his enlistment he was living with his family in Perthville, which was then a village just out of Bathurst but today is a suburb of that large regional city. Family meant his father, Edward, his mother, Laura, and five siblings. Edward was the eldest of the six Lynch children and was followed by William, Kevin, Ella, Veronica and Joan. Neither of his brothers joined him in the AIF, but they served in the Second World War. His three sisters all became nuns.

We know from his army personal service records that Lynch was a small man, 5 feet 4 inches in the old scale (1.6

metres) and weighing 9 stone 9 pounds (61 kilograms). His complexion was fair, his eyes hazel and his hair brown. A Roman Catholic, he attended mass regularly. His 'trade or calling' was given as 'student', a rare listing amidst the scores of farmers, labourers, dairymen and station hands signing up at Bathurst. He was 18 years and 8 months old – some would say still a child. Like so many young Australians at the time, called to the colours in defence of the Empire, he had led a sheltered life in rural Australia, had travelled little and never ventured out of his country.

After enlisting at Bathurst, Lynch went to Sydney by train and was sent to the Liverpool training camp. There, he received basic weapons training and instruction in military procedure. At Liverpool, he was allocated to the fourth reinforcement to the 45th Battalion, made up of 150 men and two officers. All the battalions were state-based and were often competitive with each other.

Training was traditional and tough: parade-ground drill, route marches and poor-quality, basic army food. But life in Australia was tough in those years and a young recruit would usually have been strong and physically fit for the training ahead. This would especially have been the case for country boys, for whom riding, heavy manual work and shooting would have been the norm. Edward Lynch, coming from rural New South Wales, would have been a typical strong young recruit.

It was now 20 months since war had been declared and the first men had swarmed around the recruiting tables of

Australia. Then, army regulations required a soldier to be at least 5 feet 6 inches (168 centimetres) tall, have a 34-inch (86-centimetre) chest, and be aged between 18 and 35. With so many men offering to enlist, the army could be very selective and rejected men even for having bad teeth. In the first year, they turned away about a third of all men who volunteered for service.

However, by mid-1916 and before Edward Lynch signed up, the minimum height requirement had dropped to 5 feet 2 inches (157 centimetres) and men up to the age of 45 could enlist. Lynch made it into the army by 2 inches in height; and a quick glance at the records of men in his reinforcement shows that he was not alone in falling short of the original 5 feet 6 inches standard. In April 1917, the army would so desperately need men to fill the ranks that they would lower the height restriction again, to 5 feet (152 centimetres).

While at Liverpool training camp, Edward Lynch was issued with his uniform, basic equipment and webbing. The woollen khaki AIF battledress was drab and baggy, designed to be functional and serviceable in war. There was no colour – except the small identifying unit colour patches worn on each shoulder – and there were no shiny buttons and braid. Four large pockets on the front of the tunic distinguished the Australian battledress from all others, as did the rising sun badges on the collar and the brass badges reading 'Australia' on the shoulders. Over their breeches and good-quality Australian-made leather boots they wore puttees – long strips of cloth wound around their legs from ankle to knee.

Perhaps the most distinctive feature of the AIF uniform was the slouch hat, turned up on the left side, on which it bore the rising sun. It too was designed for fighting, not parade-ground smartness and, as a result, the AIF's battledress appeared to other Allied troops as untidy, even slovenly, further adding to the Australian soldiers' reputation for being undisciplined and sloppy. Officers in the British army provided much work for the tailors of Savile Row but, in contrast, Australian officers drew their uniforms from the same Q-stores as the men, thus eliminating any obvious difference in appearance and apparent smartness between the ranks.

Another thing that differentiated the Australian troops from the British was their rate of pay. A soldier in the AIF was paid five shillings a day for active service, plus one shilling a day deferred pay he would be entitled to on discharge. This was based on the average worker's pay at the time of six shillings a day, minus something for rations and lodging, and was the highest pay for any army at the time. Even a citizen soldier in the militia in Australia was paid four shillings a day. But a British soldier on active service received one shilling a day, which increased later in the war, though only to three shillings a day. For officers, the situation was reversed. Australian officers were paid less than their equivalents in the British army, and the higher the rank, the greater the disparity.

By the time Lynch enlisted in April 1916, well into the war, the army was able to train, equip, inoculate and ship new men to the front in only three months. This required capable officers who understood the special challenges of handling men in a peculiarly Australian way, as most recruits had never been ordered around or strictly disciplined. Perhaps understandably, the British feared at the outbreak of the war that Australian troops would be so lacking in discipline and organisation that they would be ineffective and at best form reserve units or be kept to the rear of the fighting. But the landing and subsequent battles at Gallipoli in 1915, which ended in a successful evacuation but dismal withdrawal, put paid to any concerns they had. In the eight months of the Dardanelles campaign, the Australian Imperial Force, now known as the Anzacs, fought valiantly and suffered nearly 27,000 casualties, of which 8,709 died and another 18,000 were wounded or captured. Afterwards, the British General Sir Ian Hamilton, commander-in-chief at Gallipoli, wrote, 'Before the war, who had ever heard of Anzac? Hereafter, who shall ever forget it?'[1]

Despite this recently forged reputation of heroism in Gallipoli, many Australians went into the army thinking it was much like any other job and viewed their officer as simply a boss who, rather than issuing orders, should respectfully and politely ask that something be done. Soldiers had even conducted major strikes and marches in early 1916, much as they would in a normal job, to secure better camp conditions.

The relatively casualty-free period for the AIF as they regrouped in Egypt came to a devastating end with their introduction to the Western Front in July 1916, the month before Lynch was shipped over. On the front, the AIF were to endure horrific conditions and sustain casualties on an unprecedented scale. The war for Australia would never be the same again.

On 22 August 1916, Lynch and the other men rose early, were inspected and marched to Liverpool station, from which they went by train to Central station. Few knew that so many of them would never see these streets and their people again.

The tragedy of this chapter is that we know how the story will unfold for these young men, but they are not fearful, not concerned with the future. What Lynch portrays is a soaring euphoria, jubilant crowds lining the streets, laughter, a jumble of happy faces, halfpennies showering down from above, bearing the addresses of adoring young girls. Even then, though, reality does its best to intrude. Pricking Nulla's consciousness are the few 'silent women in black, mute testimony to what has befallen others who have marched before' and then, at the wharf, the mothers and wives who 'couldn't stand the pretence any longer' and have to be taken away to the back of the crowd. The men are a 'happy-go-lucky, carefree lot', oblivious to these omens of how their lives are about to change.

Unlike the wives and mothers of the first men to sail in October 1914, these women knew of the weekly casualty lists, the official telegrams and ominous names such as Lone Pine,

Quinn's Post, Fromelles and Pozières. In the dark days of July and August 1916, when the AIF was in a desperate fight to take Mouquet Farm, the Australians suffered 23,000 casualties in just six weeks. When the slaughter of the 5th Division at Fromelles is included, the total is 28,000.

In *Somme Mud*, Nulla's reinforcement is made up of 250 men and two officers, but in reality Lynch's reinforcement as taken from the Embarkation Roll comprised 150 men plus two officers. Nevertheless, Lynch's experience would have been like Nulla's, on a rowdy ship crowded not only with men from their own reinforcement, but those going to bolster other battalions at the front. Their ship, the HMAT *Wiltshire*, designated throughout her service during the war as ship number A18, departed from Dalgety's Wharf at the old shipping hub of Millers Point, whose jetties and warehouses have in recent years given way to a new development of shops and businesses. The *Wiltshire* was a steamship that had been contracted by the government for transporting soldiers, and had been part of the original Anzac convoy that assembled at Albany, Western Australia, to take the first troops to Egypt in October–November 1914. Since then, the ship had been on the Australia–UK run, transporting fresh reinforcements and bringing back the wounded, maimed, those dishonourably discharged and the venereal disease patients. The *Wiltshire* was to remain in service until December 1917.

To run your finger down the list of men who embarked from Sydney with Edward Lynch makes for interesting reading. Most of the men were young, 18 to 30 years old, though some who gave their age as 18 may well have been even younger, a common occurrence during the First World War. From the Embarkation Roll we know that the oldest man was 45 but there were only eight men over 40. They were mostly single – just 22 out of 150 men were married, and there was one widower. Only three men had what we would today term a profession: a sugar chemist, a schoolteacher and an engineer. Most were either unskilled or worked at a trade, though some of their trades no longer exist today, such as coach driver, horse breaker, carter and coal lumper, blacksmith, trapper and wheelwright.

Their shared ancestry was the British Empire, with their next of kin hailing, if not from Australia, then from England, Scotland, South Africa, New Zealand, Norfolk Island or Guernsey in the Channel Islands. Most were Church of England; about one-third were, like Lynch, Roman Catholic; plus there was a smattering of Presbyterians, Methodists and Baptists, one Congregationalist and one Church of Scotland. Everyone listed a religion – no one declared themselves agnostic or atheist. At that time it would have been considered inappropriate for a soldier – fighting for God, King and flag – to do so. But if the irreverent attitudes that Lynch describes in *Somme Mud* are anything to go by, it seems that some of the men of the 45th were religious more in name than in practice. Twenty-two men had, like Lynch, been in the Citizen Forces and so had some previous military experience before they trained together at Liverpool. Eight other men in the reinforcement came from the 41st Infantry, which Lynch had served in.

The 45th Battalion that Private Lynch and his mates were going over to join had been formed only six months before, on 2 March 1916, as part of the expansion and reorganisation of the AIF taking place at their old base camps in Egypt. With tens of thousands of reinforcements on their way to bolster the war effort, there were not enough battalions to absorb all the new recruits, and so 16 battalions that had seen action at Gallipoli were each split, forming an additional 16 battalions. Recruits from Australia would bring these split battalions up to a full complement of men. Creating new battalions this way ensured there would be a mix of experienced men, in this case from the Dardanelles campaign, and new recruits.

The 13th Battalion, a New South Wales battalion that had served at Gallipoli from the first days until the evacuation, split to form a 'daughter' battalion with half of those seasoned Anzacs forming the nucleus for the new 45th Battalion. While the reorganisation of the battalions was a military necessity, it was hard for the men of the 13th, who had survived Gallipoli together and had a strong desire to remain with their battalion and their mates. In the words of the *Official History*, the 45th had been formed by 'simply handing over two splendid companies' and 'the sight of half the old battalion marching away from the desert camps was distressing in the extreme, not only to the half that was being divorced, but to their former comrades which watched them go.'[2]

After they were joined by reinforcements from Australia and underwent training and final preparations in Egypt, the 45th Battalion sailed on the *Kinfauns Castle* to Marseilles, France, arriving on 2 June 1916. They then travelled by train to northern France, where they went into the 'nursery area' – so called because the frontline there was relatively quiet – at Méteren on 11 June 1916.

On 1 July 1916, Britain's General Haig launched his disastrous five-month-long campaign in the Somme valley, known as the Somme offensive or the Battle of the Somme. The British aimed to wipe out Germany's reserves of manpower and divert their resources from Verdun, the French fortress the Germans had beseiged since February, severely impacting the French army. But Haig underestimated the strength of the enemy's defences and the first day of the Battle of the Somme is still the bloodiest in the British army's history, with nearly 20,000 men killed and another 40,000 wounded or captured.

The first major Australian engagement on the Western Front came at Fromelles on 19 July 1916. The attack, designed as a feint to draw German troops away from the Somme offensive, was a total disaster tactically and resulted in horrific casualties for the Australians. In one night they suffered over 5,500 casualties, including more than 1,800 dead.

While Private Lynch and the men of his reinforcement

sailed out through Sydney Heads and into the cold, blustery Southern Ocean, the 45th Battalion was moving towards the front and its first major battle of the Somme offensive. The men moved through Albert, past the once grand, ornate cathedral whose Virgin Mary statue, damaged during fierce fighting, was dangling precipitously from the spire (it was known as the 'leaning virgin'). They continued through La Boisselle, towards the cauldron that was Pozières. Resting for a night, the men watched the terrific bombardment of the Pozières windmill, finally captured on 4 August by men of the Australian 2nd Division. The high ground beyond the village and the sky above was red with the flash of the guns and bursting flares, lighting the night sky.

The following night, the battalion moved forward, winding through the congestion of Sausage Valley, which had recently been the scene of savage fighting but was now the main line of communication and transport for Australian troops on this part of the front. On they filed, past shattered trenches, first aid posts, smashed guns and wagons and the bodies of the dead. On through cluttered communication trenches, until they came to what had been the frontline: the shattered remains of OG 1 – Old German trench line 1 – below the crest of the Pozières ridge and just to the southwest of the destroyed windmill and the Bapaume to Albert road. Here the battalion spread out to hold a front of about 550 metres, with Australian battalions on either side.

For the following ten days, the 45th remained in the frontline or the support trenches close to Pozières. By the time they were withdrawn, three officers and 76 men of other ranks had been killed, and seven officers and 334 men of other ranks wounded, a total of 420 casualties. As the battalion history tells us, they came under such heavy and sustained bombardment and counter-attacks from the Germans it was a wonder anyone survived. They successfully repulsed the German counter-attacks, but their time in the line took a terrible toll physically and mentally on the men, many of whom were Gallipoli veterans.

Meanwhile, the HMAT *Wiltshire* sailed on with a number of scheduled stops – Melbourne, Adelaide and Fremantle – to collect more men, before heading west across the Indian Ocean to Durban and Cape Town. Lynch portrays the voyage as one of boredom and monotony, broken by moments of hilarity and larrikin behaviour. Many of these 'men' were mere boys, full of youthful gusto. They had never travelled far from home. This was a great adventure and they were not going to miss out on the fun with their newfound mates.

When the ship docks at Durban, the men's attentions turn to the local dock workers – or, as Nulla and his mates refer to them in the pejorative language of the time, the 'niggers and coons'. Later, when they stop at St Vincent in the Cape Verde Islands, they again have their fun throwing coins for the 'stark naked niggers' to dive for. They held no respect for these poor dock workers nor indeed the English merchant seaman or people of rank and authority.

In these scenes in which the men entertain themselves at the expense of the locals, Lynch captures an anti-authoritarian, almost anarchic spirit, for which Australian soldiers were so renowned amongst other armies. In *Somme Mud*, it is mates against everyone else, whether it is the enemy, the local black populations, the British soldiers or their officers. No one is able to put a stop to the chaos they cause on shore; when they hit the streets of Durban it takes two hours to round them up from the local watering holes; by the time they reach Cape Town it seems that their journey to the battlefield is akin to a pub crawl. They play poker on board while the chaplain addresses them, pelt spuds at the dapper, cordial Harbour Master in Cape Town, and always manage to make fools of the officers and English merchant seamen.

For the men, this was a time when they could test those in authority and learn the parameters of military discipline. It was also a time to forge bonds and test friendships. A soldier could quickly gauge whether a mate could be trusted to stick by him, even if his antics were dangerous and likely to offend. For the reader, however, there is something foreboding about the men's pranks, their drunken carousing in port, their careless fun, for we know what these men are steaming towards across the ocean.

South of Africa, Lynch's ship headed north into the Atlantic, across the equator to St Vincent in the Cape Verde Islands. From there, the *Wiltshire* made for England. After seven weeks at sea, she berthed in Plymouth on 12 October.

For Lynch, Bathurst was a long way away and there was much to endure before he would again smell the eucalyptus of his native land. He was heading into a terrible and bloody war he had no way of comprehending.

# TWO

# France
and Fritz

Private Lynch was admitted to hospital with the mumps on the day he landed in Plymouth, and he remained there for 11 days. Though no mention is made of his sickness and medical treatment in *Somme Mud*, we know that on 23 October he was released and returned to the 12th Training Battalion camp at Rollestone to begin his training.

After the AIF had moved from Egypt, it had established a number of training camps in southern England, 15 to 30 kilometres from Salisbury, some within sight of Stonehenge. Initially the 1st Division had established a divisional training base at Perham Down. They were followed by the 2nd and 4th divisions, who established themselves at Rollestone, while the 5th Division had their base at Larkhill. These camps were part of Southern Command and came under the control of General Sir Henry Sclater, an officer of the British regular army renowned for firmly laying down War Office regulations about the fitness standards and training of men about to be sent to the front.

While Lynch was training in England, weekly reports were coming in as to the exact number of reinforcements needed to replenish depleted battalions in France. Losses to battalions came not only from those killed, wounded and captured but also from those evacuated due to sickness, those who were sent to attend specialist training and from those transferred to other units. Reinforcements came from the men who had been trained in the AIF divisional camps around Salisbury, generally men fresh from Australia and new to France and the war, or from those returning to the front.

Since being involved in the heavy fighting between the Windmill and Mouquet Farm, just to the northeast of Pozières, in August 1916, the 45th Battalion had travelled north into Belgium, to the area west of Ypres. Then they had gone into the line at Ridgewood near Vierstraat to relieve the Canadians and from there on to Bois Carré to relieve the Australian 47th Battalion.

On 28 October, they and all the other Australians serving in France had voted in Prime Minister Billy Hughes's first conscription referendum. Australian recruitment numbers were down from 36,600 in July 1915 to 6,170 in July 1916 and something desperately needed to be done to keep battalions at full strength. Prime Minister Billy Hughes had spent the early part of 1916 in England, where he had seen their conscription system in practice. Though conscription was politically unattractive to many of Hughes's Labor ministers, some of whom resigned rather than support him, he decided to put the idea of compulsory military service to the people of Australia and the troops overseas through a plebiscite.

All Australian troops at this time in the war were volunteers. There was a strong sense of pride in fighting for king and country without being conscripted as this, they believed, would change and devalue their sacrifice and contribution. There was also a strong feeling that only men who were prepared voluntarily to enter this hellish world of gas, mud, shelling and death should be there – a surprisingly sensitive thought given that more reinforcements from Australia in the line would have relieved their position and assisted their effort.

The issue divided the nation and split communities and families, and after the votes were counted, the 'no' vote prevailed by a narrow majority. The troops overseas voted in favour of conscription: 72,000 votes to 59,000. In Australia, the failure of the first conscription referendum had been compounded by low recruitment numbers and a general apathy among potential volunteers. The Prime Minister was, as a result, expelled from the Labor Party and, with four loyal ministers and 19 backbenchers, formed a new party, the National Labor Party, later known as the Nationalist Party. The raising of further troops would depend solely upon volunteers, of which there were only 5,055 in November 1916. The following month, total recruitment across Australia would be only 2,617 men.

Back in the training camps near Salisbury, Lynch was

preparing to leave. He made the three-hour journey by train to the southeast coast of England, where he left the port town of Folkestone on 21 December 1916 on the ferry *Princess Clementine*, escorted across the Channel by warships.

Though only a three-hour trip, it was a potentially dangerous one, as slow-moving ferries were tempting targets to German U-boats. It was also frequently a rough voyage. The journey across the choppy English Channel made many men sick, though probably as much from nerves as the sea itself. Little wonder Lynch had his character Nulla comment that the 'ship reeks with the sour stench of seasickness'.

On arrival in Boulogne, France, Lynch travelled by train to the massive British base area at Étaples, about 25 kilometres south. Here there were depots for the five Australian divisions plus an Australian General Base Depot for other branches of the service, such as the Light Horse. There were also 16 British hospitals and a convalescent depot, which collectively could accommodate 22,000 soldiers at any time. Nearby was the Étaples Military Cemetery, where today among the 11,000 graves are those of 461 Australians.

Men new to France and the front were subject to further tests, medicals and training and a 'final touch-up before facing the foe', as Nulla puts it. Within the training camp at Étaples was the famous 'Bull Ring', a circular course of training stations that had a reputation for being rigorous and harsh and overseen by bullying British NCOs – men not popular with the Australians. Training aimed to prepare the men for the practical side of fighting and for surviving the frontline trenches, and included bayonet practice drill, trench warfare, 'hop-overs' (leaving the trench and going 'over the top' for an attack), grenade throwing and the use of gas masks.

The days were long and hard and, for some, a frustrating delay, but if Lynch's account in *Somme Mud* is any indication, the men of the fourth reinforcement had lost none of their sense of humour or anti-authoritarian spirit. Nulla's mates get their own back on the training staff, making a fool of, and even injuring, the sergeant whose unfortunate job it is to teach them bayonet fighting. But at night they hear the faint rumble of the guns on the front, 80 kilometres away, which must have been sobering. Nulla reflects, 'We were not very interested as we know before we're much older we'll hear all the guns we'll ever want to hear.' [p. 35. NB These page references refer to the paperback edition]

After 10 to 15 days' training at the Bull Ring and then being passed medically fit, men were sent to join their battalions. Some were sent to nursery areas on the frontline which ran from Armentières southeast towards Lille. Here the country was unsuitable for active operations and both the British and the Germans had a tacit agreement to let it remain quiet, which provided good experience for newly arrived troops.

Lynch was not to be so lucky. He was destined for Dernancourt – a 'scene of filth, mud and misery' according to his narrator, Nulla – and then the far-from-quiet Gueudecourt. It is likely Lynch's journey from Boulogne to the front was similar to the one he describes in *Somme Mud*, and that after about ten days' training at the Bull Ring he had three days' travel, stopping in a couple of villages on the way.

In *Somme Mud*, Nulla tells us:

> For two days we journey slowly towards the Somme. The train stops at night in pouring rain and after marching the wrong way, we arrive just after daybreak at the tumble-down village of Brucamps where our own battalion is billeted. [p. 40]

Going by the battalion's published history, Lynch's battalion was in fact probably not at Brucamps. Although there is a brief reference to 100 reinforcements joining the battalion there in October 1916, Private Lynch did not land in France until 21 December, when the battalion was north of Amiens at Flesselles, about 22 kilometres closer to the frontline. This is one of very few instances in the book where the life of Private Lynch and his character Nulla diverges and was probably a simple mistake in dates.

Australian troops were often billeted in French farms and houses well behind the line. Nulla describes a typical farm layout that has been used to accommodate Australian soldiers.

> Our platoon is in a big shed where fowls once camped before the Australians, part of a large farmhouse. The centre is a great, smelly manure pit round which the buildings form a quadrangle. On one side is the residence, whilst barns, stables

The ruins of the Cloth Hall, Ypres, taken by Frank Hurley in September 1917. *Courtesy of Australian War Memorial (E00717)*

The new Cloth Hall was not completed until 1962. On the right you can see the rebuilt cathedral. *Copyright Will Davies*

Hyde Park Corner in the Messines Sector, near the entrance to the Catacombs at Hill 63. Ploegsteert Wood is in the background. *Courtesy of Australian War Memorial (E01588)*

The Messines–Ploegsteert road today. As you can see, the trees have regrown in Ploegsteert Wood. Copyright Will Davies

*Top left*: Two message runners proceeding toward Hill 63 during the battle of Messines. While this photo was being taken three shells burst: one on top of the hill on the left; one on the extreme right of the picture, near Ploegsteert Wood; and one uncomfortably close to the camera. *Top Right*: Another shell strikes the road in an attempt to stall the movement of troops and transport. *Courtesy of Australian War Memorial (E00599 and E00480)*

Today a farmhouse sits on the corner of the narrow road to the west of Ploegsteert Wood, Messines. *Copyright Will Davies*

Huns Walk, Messines, where the 45th Battalion attacked towards Owl Trench. *Courtesy of Australian War Memorial (E01295)*

The Messines–Comines road today, a kilometre east of Messines village. A farmhouse has been built where the blockhouse was once situated. *Copyright Will Davies*

A German blockhouse at Owl Trench, Messines, which was one of two attacked by a 45th Battalion patrol. Nulla was wounded here on 10 June 1917. *Courtesy of Australian War Memorial (E01366)*

The remains of one of two German blockhouses along the line of Owl Trench. Today it is used as a barn for cattle. *Copyright Will Davies*

Hellfire Corner on the Menin Road, Ypres Sector. At one point this was the most dangerous spot on earth. *Courtesy of Australian War Memorial (E01889)*

Hellfire Corner is now a busy junction on the outskirts of Ypres. *Copyright Will Davies*

The Menin Gate and forts in Ypres before the First World War. *Courtesy of Australian War Memorial (P04760.001)*

The Menin Gate Memorial to the Missing contains the names of 54,896 men whose graves are not known. *Copyright Will Davies*

A motor ambulance and other vehicles on the Albert–Bapaume road near Le Sars, March 1918. Private Lynch would have travelled this road on the way to the frontline. *Courtesy of Australian War Memorial (E04657)*

The Albert–Bapaume road today. *Copyright Will Davies*

and sheds complete the other three sides. The pit is fed with every bit of manure dropped on the farm; rotten vegetables, waste straw, potato peelings, feathers and rubbish of all sorts go into it, to be used by the farmer as fertiliser. [p. 40]

In France today you can still see farms laid out this way – the barn, sheds and storage areas forming the four sides of a quadrangle. Sometimes entry is through an arched doorway to a paved or cobbled courtyard area. During the First World War, French farmers were not only paid for billeting Allied troops, but for any food they provided like eggs, milk or fresh vegetables. They were also compensated for anything 'used' or stolen by the troops during their stay. Nulla mentions a number of times how French farmers would claim inflated losses:

> Our billet tonight is a disused pigsty, so we 'rat' a lot of
> hay from a shed to sleep on. The old podgy Froggie farmer
> pretends not to see us taking the hay. We remark upon this,
> but a wise-head tells us, 'He sees all right, the lousy cow, but
> he won't complain for fear that we'll be made [to] put it back.
> He'll wait till we're moving out tomorrow and then kick up a
> shindy and get paid for three times the amount we've used.
> All these Frogs do that.' [pp. 40–41]

These claims were rarely contested or disputed by the Allied authorities, but paid for through the Anglo-French compensation system.

Thanks to an especially wet autumn, the battlefields and trenches had turned to slimy mud, slowing down the Somme offensive. The Allies were held back by logistical problems, too. Late in October 1916, the vital Mametz–Fricourt road was forced to close because heavy military traffic had badly damaged it. Surrounding roads were blocked, too, and much-needed supplies could not get to the front. Those left waiting on the roads were enticing targets for German artillery or air attack. Ambulances took hours to travel a few miles, men died in need of medical help and there were fears that the troops on the frontline might run out of food. As a consequence, repairing the roads became a first priority, for without roads to deliver supplies to the front, the men there would have no chance of rebuilding the frontline trenches.

At Longueval in early November, an attack by a number of battalions even looked in jeopardy because of transport problems. Because the men had been constantly removing the mud from the trenches, they had become too deep to perform the usual 'hop-over', so scaling ladders, which the troops would use to climb out of the trenches, were needed before the attack could take place. But as the time of the attack drew near, few ladders had made their way to the front. Field ambulance horses and sledges designed to take the wounded from the battlefield had to be requisitioned to fetch them. Such a small thing as 600 scaling ladders could ruin the timing of an attack, costing lives.

The main Australian operational area was around Flers, to the east of Pozières and just south of Gueudecourt; a number of futile attacks around Flers were launched in November, but as winter approached, the offensive was halted. On 18 November, the Battle of the Somme came to an end. The Germans fell back from Verdun, thanks to successful French counter-offensives. Both the French and the Germans had appalling casualties at Verdun, but in the end this frightful battle had achieved very little for either side. French casualties alone numbered 377,000 men, while British casualties on the Somme numbered some 432,000. The Germans had an estimated 567,000 casualties on the two fronts and, in most places, the frontlines had changed very little.

The men of the 45th Battalion were active in their patrolling at night, but the German artillery was alert to this. Their unit history says that on 27 November 1916, one officer and seven men were killed and one officer and 28 men of other ranks were wounded – a lot of good men. After this time in the line near Gueudecourt, they moved back to New Carlton camp near Bazentin, 10 kilometres behind the line. The 45th then established themselves at Flesselles, north of Amiens, where they enjoyed Christmas and were granted leave to visit the city. Though far from the warmth of an Australian summer, the men of the 45th Battalion enjoyed a quiet Christmas behind the lines. The men's ordinary food ration was supplemented 'by the purchase of certain delicacies', according to the battalion history, and each man received a parcel from the battalion Comforts Fund, including a pipe and tobacco, cigarettes, socks and sweets. The battalion history goes on to say: 'These simple gifts had a special significance to soldiers fighting thousands of miles away from their own folk and they were valued because they were packed with loving care and the best of good wishes.'[1]

In Australia, the hot, dry summer was in great contrast to the northern winter. Christmas for many families was a sombre affair with celebrations and the usual ceremony far from their minds. Of more concern were their menfolk, how they were faring; if indeed they were still alive. On 1 January 1917, daylight saving was introduced under Common-wealth legislation as a wartime fuel-saving measure which, due to wartime emergency regulations, was binding on all the states.

In early January 1917, the 45th Battalion were met by their reinforcements, including Private Lynch, and marched to Dernancourt. There, Nulla and his mates are like visitors at first, inspecting 'souvenirs' in chalky old trenches, seeing their first dead man, wandering off to look at an anti-aircraft battery, before they 'make off for fresh excitement'. Nulla watches the firing of the big guns and speaks to the gunners about their targets. The gunners explain that each gun, when not firing on a specific target, is ranged on the Australian SOS line – an area in front of the Australian frontline in no-man's-land and extending back into the German positions. Should there be a surprise attack upon the Australian line, the defending troops would fire a coloured flare or series of coded flares so that the guns, already registered on the likely area of attack, could be quickly brought into action. The Germans did the same and many times in *Somme Mud* we read of German SOS flares being fired once any disturbance was detected from the Australian front.

For Nulla and his mates, it is only when they see the first casualties come in, 'the mud-stained, blood-sodden bandages and the frail white faces', that reality begins to sink in. But there is no time for pondering: that afternoon they move off for the frontline.

Moving towards the front 'through absolutely unbelievable conditions', Nulla passes through Bernafay Wood:

> On either side stretches a quagmire, a solid sea of slimy mud.
> The roads are few and narrow and only distinguished from the
> surrounding shell-ploughed mud by an unbroken edging of
> smashed motor cars, ambulances, guns, ammunition limbers
> and dead horses and mules. [p. 43]

Bernafay Wood had been a British objective in the July 1916 offensive and was the scene of savage fighting. The Germans had set up well-sited machine-gun positions in the shattered wood and inflicted high casualties on the advancing British, but the wood was captured on 4 July. Today this wood, as with others in the immediate area like Delville Wood, Trones Wood and High Wood, shows the scars of the heavy shelling and fighting during the First World War.

This is the same across many of the old battlefield areas of France and Belgium. After the war, the trees grew back, creating woodlands once more, but nobody cleaned up the area and filled in the shell-holes. And so today, once you walk into the tree line, the ground is rough and churned up and both the trench-lines and the shell-holes are clearly visible, though overgrown with blackberry bushes and other weeds. The boundaries, however, remain virtually the same as they were for hundreds of years before 1914.

The men press on. Nulla notes that bogged vehicles are being dug out and 'patches of corduroy are being placed over the worst places' in the road, referring to the common practice during the First World War of laying down logs side by side to make a roadway. The existing roads had not been built to take the enormous amount of traffic and the heavy weight of gun limbers (carts for guns and ammunition) and supply wagons. They were farm tracks or narrow country laneways between villages, unsealed and with no firm foundation or base. For the men stumbling forward, they were now covered in slippery logs or lengths of sawn timber; broken, irregular and hazardous underfoot. Men slipped and twisted their ankles, slid between the logs or stumbled on exposed roots covered by a layer of sticky mud.

Because of the accuracy of the German artillery, these roads were continually under fire, so that the sides of the road were littered with upturned wagons, dead horses, smashed timber and the stores and supplies that had been spilt from shell-shattered wagons. Among this debris would have been the bodies of men and horses, mud-splattered and bloated and left where they had fallen.

Nulla trudges through mud, lies in the mud in the rain with the other men for over an hour and then, when darkness falls, files on towards the frontline. He and his mates want to shelter from enemy shelling while the experienced soldiers, who have 'been through Gallipoli, Fleurbaix and Pozières', seem to barely heed it. The young reinforcements do their best to hide their fear. And then comes the 'strangled scream and the rushing air of an approaching shell' and Nulla witnesses his first death in battle, before he has even made it to the frontline.

> With a mighty roar the shell explodes spouting flame and
> phosphorus fumes everywhere. Mud is showered over
> everyone as pieces of shell fly over our prone bodies. A man
> five feet ahead of me is sobbing – queer, panting, gasping sobs.
> He bends his head towards his stomach just twice and is
> still . . . We've had our baptism of fire, seen our first man
> killed, right amongst us, and hurry on before another shell
> comes. [p. 44]

Finally they reach the front. We know from the battalion history that, just as in *Somme Mud*, at the frontline the 45th Battalion took over the 46th Battalion's trenches – Grease Trench and Goodwin's Trench – where the men were up to their knees in mud. These trenches were part of a complex of trenches including Lard Trench, Petrol Lane, Whale Trench and Oily Lane, near Gueudecourt to the northeast of Pozières. Trenches were given names in various ways. Sometimes it was after an officer who commanded a section of trench or ordered it be dug. At other times a theme was used, such as the trench system northwest of Gueudecourt, which was named after various grain crops. Hence you have Barley, Wheat and Malt Trench. Sometimes places were named after popular landmarks such as Hyde Park Corner and Piccadilly in Ploegsteert Wood, and Collins Street in Gueudecourt.

Gueudecourt was the scene of heavy fighting for the Australians and the 45th Battalion until early April, when they moved north to Bullecourt. The British front at this time was trying to continue the push in a northeasterly direction and Dominion forces were everywhere in this part of the line. The South Africans had suffered badly at Delville Wood just to the south and the New Zealanders had a similarly costly experience at nearby Longueval.

Gueudecourt is today a typically sleepy French village surrounded by green fields and quaint little farms. One place easily identified on the outskirts of the village is Fritz's Folly, which still remains a sunken road. The stark black and white photographs of Fritz's Folly show a desolate landscape bare of trees, but you can make out the snaking lane and the high ground occupied by the Germans a kilometre in the rear.

Also near Gueudecourt is what is known on the trench maps of the time as 'Cheese Road'. This too is a sunken road which starts a kilometre out of the village near the AIF Burial Ground, Grass Lane. This cemetery was in dead ground, well out of sight of German artillery observers, and was the location of an Australian Field Dressing station in 1916 and 1917. Men who died while receiving treatment were buried there. Naturally there are a number of men from the 45th Battalion interred there, such as Private Walter Leo Lussick, a New Zealand-born member of the battalion who died aged 20 on 19 January 1917. Like Private Lynch, he had enlisted in Bathurst in February 1916 and had arrived in the third reinforcement of the battalion.

Nearby are the graves of two other 45th Battalion soldiers who died on the same day – 6 August 1916 – fighting near Pozières. The first is of another Bathurst boy, Spencer John Letcher, an apprentice painter. He had enlisted in October 1915 and had sailed as part of a reinforcement for the newly formed 45th Battalion then in camp at Tel-el-Kebir in Egypt. From there he had sailed on the *Kinfauns Castle* to Marseilles, arriving in early June 1916 and, like so many others, took the train north to the battlefields. After his death, his personal effects were sent to his father and comprised '2 wallets, belt, note book, cigarette case, letters, gospel, tracts'.

In the same cemetery is the grave of Lance Corporal John Stewart Mulholland, aged 33, who was also killed in action on 6 August 1917. He was born in New Zealand, landed at Gallipoli five days after the initial landing and also sailed to Marseilles on the *Kinfauns Castle*. He was killed during the fighting around Flers and Gueudecourt in early 1917.

Private Lynch's luck held and his war continued. On his first night in the line in Grease Trench, his character Nulla experiences the German heavy mortars known as *minenwerfers* ('mine throwers') as they bombard the trench, making the ground shake. These weapons came in a range of calibres, but the most common was the 'light' *minenwerfer*, which fired a 7.6-centimetre-calibre explosive-filled projectile weighing 4.5 kilograms. It had a range of up to 1,300 metres but was very effective in close trench fighting because it could send a projectile high into the air so that it dropped on the Allies' line only 300 metres away, demolishing a section of trench. Though they were heavy and difficult to handle in muddy conditions, they were used extensively from the beginning of the war. At the armistice, there were 10,000 still in service.

While the Germans had developed the *minenwerfers* before the outbreak of the war, the British were slow to introduce an equivalent. The British engineer Wilfred Scott-Stokes set to work designing a 3-inch mortar, however, the first Stokes mortar did not see active service until September 1916.

While in the frontline at Grease Trench, Private Lynch was part of a wiring party sent out at night to strengthen the barbed wire defences in front of their position. This involved screwing in iron pickets, twisted iron stakes (also known as a 'screw picket') to act as a post onto which the wire was secured. This was dangerous work in no-man's-land in front of the Australian trenches and close to the German frontline. As Nulla tells us:

No one speaks as everyone knows that half a dozen
machine-guns are on the enemy parapet just a hundred yards
away. Quietly out, our footsteps sound like thunder to our
excited minds. [p. 45]

At this time, screw pickets were made in Sweden and the
company supplied both the German and Allied armies. Today
in France and Belgium, you can still see First World War screw
pickets being used by farmers to hold up fences to keep in
their cows. You can also find them dumped with other rusty
war detritus.

As Nulla recounts, his half hour with the wiring party and
coming under fire did more to accustom him to the frontline
than a week standing in the mud. He and his mates had been
blooded. They were not quite the same fresh-faced, carefree
larrikins who steamed across from Australia on the *Wiltshire*.
We can only imagine that Private Lynch, like so many
Australian soldiers, experienced a similar dramatic change on
entering the frontline.

For almost the next three years, Lynch would go through a
cycle of spending a few days in the frontline, or in support or
reserve lines, then being marched out to a rest area for a spell
or to a hospital for treatment of his wounds, only to then
return to the frontline to face death and the horrors of battle
once again. Just like his narrator, Nulla, Private Lynch's war
was to centre for months on a small area no bigger than 10 or
12 kilometres by about 6 kilometres across; from
Gueudecourt in the north, to the divisional baths in Fricourt

further south. From early January until the move north in April 1917, he was never far from the sounds of war and, for most of this time, within artillery range of the heavier German guns.

# THREE

# Holding the Line

The winter of 1916–17 was the worst in living memory, and the snow and icy conditions were something totally new to the Australians. The earth froze for a time and, while this was easier to deal with than mud in terms of moving troops and supplies, it increased the risk of hypothermia for the men and made attacks impossible. Weapons and machinery froze because oil could no longer lubricate them; guns did not fire. Men took to loaves of bread with axes and slept in their boots, as they would be unable to pull them on in the morning because they would be frozen and brittle. The earth was rock hard, impossible to dig into.

The weather slowed operations and the mounting of offensives would have to wait until the spring thaw. The war had become one of survival against the elements more than the Germans. In Egypt, the British were preparing to push into the Sinai Peninsula to clear out Turkish forces before their planned invasion of Palestine, which had Jerusalem as its ultimate objective. In Mesopotamia, British forces were pushing towards Baghdad. On the Western Front, the Australian divisions were concentrated in a 5-kilometre front in an arc around Gueudecourt.

Lynch's first experience of the frontline had lasted an exhausting eight days, and following three weeks' rest at Mametz Camp, he returned with his battalion to the trenches near Gueudecourt. On 8 February they moved into the support positions in Gap and Switch Trench and relieved the 14th Battalion. Eight days later, they moved forward into the reserve trenches at Pilgrims Way, before moving into the frontline at Stormy Trench on 17 February.

It is in the village of Bazentin – by now just a 'pulverised brickyard' – that *Somme Mud* picks up the story. That night it starts to rain and, weighed down by heavy greatcoats, equipment, rations, ammunition and a wet blanket each, they march to the line. Nulla mentions that the guide who is to lead them to their positions calls to them when they reach 'the sunken road'. Sunken roads, which are still common in this area, are roadways that have, as a result of constant use over a long period, cut themselves into the landscape and hence appear 'sunken'. They may be a metre or more beneath the level of the surrounding countryside, often with steeply angled sides. Within the deeper sunken roads, men were able to burrow into the sides and make temporary shelters. Battalion headquarters, always somewhere just behind the frontline, were often situated in the protection of a sunken road, along with support units such as field kitchens, first aid posts and communication centres. Today they are popular with military archaeologists who, with the aid of metal detectors, often find interesting war relics in and around them. Many sunken roads have been widened to allow two lanes of traffic and their profile is very different from what it would have been in 1917.

Naturally, changeovers were done at night, but any sound quickly summoned an enemy barrage on the frontline and the support trenches, risking the lives of double the usual number of men, as one battalion left and the new one came in to replace them. If German intelligence received word of troop movements in and out, they became an attractive target for the gunners – men massing in narrow, unprotected trenches, with nowhere to run.

Nulla and the other men climb up out of the sunken road and walk across the mud to their guide, who is waiting for them in Eve Alley, a communication trench leading to the frontline. The trenches around Gueudecourt were in very poor condition, especially Eve Alley. The mud there was knee deep and the men preferred to walk in the open above the trench, exposing themselves to enemy fire, rather than struggle through the mud and become exhausted. Nulla himself does this, risking the German machine-gunners and snipers about 200 metres away. Conditions in the reserve lines were no better. According to Charles Bean, Gap and Switch Trenches, near Gueudecourt, were 'merely an open muddy drain in which men suffered almost as severely as in the frontline'.[2] Looking at the open, undulating countryside today, so windblown and exposed, it is clear the men had little protection from the elements and it is easy to imagine how terribly cold they must have been.

This part of the frontline had been so heavily shelled that long sections of trench had been obliterated. Soldiers were manning shell craters and short sections of trench and there were gaps between their isolated posts. There was a large gap in the line between Lynch's 45th Battalion and the 48th Battalion some 100 metres away and this gap needed to be patrolled regularly during the night, with men from each battalion taking turns to make the dangerous trip between outposts.

One can imagine the fear of a man having to sneak out alone and make his way across 100 metres of muddy, shell-blasted battlefield at night with nothing to guide him but his sense of direction and rat-cunning. There were no landmarks in this flat, desolate landscape, no hills or even trees to act as reference points, just a trust in your sense of direction and a lot of courage. You were on your own. In the blackness, somewhere over there, you would have to find the Australian frontline, knowing that the men there were silent and alert, staring into no-man's-land, ever vigilant in case of a surprise attack. The chance of a nervous or trigger-happy sentry firing on you would prey on your mind, especially as you needed to crawl close to the Australian position before whispering the password, so that the Germans, a short distance away across no-man's-land, could not hear.

Over 100 metres, if a man strayed off course by only a few

degrees, he could suddenly find himself in the enemy's trench or caught in their wire. As trenches were built and destroyed, saps were pushed forward and trenches weaved and twisted in all directions, it was very easy to take a wrong turn. Later in this chapter, Nulla's mate Yacob makes himself very unpopular both with the men and his officers when he nearly guides the relief troops into the enemy line – and from what history tells us about the trenches around Gueudecourt, particularly the nearby area of the 'Maze', this was easily done.

Nulla knows the danger involved in doing the first patrol, but is 'prompted more by nervousness than anything else'. He likens it to the nervousness descending over a batting side in a game of cricket, before the wickets begin to fall. It is a simple comparison that highlights the limited experiences of a 19-year-old. As he leaves he is warned about wandering too far and getting lost, because two nights before a man disappeared on a similar patrol. Had the man wandered into the German lines and been captured? No one had heard a shot. Had he been silently garrotted or stabbed somewhere out there in the darkness, bleeding and dying alone, his body sinking into the seemingly bottomless mud of a shell-hole, lost forever? How would his mother ever find his grave in a place like this?

Fortunately for Nulla, he doesn't allow this fear to be augmented by the story told by the 48th Battalion men that the Germans had a secret and silent killing weapon; a bow that fired steel arrows carrying an electric current. The tale went that it was this weapon that probably 'got the cove on Friday night'. Nulla seems, however, to have picked this for what it was – a joke for new men in the line. There would have been many new men who were not as educated or astute as Nulla, who would have believed this tale and worried unnecessarily about it.

Nulla does have a truly frightening experience on his first lone patrol, however, and must wonder for a moment whether he is about to disappear, just like that other Australian the night before. He is confronted by two Germans, lying in wait in a shell-hole. As flares light the sky, they appear to fly straight for him. He bounds sideways out of their line of attack, and as the flare dies so the Germans disappear back into the jagged landscape. Then, another flare and there they are, not 3 metres away, staring at him – dead. As Nulla puts it, 'No six live Fritz have ever given me the awful turn those two dead ones did.' [p. 52]

Lynch evokes the surreal nature of the battlefield at night, a time when imaginary danger can be even more terrifying than the real. Nulla needs his mates; sick from fear, he hurries to the trench. Over the course of *Somme Mud*, it becomes ever clearer to the reader just how crucial mateship was to the Australian war effort, and here Nulla says of the trench, 'It's not its protection so much as its companionship I seek . . . At last I'm back with my mates.' [p. 52]

Undaunted, Nulla is soon volunteering again, this time to replace a runner who had to be evacuated. Radio communication would not arrive on the battlefield until

1918. Until then, the most efficient way to communicate was by field telephone, but the telephone lines were easily damaged during bombardments. More often than not, a man had to run with a message between the forward areas and the headquarters at the rear, or between units spread along the line. The runner took messages between officers and NCOs, sent reports back to headquarters and delivered requests for supplies and ammunition. (In the absence of a working telephone line, artillery bombardments were ordered not by runners but by the firing of coded signal flares in the air.) Runners also acted as guides, leading incoming units through the maze of trenches and over the blasted ground to their forward positions, leading exhausted units out of the line to the rear, or leading men carrying supplies.

On his first mission as a runner, Nulla is ordered to go down the trench and tell the men to prepare for rifle inspection in half an hour. He notes the casual attitude of his fellow men, some of whom have useless rifles caked with mud, others with their mechanisms frozen even though non-freezing oil has been issued. Some men would keep their rifles wrapped in protective material, and would therefore have 'yards of blanket to unwind before they can use [them]'. 'We're a pretty casual sort of army all right,' says Nulla, and continues:

> The battalion has never lost a position to the enemy and much
> of their worth lies in this casual-going attitude. They'll stand

amidst a tornado of screaming, crashing death and pump
bullets into an enemy attack . . . with the same casual air that
they'll chuck, or fail to chuck, an off-handed salute to the
British staff officers on the Strand. [p. 55]

The Australians' casual attitude may also partly explain the
trench humour that Nulla finds hard to become accustomed
to. Though every effort was made to bury the dead where they
fell, bodies were often disinterred by shellfire and their
remains scattered. Some killed in attacks lay where they were
hit, especially if they fell between the lines, like some
Australians who died at Fromelles who were not recovered
until 1919. Nulla is aghast when he sees a dead man's hand –
'bleached white from exposure to the weather' – protruding
from the side of the trench. No one knows whose hand it was.
He speculates, 'Maybe a musician, a Fritz, as the trench had
lately been captured . . . Poor beggar!' [pp. 57–58] The hand
has been used as an ashtray and a small cardboard sign reading
'Gib it bacca, boss' hangs from it by a piece of string. To young
Nulla – and indeed, to us readers – it seems callous, but a
corporal explains that humour is a survival technique for the
seasoned soldiers. He advises Nulla that the best way to cope
is to 'give up thinking too much' and to 'treat danger as a
humorous episode'. Nulla seems to heed at least the latter
advice, as he and his mates do come to see the lighter side of
grim situations.

There are abundant wartime stories similar to the one
about the fun being had with the unknown soldier's hand,

and such things were common occurrences. Charles Bean mentions that troops were helped by looking upon hard times as a joke, and by dismissing and covering their inner feelings with wittiness and hilarity. There is much evidence of this tendency in their letters home, in poems and diaries and even in official dispatches and reports.

Nulla's next job as a runner is to guide into the line men carrying supplies designed to help the battalion cope with the cold, muddy conditions: sheepskin gloves and whale oil. By mid-January 1917, the snow had turned the battlefield into deep, clinging mud. Trench walls collapsed and the trench bottom was deep in mud, which went up to men's knees. Men tried to get some sleep standing with their backs against the wet, muddy trench wall but they would simply slide into the mud as soon as they nodded off. Just as Lynch describes in *Somme Mud*, some men would spread a blanket, hoping that this would keep them out of the mud, but their weight would soon cause it to sink and they were left with a cold, muddy blanket to keep them warm.

It was the depths of winter and the clinging mud was as cold as ice. This caused hypothermia, which itself sent many men to hospital; with the continual exposure of the men's feet to moisture, it also led to the dreaded 'trench foot'. This was a form of frostbite and was caused by bad circulation in the legs and feet due to the cold and damp. It was exacerbated by the men's tight boots and puttees. As with hypothermia, blood from the heart ceases to flow to these frozen extremities, the limbs freeze solid and frostbite begins to set in. Hands and ears could also become frostbitten, but this was far less common as they were clear of the mud and the men could cover them or rub them to keep the circulation going.

It was impossible to keep their feet out of the icy mud, though, so their circulation was reduced and if they did not receive treatment, gangrene would develop. Their feet would go black and the tissue would die. Nulla describes how 'huge water blisters appear and when these burst, a painful raw sore is left . . . men . . . endure great agony, can't stand and must be sent out of the line to have their feet amputated' [p. 56]. The problem was endemic to the Western Front and Bean noted on a tour in the frontline during the 1916–17 winter that 'practically all the men in many Australian battalions were suffering from trench feet at least in its incipient stages'.[2]

Attempts were made to prevent trench foot by encouraging the men to regularly massage whale oil into the skin of their feet and then put their boots back on, unlaced at the top. Instead of winding puttees tightly around their legs from the tops of their boots to below the knee, they were to wind sand-bags loosely around their legs, to allow blood to circulate more freely. You can imagine how hard it would have been to put this advice into practice. Standing in a cramped trench, you would have to take one boot off while balancing on the other foot sunk deep in mud, then clean, dry and rub whale oil – which Nulla says has 'an awful smell like nothing we've smelt before' – into your foot. Then you would need to put on a clean, dry sock – not such an easy thing to find – and struggle to get your boot back on again, only to sink it straight back down into the mud. The officers who gave such instructions had little knowledge of conditions in a frontline trench and they compounded their ignorance by threatening military discipline on men who got trench foot. They ignorantly believed that it was a self-inflicted wound that should be punished harshly.

In an effort to keep the AIF warm, men were also issued with a pair of Australian sheepskin gloves with the wool inside and a long cord that passed around the neck to join the gloves together and prevent them getting lost. Though it is not mentioned in *Somme Mud*, woollen sheepskin vests were also distributed to men on the Western Front.

These sheepskin gloves and woollen vests were greatly appreciated by the men freezing in the frontline. At this stage of the war, the cold weather and mud were causing more casualties than the Germans. This, of course, required stretcher-bearers to carry them out, but carrying stretcher cases in deep mud was an exhausting and near impossible task in itself. Normally it took two men to carry a stretcher, but here you needed 10 or 12, who, after 50 metres, needed to be relieved. To get a soldier with trench foot to the rear, just 4 kilometres or so away, took 12 hours and many relay teams. There were cases of men with trench foot crawling back to aid posts to allow valuable stretchers to be used for wounded men more in need than themselves. However, casualty clearing stations were often exposed to the weather, so were wet and freezing and provided little shelter, comfort or any real relief for the wounded and sick.

After four nights and days, only half of Nulla's company remains holding the line. Even his corporal has been carried out with trench foot, and so Nulla is taken off runner duties and put in charge of his old post. A young and inexperienced soldier – albeit one who has already displayed courage and dependability – now finds himself commanding his fellow men. Similar scenes to this were being played out across the front as Australian battalions became severely depleted through illness. Soon after being told to take charge, Nulla is put to the test.

On 16 January 1917, while in the front line near Gueudecourt, the 45th Battalion was attacked by a German raiding party of approximately 50 men. The battalion diary states:

> At 3 a.m., a raiding party of about 50 or 60 raided our trench at [grid reference given]. This party was repulsed suffering four OR's ['other ranks', meaning gunners, privates, drivers or sappers] killed and a number wounded. Our casualties as a result of the raid nil.[3]

Nulla makes mention of this raid in *Somme Mud*:

> Suddenly the stillness of the night is broken by a whispered 'stand to' passed down the trench . . . Men scramble up and line the parapet, eyes peering into the darkness ahead. [p. 62]

Later, we are told by Nulla:

> The prisoners say about fifty men attempted the raid and that
> very few escaped unwounded, but most of the wounded
> crawled back to their own trench. [p. 65]

This is a typical case of an incident report being written up in the battalion history and then included in the narrative of *Somme Mud*, providing the historical accuracy that is evident throughout the book.

# FOUR

# Making Back from the Line

In the First World War, killing was very efficient, very accurate and very destructive. Although there were failings in the Allies' operations, overall tactics had improved since the battles of the nineteenth century, as had weaponry, uniforms and equipment, systems for resupplying the front, medical services and communications.

Many people imagine that soldiers during the First World War faced danger only when they were close to the frontline, but the reality was entirely different. First World War artillery had a range that extended well into reserve areas behind the front and into what might have been considered safe billets in the rear. Even a small artillery piece could fire 20 shells a minute at a range of 5 or 6 kilometres. The range of German and Allied artillery was such that generally anyone within 20 kilometres of the front was in danger, but the German 'Amiens gun', captured by the Australians in August 1918, was able to shell the city of Amiens from 25 kilometres away. Any place that personnel were likely to be found was targeted: crossroads and junctions, supply lines, towns, observation posts and high ground, known artillery positions, troop concentration areas including forming-up points and start lines, headquarters and cookhouses. With accurate range-finding and communication, artillery could follow and attack single vehicles and trenches in the support lines, or even hunt individual men.

A notable, tragic case of this came later in the war, on 31 May 1918, when the Germans shelled the rest area in the small village of Allonville, just north of Amiens. The Germans had learnt from Australian prisoners that the village contained a Divisional Headquarters, a training area and a rest area. At 1 a.m., they fired on the village from 10 kilometres and, with the aid of an aircraft to pinpoint the exact range, succeeded in landing shells on two barns where members of the 14th Battalion were sleeping, killing a total of 18 men and wounding a further 68.

As men left the frontline, they knew they were in danger, with the ever-present risk they might draw fire from German artillery and snipers, or from German aircraft. Exhaustion and cold, shell shock, minor wounds and fear went with the men, their faces hollow and bearded, their clothes often shredded, muddy and bloodstained. Staggering back to rest areas and billets, they at last had the chance to bath, repair and clean their weapons and sleep in warm beds. This was the cycle of war.

Getting back out of the line was as dangerous as coming in. It was always carried out at night, in the pitch black. When the 45th is finally relieved on the frontline near Gueudecourt and head back to the support line, Nulla and his mates Yacob and Dark are separated from the rest of their battalion – Nulla and Dark because they have been given jobs to do, but Yacob because he has been detained for nearly leading the relief into the enemy's line.

They try to save time by making their way back to their battalion across open ground. Suddenly, however, the night is shattered by a series of shells, randomly fired onto likely targets, so they seek shelter in a sunken road. They make for a deep underground shelter, probably constructed by the Germans when this part of the line was in enemy hands. Fifty feet below ground, men could warm up, wounds could be treated and they could grab a little sleep.

But for Nulla and company, there is no room at the inn. After seven nights standing up in a frontline trench, catching only a little sleep, they are exhausted and soon fall asleep on the top step at the entrance of the dugout, with no shelter from the freezing conditions. When they wake the following morning, 'cramped and shivering', they are covered in 15 centimetres of snow which fills every crease in their uniforms and completely covers their rifles and other equipment.

Around them, the landscape has taken on a new and unfamiliar look as many Australians would not have seen snow before, except perhaps the Gallipoli veterans, who had suffered on the peninsula with the snowfalls in November 1915. Snow now covered the pitted, shell-smashed ground, the bodies of the dead, the duckboards and tracks – making the trip to the rear even more difficult. And it also made men and movement in the white landscape far more visible. Far out across no-man's-land, German eyes on higher ground would be scouring not only the frontline trenches, but also the rear area for any movement whatsoever and any tell-tale sign of men, equipment or stores.

Normally, men only tried to make it back from the frontline under cover of night, but as the sun is only now beginning to rise and snow is falling again, reducing visibility, Nulla and his mates set out across the open ground, safe in the belief they cannot be seen by the ever-watchful Germans.

First, they come upon some officers' gear that has been left unattended and collect a bundle of clean, dry blankets that have been rolled and tied with pack straps, 'the work of some neat batmen', or officers' servants. Nulla even swaps his muddy rifle for a clean one.

Weighed down with their bounty of fresh blankets hidden under a greatcoat, they set off, but the sun suddenly breaks through and they are caught in the open. They are now even more visible: clear black, moving specks in the vastness of the dazzling white landscape. At that very moment, probably half a kilometre away, a German *minenwerfer* crew receives their coordinates and races to fire their weapons. Seconds later, three whiz-bangs (shells) crash 20 metres behind the three men, frighteningly accurate for a first salvo.

'Swing to the right,' calls Dark, a smart move, for the Germans would have quickly corrected their range, added the 20 metres plus a further 20, hoping to land their next shell on the running men. Sure enough, three more shells land exactly where they would have been had they not made their right turn. Running on, the men would have been very obvious to German forward observers, who would have signalled to their own men the Australians' position, allowing the quick re-registering of the German mortars and the change in the type of ammunition they were firing.

> *Cr-up!* and a big shrapnel bursts high up just to our right and we see the mud and snow kick up in fifty places where the deadly pellets drive into the ground. [p. 74]

Shrapnel was greatly feared by men in the open. It had been invented in 1784 by a British Royal Artillery officer, Lieutenant Henry Shrapnel, who took the existing technologies of canister shot or grapeshot to a new level. Grapeshot comprised multiple iron balls that were fired by a cannon; in canister shot, smaller lead balls were encased in metal, which burst open when fired. Shrapnel's innovation was to place lead shot in a shell casing along with a crude timing device that allowed the shell to explode much further away, increasing the range from about 300 to 1,100 metres.

Shrapnel was used extensively by the Duke of Wellington against Napoleon's troops in the Battle of Waterloo in 1815. The German armament manufacturer Krupp further developed it by incorporating.TNT, but the use of shrapnel in the First World War was limited, because it was ineffective against men in trenches and with overhead cover. It was also ineffective against barbed wire, as seen in the Somme offensive in July 1916, when even after intensive use of shrapnel, the German wire was left intact. But for men in the open and unprotected, it was deadly.

In response to the air-bursting shrapnel, Nulla and his mates change tactics. They run an erratic, zigzag course and spread out to make the gunners' task more difficult and head towards some old trenches. By doing this, only one life is risked with each shell, rather than three. The Germans target first one man, then another. At the sound of an incoming shell, the targeted man flings himself to the ground, hoping the explosion will not kill him outright and that he can get low enough to the ground to avoid the flying shrapnel balls and shards of metal from the exploding shell. The other two slacken their pace until they know the man is not wounded and can get up and run on. These small acts of bravery in very dangerous conditions were common among the men in the line. A fellow Australian rarely left a wounded man behind, even if his own life was endangered.

Stories like this abound, such as that of Corporal Fred Nicholson, a Gallipoli veteran and an orchardist from Hobart. He was one of a party of 14 men of the 12th Battalion bringing forward rations when his group crossed their own frontline and found themselves on the enemy parapet. Dropping the rations, they ran back, but two men were killed and two fell wounded. Corporal Nicholson went back for one of the wounded, but was killed himself in his selfless attempt to save a mate. His grave is at Bulls Road Military Cemetery, Flers.

Nulla and his mates, though, are lucky. They find their way to the shelter of the old trenches and, from there, back to their battalion on the support line. The purpose of the support line was to provide reinforcements if a German attack on the Australian frontline trenches broke through. The frontline was connected to the support trenches with communications trenches, which zigzagged to make it harder for enemy infantry to fire on them or for enemy aircraft to strafe a line of troops in them. Troops used angles and bends in trenches to build 'blocks', barricades where men could defend the trench while still being afforded some protection.

Reaching the support line, Nulla and his mates' minds are on food and at the end of the trench the cooks have prepared plenty of hot Maconochie rations – a soup-like stew made from canned meat, gravy and small pieces of vegetables such as carrots.

Hot food was very important during the terrible winter of 1916–17, both for the strength of the men and for their morale. Battalion cookhouses were set up as close to the frontline as possible, so hot food could be taken forward in insulated containers to men occupying even the most forward positions, but in many cases the food was cold by the time it got to the men.

It was very difficult to carry containers of food over terrain churned up by shelling or covered in mud, snow or ice and then along narrow, clogged and broken-down muddy trenches. Sometimes it was impossible, in which case the men had to make do with their cold rations. These consisted of canned meat known as 'bully beef', hard biscuits and possibly cheese or jam. When they could get bacon, it was popular on bread or a biscuit. The Maconochie rations were famous for their tendency to induce severe flatulence and for their disgusting taste, especially when cold.

To wash down these indigestible meals, the men drank tea from a mess tin or dixie. Hot tea was sent to the front in drums, but often it was cold by the time it got there and tasted like the petrol the drum had once held. The tainted brew forced a difficult choice on men: refuse the tea and freeze, or drink the tea and vomit. Bean mentions tea that so reeked of petrol the men dared not light a cigarette for fear of it exploding, so bad was the taste. To compound this, cooks collected ice from shell-holes and boiled it for making tea and for cooking, probably believing that boiling the water would kill any germs, but these shell-holes often contained dead horses and men and other detritus of war, so it was an unhealthy practice that led to disease and infection.

After their breakfast, Nulla and his mates seek a dugout or 'funk hole', an alcove cut in the side of the trench as somewhere to sleep. After a week on the line with virtually no sleep, their respite is a cold, wet, muddy hole only 1.5 metres square. They do their best to make it comfortable – 'arranging the interior decorations' – and even see themselves as fortunate compared to the others because they at least have clean, new blankets. Crude shelters such as this gave men not far from the frontline some protection from the wind and snow and a chance to dry their wet, muddy clothes and sleep.

Before settling down, Dark and Nulla turn their underpants inside out in a futile effort to 'trick the chats', or lice. In his characteristic style, Nulla makes light of the lice problem: 'They've had a pretty fair run now, a whole week of undisturbed freedom in which to play and eat us.' [p. 77] But Lynch, like all the men on the Western Front, must have found them nearly intolerable. Lice caused severe itching, which created welts and lacerations, which in turn became infected and sore. Worse, lice caused trench fever, a debilitating flu-like illness contracted when louse faeces entered the bloodstream through a cut in the skin or a louse bite.

With lice a major concern for officers and medical authorities, soon after their arrival in France, the AIF had established divisional baths where men returning from the line could have a hot bath or shower and hand in their clothes and underwear to be disinfected. They were then issued with clean, vermin-free clothing. But visits to the divisional baths were few and far between. The efforts of the men to search for and kill lice in their clothing were a waste of time, but provided amusement during long spells of boredom and inactivity.

Another problem was rats. They grew fat on the bodies of the dead and then ran around through the trenches, over sleeping men, in their endless search for food. Rats spread disease, but there was little the men could do to curb their numbers, for they multiplied quickly and had an endless supply of rubbish and corpses to feed on. A favourite pastime for many men, and something that Nulla does mention, was to skewer a piece of food on the end of a bayonet and wait for a rat. Then, once they were blissfully enjoying their meal, to pull the trigger and send the splattered rat off into no-man's-land.

So the war was not only fought against the Germans. There were many other enemies to consider: the weather, disease, fatigue, poor living conditions, vermin and parasites, poor sanitation and, of course, the terrible Somme mud.

# FIVE

# In Support

The Germans held much of the high ground on the Somme. This was a major advantage, because it allowed them to more easily observe the Allies' positions. To counter this, the British regularly sent up observation planes and balloons to photograph and map the opposing lines and used the information to plot German artillery positions and subject them to accurate counter-battery fire. Many German guns were put out of action this way. The Germans were well aware of the value of this intelligence, and so were equally active in trying to destroy Allied observation planes and balloons. The British therefore massed fighter aircraft to protect the observers and continue the flow of vital information to Allied High Command. German aircraft, although more numerous, seldom flew deep behind the British front, restricting their activity to strafing the infantry in frontline and support trenches rather than seeking out and directing counter-battery fire onto the Allied gun emplacements.

This is what Nulla and his mates observe from their position in the support line – a British fighter plane protecting an observation plane from a German Taube. It is a kind of frightening entertainment that momentarily shifts their attention away from the messy, muddy ground war onto a different, yet just as deadly, kind of fighting. There is no talking, no joking, amongst the men as they watch the struggle, and as readers we can feel their relief when the Allied pilot sees off the enemy. He sweeps past and waves at the men on the ground, who are calling up and waving to congratulate and perhaps thank him for his efforts – a brief moment of contact between these two diverse but integral fighting forces.

And then, for the men, it is back to *their* war, a war of long days and nights in the cold mud. Though the winter had slowed down the fighting, there was still plenty of work for soldiers on the Western Front, as there was much infrastructure that needed to be built or repaired before the recommencement of hostilities in the northern spring. The lull in active fighting meant High Command could put the men to the urgent tasks of road building, repair and extension of light rail lines, and rebuilding trenches, underground shelters and lines of communication.

Ammunition had to be brought to the line, as did duckboards, to be laid on trench floors or muddy tracks. Nissen bow huts – prefabricated semi-circular steel structures that were designed as an alternative to tents – had to be erected in rear areas. By the end of the war, over 100,000 bow huts and

10,000 hospital huts had been built and these were seen as the leading hut technology.

Brigade camps, where men would rest and train when they were out of the line, also needed to be completed. Engineering units and labour battalions did some of this work, but 'fatigues', parties of men from the fighting battalions who were now in the support lines or rest areas, were also given this kind of work.

Nulla mentions that his platoon is sent out on a fatigue, a 'dangerous trip to Gueudecourt to gather up old iron'. The iron is no doubt to be recycled for use in the war effort: as the conflict drags into its third year, every resource the Allies can get their hands on is valuable. The reason Nulla describes this seemingly innocuous fatigue of picking up scrap metal as 'dangerous' is that the village of Gueudecourt was no more than a kilometre behind the frontline at this time and was being shelled by the Germans at a rate of one shell per minute, day and night. Later in *Somme Mud*, Nulla surmises that the reason for this intense shelling is that when the Germans retreated north, they left behind a large dump of shells in Gueudecourt and were trying to destroy them before the Allies got them. This may have been one of the many 'furphies' or rumours Lynch heard on the front, but the real aim was to prevent the town being used by the Allies as a billeting or staging area from which operations could be launched.

Nulla and his platoon make it back from their fatigue to the support line, and as the morning breaks they see a small party of men coming along the duckboard track from Delville

Wood. When fired upon with shells, the men instinctively run for the shelter of a disabled tank nearby, not knowing what Nulla and his mates know: that the Germans, realising men will do the obvious thing and seek shelter beside it, have the range of this tank accurately. As they hold the high ground south of Bapaume, it is also likely that the Germans can see men moving in this area.

Lynch vividly captures the randomness of the battlefield in a scene where several of the men are killed even though they run from the tank to the support trench, while one man who 'moves slowly, without a duck or a flinch' survives. Rather than rush to the relative safety of the trench like the rest, he stops to bend over one of his fallen mates to remove his personal belongings, no doubt to send home to his family. As shells burst around him, he slowly walks on, unscathed. 'The luck of the game,' Nulla concludes.

So much of the world Nulla finds himself in is random, devoid of reason. All the old certainties of life seem to have gone. One of the men injured on his way from the abandoned tank, who has serious wounds to his head and body, and a smashed arm, somehow survives, while another, with a single finger shot off, dies of shock on his stretcher. Nulla supposes it must all come down to a 'matter of constitution'.

In many instances, men were buried where they fell. Though their grave would have been crudely marked and a record possibly kept of its location, bodies were often turned over in the subsequent shelling of the area, blown apart and lost forever. Others might appear in a trench wall, such as the hand in the previous chapter and the top of a skull as described by Nulla in this chapter. Polished like a billiard ball, someone had written 'The Dome of St Paul's' and beneath it 'drawn a fine fat spider'. The spider, we are told, is 'to keep the flies away'. Typical trench humour, though it did of course disgust some men.

Today, all along the frontline are cemeteries; literally hundreds of them. The condition in which they are kept is remarkable thanks to the meticulous care of the staff of the Commonwealth War Graves Commission. The row upon row of standard white headstones are such a powerful and sad reminder of the war.

Back in Switch Trench, Nulla has just enough time for some warm bully beef stew when German shells crash along the frontline. Switch Trench had been part of a long German line that was now held by the Allies. Its western end intersected the Albert–Bapaume road above Pozières, just near the windmill, and the eastern end was near Péronne. Although smashed by shellfire, it provided a rear rest area with cookhouses, stores dumps, aid posts and company headquarters. And it was also a favoured target for the German artillery, who knew exactly where the trench-line ran – given they had built it – and had their guns ranged on it to the metre.

Under enemy shelling, the cosy, once protective hollows in the sides of trenches, not a metre below the surface, became a death trap for the Australians. Long sections of trench-line would be blown away and walls would collapse. Men were regularly buried, if not killed outright, by the explosions, flying fragments of metal, or concussion. The desperate calls for shovels or stretcher-bearers or, as Nulla recounts, of 'Dugout blown in!' were a chilling reality for men in this part of the support line. With shells landing randomly, remaining to dig to save a man's life must have taken exceptional courage.

Amidst the terrible shelling, in this chapter Lynch tells one of the most moving stories of mateship in all of *Somme Mud*. Scotty and Blue, both terribly wounded in the same part of the trench, think not of themselves but of each other. Blue, sodden with blood and 'dragging his shattered legs after him', tries to refuse help, telling the uninjured men to find Scotty. When they find Scotty, he has horrific injuries to his face – 'his top lip is slit clean back from his teeth' and 'blood is pouring from his face and filling his gas respirator bag'– yet he manages to ask after Blue. Throughout *Somme Mud* we are constantly reminded of the compassion and unselfishness of the diggers. Nulla, understanding these mates' bond, gently reassures Scotty about Blue's condition. '"Yes, got a Blighty. Coupla leg wounds," I lie to him . . .' The phrase 'got a Blighty' was widely used at the time, meaning that a man had received a wound not bad enough to kill him but to get him evacuated to Britain.

And indeed, it turns out that despite the horrific appearance of his injuries, the doctors believe Blue will live, though he will lose his left foot. It is a terrible price to pay, but seven of his fellow men have lost their lives. Carnage has now become so commonplace that Nulla and his mates crawl back into their dugout and shiver themselves to sleep.

# SIX

# Fallen Comrades

Once again in the support line, probably in Switch and Gap trenches, Nulla is confronted with the violence of war when he is sent out to salvage anything useful that can be recovered from former battlefields now well behind the Allied lines. This war *matériel* comprised weapons, ammunition, barbed wire, picks and shovels that littered the ground after the extensive fighting in 1916. Places such as Delville Wood, High Wood and the villages of Fricourt and Mametz had been viciously contested, won by the Allies, lost and then re-won.

Nulla's scavenging journey takes him via the Pozières chalk pit. This lay about 1.5 kilometres southeast of Pozières and was behind the German lines before the Somme offensive of July 1916. Once captured by the Allies, the chalk pit became an important storage and depot area, and was where the Australian medium and heavy trench mortars were located. The chalk pit and the road that ran through it were regularly shelled and men passing along it did so as fast as possible. Today the chalk pit is the site of the town's rubbish tip.

Nulla enters 'the back part' of Delville Wood, presumably the southern side, somewhere near where the South African National Memorial is today. The area had been the scene of savage fighting by British troops in early July 1916 and was a killing ground for the South Africans from 15 to 20 July 1916. It would have been a churned-up wasteland of shattered trees and abandoned military equipment as far as the eye could see, as in the typical black-and-white battlefield photographs we all know from the First World War. From the outskirts of Albert nearly to Bapaume, a distance of 19 kilometres, the landscape was totally devastated from the fighting that had raged for five months.

In the wood, Nulla comes upon a scene of slaughter and death, the undisturbed aftermath of a battle fought months before. He describes the slaughter of the men from both sides in what is a very detailed and rare depiction of the aftermath of battle and tells a frightful story of the life and death struggle that went on.

Just outside the wood, we come to a well-constructed trench. In it there's a British soldier to every yard, killed on the parapet in trying to hop-off. Twenty yards in front, a row of dead Tommies in perfect line as if on parade; NCOs in position and a half-dozen paces ahead, their platoon officer, a rusty revolver in one outstretched hand, his whistle still clasped in the other, mowed down by machine-guns. [pp. 89–90]

The violence of trench warfare is captured graphically, but Nulla recollects with a clarity and observation unique in the writings of the First World War:

> In a wide part of the trench we find a big Tommy sergeant. Across him are sprawled two Fritz and their bayonets are driven through his body. No less than seven Fritz lie nearby with their necks horribly gashed, whilst one has been opened from his shoulder halfway down his chest. Between the sergeant and the side of the trench is an enemy officer whose steel helmet, head and face are cleft by a Fritz trench-spade, the blade of which is still in the opened head, whilst the broken handle lies near the British sergeant. [pp. 90–91]

Whether this account accurately reflects a real event is a matter for speculation. If Lynch himself came upon a scene such as this, it would have to have been the result of the fighting in July or August 1916, some six months before. While Nulla mentions that the bodies are shrunken, perhaps one would expect them to be more decomposed, or in fact to have already been buried. It was not as if these bodies were in no-man's-land and hence unrecoverable.

These question marks do not detract from the essential truth of his description of close-range combat and the routine heroism on the Somme. In the grim days in Delville Wood, when thousands of lives were lost taking ground from the Germans and then fending off their counter-attacks, the bayonet did see action. When we think of First World War weaponry we are more inclined to think of shells, grenades, machine-guns and mustard gas, but when a man found himself face-to-face with the enemy in a narrow trench, the bayonet could prove invaluable.

How many men were killed with the bayonet has long been argued about and there are no precise figures. We do know, however, that for the Australians, it was a favoured weapon – men trained hard with the bayonet and it became a feared skill. Australians used to slash sideways with it, rather than parry and stab, as this would open up the stomach and give the victim a frightful wound (if it did not kill him outright) requiring four men to carry him out. Wounding a man would drain resources more than outright killing him – a chilling reality in the quest to win the war.

For the most part, Nulla's war is filled with dreary boredom and strenuous labour, just as Private Lynch's would have been. One day, the monotony is broken for Nulla by a delivery of mail from Australia, including three-month-old newspapers that the men think will be great to burn so they can thaw out their frozen boots in the morning. They also get their news when reinforcements arrive who are fresh to the front, including Jacko, who's 'a real newspaper, a whole newsagency in fact to us'. Meeting Jacko and hearing about home makes Nulla realise that trench life has replaced the reality he once knew; the new man is a link to his old life across the other side of the world. Jacko's entry into Nulla's circle of mates brings the men a feeling of optimism because it causes them to think about the future, when the war will be a memory 'blanched by the sunshine of our own land, our own Australia Fair'.

Nulla and his mates take Jacko under their wing and teach him the ways of life on the front. Although he is in fact older than Nulla and Snow, he is 'young Jacko' to them; they have been seasoned by their time at the front and they cherish the opportunity to pass on what they know. They instruct him to freeze when an enemy flare is fired, so that he will not be seen; they take care to make sure that he and the other reinforcements keep well down when they are fired on by an enemy machine-gun. Perhaps Jacko represents to Nulla and his mates not only the opportunity to pass on their knowledge and experience of warfare, but the chance to care for someone, look after someone's welfare, and be responsible for them. In a world of killing and hard, dangerous graft, a chance to care for another person could have been one small way to recapture their humanity.

When Nulla first entered the line, he was young and inexperienced and wanted to hide when they were shelled, astounded that experienced soldiers walked on, unfazed. Now, after only a couple of months in the trenches, Nulla *is* one of those experienced soldiers, able to explain to Jacko why the other men don't flinch when they hear the sound of gunfire (they can tell from the sound that the enemy isn't firing in their direction) or why they reach for their gas masks when they hear dud shells that have failed to explode (they sound a lot like gas canisters). All across the Western Front, the war was turning Australian boys into men at a vastly accelerated pace.

Young Jacko is lucky to have the support of Nulla and his mates, particularly when they are out on a fatigue digging a trench and the Germans mount an attack. They are called back to the support line and must pass through an area of heavy shelling to get there. In the trench, they watch for the SOS signal from the frontline – a red flare followed by a green followed by a red – which thankfully never comes. The attack is fought off, but with many casualties amongst the gunners, drivers and horses. Though the men can find humour in such sights as human hands and skulls protruding from trench walls, the misery of wounded horses – such dependable, innocent and defenceless creatures – is something they'll 'never get hardened to'.

Since arriving at the front as a fresh reinforcement, Nulla has been, by turns, scared, shocked, appalled, disgusted, cold, hungry, miserable, amused – and now, for the first time, he is reverent. Confronted by the sight of Australian bodies lined up in rows on the snow, today fallen comrades but only yesterday mates, sombreness falls over not just Nulla but all the men. There are things, it seems, that even Australian soldiers can't laugh off.

Lynch, as a private who had seen countless men die and countless bodies lying in the snow or mud, is able to take the reader deep into the psychology of every soldier who ever saw a mate fall:

'Cripes, mate, you'll sleep cold tonight,' a man remarks as he tenderly straightens the poor broken body in its grave of mud. There's nothing irreverent or callous or frivolous in the remark. It's just familiarity, the sorrowful, friendly familiarity of the sad side of soldiering. [p. 102]

# SEVEN

# Straightening the Line

The routine of a soldier on the Western Front was one of being rotated through the different stages of the trench system, with occasional trips to rest areas at the rear. After a stint on the frontline, a battalion would be moved to a trench in the next line back, the support line, or the furthest one, the reserve line. When a battalion wasn't in one of the lines, they were sent back to their rest area at the rear. There wasn't necessarily much rest to be had in a 'rest' area, as the men could be sent out for fatigues or given training to prepare them for future operations. Then, after a stint in the rest area, it was back into one of the lines.

Each AIF division, comprising between 10,000 and 20,000 men, was designated a locale in the areas well behind the lines in which to rest their 12 battle-weary battalions. As part of the 4th Australian Division, the 45th Battalion's rest area was Mametz camp, about 12 kilometres south of the frontline at Gueudecourt. The 45th Battalion history describes it thus:

This was a comfortable place and as each hut had a couple of braziers, the men used to augment their daily issue of fuel by bartering rum and cigarettes for supplies from the Tommy sentries on the coal dump at the railway siding. Whilst at Mametz, numerous working parties were sent out. Full use was made of the Divisional baths at Fricourt, and the opportunity was taken to disinfect the blankets and uniforms, as it had been proved that lice were responsible for disseminating trench fever.[1]

In the chapter 'Straightening the Line', we find Nulla and his battalion back in the support line after a rest in the huts at Mametz. They're about to be sent up to the frontline for a 'stunt', the men's term for an attack on the enemy. This is a tense time, the men knowing that once over the parapet and walking across no-man's-land, they will be easy targets. As soon as the Germans detect an attack, their artillery fire will come down with devastating consequences; the air will suddenly be filled with bursting shrapnel, exploding grenades and the whine of bullets. Men will be falling everywhere and the call 'Stretcher-bearer!' will be heard all along the front. Men will be surrendering, the wounded will be screaming, the air will be thick with the explosive cordite, and the smoke of battle will be lit in eerie confusion from flares and exploding shells.

Lying in cold dugouts writing letters home, the men cope with the awareness of what is to come by hiding their own fear from themselves. The 'depressive knowledge' that for some men these will be the last letters they write to their loved ones is what makes them 'write so cheerfully'. Simply in order to keep going, each man needs to kid himself that it will not be him who is killed.

Nulla is called upon to be a runner, a very responsible and dangerous job, entrusted to few men and crucial to the success of their operation to 'straighten the line'. Military planners on both sides were always keen to 'straighten' a frontline to avoid bulges or salients. These would provide the enemy with an intrusive wedge into the other's front, allowing them better observation and, most importantly, allowing them to enfilade the other's trenches from the side, or fire into and across rear areas.

Nulla's task is to lead 400 men and an officer through a maze of support trenches to collect bombs and then to Fritz's Folly, a sunken road where the men will be met by the officers and the handover completed.

It may seem extraordinary that a 19-year-old private who has only been in France a couple of months would be given responsibility for getting 400 men safely to the frontline trenches prior to an attack, but young men on the Western Front routinely found themselves in situations requiring bravery, skill and maturity. There was a maze of trenches and saps leading off in all directions that needed to be negotiated, there were no torches or lights of any kind, few trench signs, and this relief needed to be done silently and carefully, because any noise could instantly bring a German bombardment along the crowded frontline trenches.

The night is 'as black as an infantryman's future' and Nulla can see little, but he bluffs when an anxious officer asks him if he can see any landmarks. 'Yes, plenty of them,' he says, though he recognises nothing in the blackness. He understands enough of a soldier's psychology to have the sense to keep this to himself; 400 men finding out they are being guided by the distant horizon or, when Nulla cannot see that, by a sense of direction and luck, could perhaps turn into an angry mob.

Nulla successfully guides the men into the frontline and returns to his company, who are anxiously awaiting the 'hop-over'. He attributes his ability as a guide to an 'instinct inherited from my pioneer ancestors'. In reality, according to Lynch's children, when he was around eight to ten years old his uncles would take him into the bush and leave him to find his way home. Tough love, but something he would have been grateful for at this time.

Nulla is ordered to take part in the attack alongside his commanding officer so that he can send messages from him back to the battalion commander, or forward to officers or men ahead should this officer become a casualty. The stretcher-bearers begin to assemble, met with an ambivalent attitude from the men: no one wants to be reminded that they may soon be carried off on one of those stretchers, yet they are thankful the stretcher-bearers are there, waiting. The stretcher-bearers move along the trench handing out extra field dressings. Men also carried small glass vials of iodine to tip straight into a wound, as an antiseptic. Bandages and iodine were useful for minor wounds, but not for the horrific injuries often sustained on the frontline – nevertheless, they helped reassure men.

Five minutes before the attack there is an unnerving silence in the trench as men ready themselves for the assault. Some pray, making their peace with God; others wait nervously, jaws or hands quivering. We know from many written accounts that Lynch's portrayal evokes a common reaction amongst men on the line in the moments before they were to hop over a parapet. Some would wet themselves in fear.

Everyone counts the minutes, wondering if these will be their last on earth, thinking of home and their loved ones oblivious to their peril. The tense quiet is shattered as the officer calls, 'Come on!' and the men leap out of the trench into the nakedness of no-man's-land. The Allied artillery barrage crashes on the German frontline and the men run, half doubled over, towards the line of exploding shells. The euphemistic terms 'hop-over' or 'stunt' belie the horror of men dropping every few yards while the remainder charge on through a stream of bullets.

When they have nearly reached the enemy's trench, they throw themselves on the ground. The Germans are shelling the Australian frontline, but Nulla and the men around him are close enough to the enemy trench to be safe from their bombardment. In another example of the randomness and mercurial nature of war, only moments before it was the men dashing across no-man's-land who seemed to be in the most unenviable position; now, they 'heave sighs of relief' that they aren't still in their trench.

What Lynch described was typical of an attack on the German line. First an artillery bombardment was launched on the German trench and then, while the enemy was reeling from that, men charged across no-man's-land to take the trench. Part of the first wave were Lewis gunners. They would set up their guns immediately in the captured trench, in readiness for a German counter-attack. What had been the parados (the back of the trench) to the Germans was now the Australians' parapet and so its defences needed to be bolstered. Men busied themselves with their spades to fill sandbags to defend the Lewis gun emplacements and build up the parapet, and they repaired other parts of the trench that had been damaged by their own artillery bombardment.

Attacks on enemy trenches were frightening and dangerous operations that the men never got used to. The confusion, the noise, the stench and the fear made it the most surreal of experiences. Some fell, yet many men went into these actions time and time again, dodging the bullets and the bombardments, to come out alive.

It is not known whether Private Lynch was a runner, but what is clear is that giving Nulla that job and making him privy to the communications of officers and battalion headquarters, he had the opportunity to comment on army command. Until this point, Nulla has been learning how to be a soldier, discovering the value of mateship and understanding the supreme sacrifices that men make for their country. In

'Straightening the Line', he learns a different, darker, kind of lesson: the scant value the army command puts on the individual lives of men in the line, and hence his own life. In the previous chapter, solemnity falls upon the men for the first time as they come to terms with a large number of fatalities, their mates lying dead on the snow. Here we see a very different perspective on the death of men, the perspective not of mates but of the officers who command them.

Once the German trench has been taken, Nulla is instructed to go back to the rear and tell the colonel that they took their objective 'with small loss'. Nulla laments the army's sense of proportion, given that at least 20 of his own company's men lie dead. The colonel 'seems happy' and declares to the brigadier by phone, 'The stunt is over.' Nulla, who experienced the attack and saw men fall around him, cannot share in the colonel's happiness. All he can think of is the dead for whom it really is over, forever; the men so badly wounded that they will be disabled for the rest of their lives; the women who are 'doomed to long, lonely years ahead with nothing but a memory to cherish'; the children who will never again see their fathers.

# EIGHT

# A Night
# in the Line

Taking the German trench, which the Allies dubbed Hoop Trench, was a positive step forward in this winter of little movement on the frontline – but it put the Australians in danger, for it meant that the German artillery now knew their exact location. So it was decided to move the line forward 50 metres into the 300-metre-wide no-man's-land.

This was dangerous work that required a great deal of organisation and resources. It meant bringing up to the frontline entrenching tools, picks, shovels, barbed wire to be laid to protect the new trench, timber for shoring up the walls and duckboards to raise the bottom of the trench above the water line. It also meant bringing in additional men and ammunition, to ensure that those doing the digging were protected and the present frontline trench could be defended from an enemy attack.

In the chapter 'A Night in the Line', Nulla's battalion assisted the Pioneer battalion, something commonplace on the Western Front at the time. There was so much infrastructure to be built and maintained during the First World War – everything from trenches, duckboard tracks connecting the frontline to the rest areas at the rear, roads, bridges and railways – that five Pioneer battalions were raised by the AIF in 1916 to support the work of the engineers and the infantry. Digging was often done by sappers – a rank equivalent to private – from Pioneer units. Labourers imported from China and India were also sometimes employed for trench building.

First a rudimentary trench, known as a sap, had to be dug towards the German lines, from the head of which the new trench-line would spread out, left and right. So that men knew where to dig, first a team of Pioneers would creep out across no-man's-land under cover of darkness to lay a white tape, pegged into the ground, to show the zigzagging course of the new trench.

The tension during such an operation was high because all of this had to be done without alerting the enemy less than 300 metres away. All the while, German artillery continued their occasional firing on Australian positions. And in the case of Nulla's battalion, a lone enemy machine-gun that caused many fatalities during the taking of Hoop Trench is still in action, sending out a burst of fire along the Australians' parapet every now and then. In his job as runner, Nulla suddenly finds himself going out on a raid to try and take out the German gun.

Their small party crawls out into no-man's-land to try to

surprise the machine-gunners. The type of scene that Lynch describes here was repeated across the front during the war and numerous Victoria Crosses were awarded to men who put their lives on the line to eliminate an enemy machine-gun holding up an Allied advance.

Nulla's party does manage to capture the gun, but Nulla has to shoot one of the enemy – if not the first casualty he has directly inflicted on an enemy soldier, at least the first he has shared with the reader. The man groans, badly wounded in the arm, inspiring Nulla's pity for a moment. Despite being surrounded by unrelenting carnage for so many weeks and despite having been under threat himself from the German machine-gun, he has not yet lost his compassion and humanity.

He soon learns another important soldier's lesson: that compassion and humanity are not necessarily repaid in war. Hidden under the man's legs is a fully loaded automatic pistol with the safety catch off, and it is only through Dark's careful spotting that Nulla has a narrow escape. It is another reminder that the dividing line between life and death, and between being a man and being a ruthless killer, is razor-thin on the Western Front.

Nulla's next task is another dangerous one. Lewis gunners have been sent out a few metres ahead of the tape line, to protect the men who will be digging the trench. Now he has to guide seven men out into the blackness of no-man's-land to set up listening posts in between the guns, which are placed at about 50-metre intervals. The job of each man at the listening post is to be alert for any sounds of movement by the Germans; at the slightest sound, they are to report back.

The gunners that are posted in front of the new trench-line are manning Lewis guns. The Lewis gun, considered the best, most efficient light machine-gun available at the time, was invented in 1911 by an American army colonel, Isaac Newton Lewis, but was not issued to British and Australian units until late 1915. It weighed 12 kilograms and had a rate of fire of 500 to 600 rounds per minute. Supported on two legs and with adjustable sights, it was effective up to 600 metres. Its introduction into the war revolutionised Allied tactics because one Lewis gun had the same firepower as fifty riflemen.

The only solace for Nulla in his night as a runner is the swigs of SRD rum he is offered. The initials stood for 'Service Rum – Dilute', meaning that it was concentrated and was intended to be watered down before drinking, but the troops coined their own explanation: 'Seldom Reaches Destination'. Though it may be hard to imagine in today's military that men could be sent out in the dark amidst tortuous trenches after drinking alcohol, in the British and Australian armies during the First World War, rum was a staple ration. Shipped to the front in one-gallon pottery jars, the rum brought a feeling of warmth and comfort to the men in the freezing trenches, and perhaps gave them a touch of 'Dutch courage' and the will to go on. As Nulla says after he accepts his CO's water bottle, to find that it contains not water but rum, 'I begin to feel it's not such a bad war after all.'

The men are moved into their new frontline trench. It is only 4 feet (1.2 metres) deep, so they have to walk bent over to avoid being shot at by the enemy, but nonetheless it is quite an achievement after one night's digging. In the following week, as was customary in this kind of operation, the men would deepen the trench, cut fire steps into the sides on which they could stand high enough to see and fire their rifles over the parapet, shore up the sides and lay duckboards on the floor.

Nulla settles down in a dugout with two signallers and offers to take a shift on the phone, allowing them to sleep. Signallers were of an equivalent rank to privates, but were part of the Corps of Australian Engineers. On the Western Front, they upheld their motto, '*Certa Cito*' or 'Swift and Sure', under very trying conditions, continuously carrying out repairs to lines blasted apart by artillery bombardment.

The signallers are pleasantly shocked to discover that Nulla has had signals training and can communicate in Morse code, which the signallers use to communicate with the battalion headquarters behind the line. At regular intervals, signallers on each end of the line would 'sound through' to ensure the line was undamaged and they still had communications.

Lynch's records show he attended a signaller's course late in 1918, and no doubt this training informed his portrayal of a night in signaller's headquarters. Certainly it must be behind his deft translation of some joking Morse code from the battalion headquarters explaining the dreadful sound coming down the phone line: the snoring of the colonel. It is a moment of levity that gives Nulla a much-needed chuckle after a night of relentless danger.

# NINE
# The Carrying Party

Although major advances were not planned until the spring, the Allies did launch minor attacks throughout the winter, in order to keep up the pressure on the enemy. The advancement of the line at Hoop Trench near Gueudecourt was one such example.

Among the attacks the Allies planned in the closing stages of the 1916–17 winter was an assault on the German stronghold at the Butte de Warlencourt. It was a 20-metre-high ancient Gallic and Roman burial mound to the east of the Bapaume–Albert road, just to the north of Le Sars. For the Allies, who had been fighting to wrest the Butte from the Germans for months, it had become something of an obsession. The Australian 2nd Division were positioned there, as they had been tasked with the job of helping to capture the Butte.

Though it is just off the Le Sars to Bapaume road and well signposted, like many significant places on the Western Front, the Butte de Warlencourt is easy to miss. Its mound shape has been hidden under trees, weeds and privet and for all the lives lost in trying to capture it, the Butte is a fairly unspectacular feature of the landscape. But if you take the time to stop and walk the winding path to the top, you can appreciate its military significance as a high point, with a view to the north extending beyond Bapaume, to the west out to Loupart Wood, south to the high ground at Le Sars and southwest to Pozières.

The Australian front was about 4 kilometres long. Next to the 2nd Division AIF, to the southeast, or the right when facing across no-man's-land, was the 1st Division. In front of them was the 'Maze', a heavily defended section of the German line protected by three lines of barbed wire and a tortuous series of trenches. In November of the previous year the 2nd Division had unsuccessfully tried to take the Maze; now a new attack by the 1st Division was planned towards the end of the winter. To the east, or the right, of the 1st Division was Stormy Trench, a former German trench that the 13th Battalion (the 'sister' battalion that had split to form the nucleus of the 45th) had attacked on 4 February. In that action, Captain 'Mad Harry' Murray had added a Victoria Cross to his fistful of decorations; he was to become the most decorated Australian soldier ever and survived the war. Parts of Stormy Trench remained in enemy hands, though, and it was decided to push into the German stronghold in the western part of the trench towards the end of February 1917. That job was given to the 45th Battalion.

As 'The Carrying Party' opens, we find Nulla in the war-ravaged town of Dernancourt, just south of Albert and about 17 kilometres behind the frontline.

> We're living, or rather existing in the dirty damp billets of the shell-torn, rat-infested shambles that was once the French town of Dernancourt . . . And how we hate this hole, its dirty dilapidated dwellings, remains of sheds and damp, foul-smelling cellars which house our battalion. [p. 146]

Hiding from German observation balloons or aircraft, they are cautious about unnecessary movement during the daylight hours, only able to come out at night to work on various fatigue parties such as grave digging, repairing roads or rebuilding bridges. Nulla complains that German prisoners are brought in from their work details when the rain starts, to be replaced by the men of the 45th, even though that night they are marching back into the line to help the push into the west of Stormy Trench.

In reality, according to the 45th Battalion history, prior to being moved up to Stormy Trench the men were resting at Bécourt, on the outskirts of Albert:

> Some much needed reorganisation was carried out, and the mornings were devoted to training which consisted chiefly of route marches, or else of lectures and specialist training given indoors owing to the inclemency of the weather. In the afternoons, organised games were held and, as an indication of

the good feeling which always existed between officers and men, a football match between the officers and other ranks was played.[1]

The conditions the men of the AIF had to endure that winter had led the High Command and the Australian quartermasters to encourage officers to make extra effort to look after the comfort and wellbeing of their men. At the time when trench-foot cases were at their worst and instances of 'lack of care' of the men were observed, commander of the AIF Lieutenant General Birdwood issued a circular to every officer, 'to put all thoughts for himself, his comfort and his wellbeing, far in the background, and to . . . always look after the men first and foremost and sacrifice himself completely'.[2]

With its references to football and the practice of keeping the men indoors during bad weather, the official battalion history may have been making a conscious effort to paint a rosy picture of the 'good feeling which always existed between the officers and men', but there is no doubt that in such trying times, the men generally appreciated the concern of their officers. To provide entertainment, in rest areas behind the lines regimental brass bands were revived, concerts and film screenings were organised and a newspaper, *Rising Sun*, was produced by the AIF hierarchy. Sports meetings were held, as happened on Anzac Day 1917 in Hénencourt Wood, where the competition between the battalions was keen. (Anzac Day was already being observed and celebrated.) At certain times, men were given leave to visit nearby cities and towns. Time in back areas also allowed men to have hot baths and get clean clothes, de-louse their blankets and repair equipment and weapons. Men spent their free time writing letters home, playing two-up and card games and generally amusing themselves as best they could.

While Lynch chose to diverge slightly from history by placing the 45th Battalion in a rainy, shell-torn French village, the official histories tell us that Lynch's 45th Battalion certainly *did* go up to the line to help the push into Stormy Trench, just as Nulla does in this chapter. And just like Nulla's journey, Lynch's trip into the line would have been horrendous. The narrow roads were clogged with vehicles of all sorts, including horses dragging wagons and gun limbers, artillery and ambulances, all in a continuous stream. Men were forced to the sides and into the mud or, at best, left to stumble along broken and splintered corduroy roads.

Nulla and his mates find themselves in Grease Trench, part of a series of trenches near Stormy Trench with names such as Lard, Bacon and Ham. On this stint in the line their job is to be carriers. Their first task is to carry a hot stew in containers on their backs from a support trench up to the frontline. The Germans start shelling so the men begin to jog – and Nulla's mate Longun slips in a shell-hole. There's burning hot stew in his pockets and his respirator bag, down his pants legs – naturally a cause of great mirth for the other men. But as could happen on the battlefield, mirth soon turns to terror as 'there comes a high-piercing scream of an approaching shell'. A mate is hit – the Prof, whose shoulder is gashed and whose side is 'a mangled mess, bleeding profusely'. He will live, but will be away from the line for some time. Nulla's little band is shrinking one by one and he knows the odds are that 'some of the rest must follow soon'.

Their next job as carriers is to supply bombs to other members of the battalion who will be attacking Stormy Trench. From Bean's official history we know that the attack was scheduled to take place on 19 February 1917, but the ground, which had been frozen, thawed and the trenches were once again horrendously muddy. The men became bogged down and fatigued trying to get to the frontline along the communication trenches and the attack was postponed. Lynch did not include this detail in 'The Carrying Party', but he does refer to the 'unbelievable' conditions in the trenches at this time:

> We live in a world of Somme mud. We sleep in it, work in it, fight in it, wade in it and many of us die in it. We see it, feel it, eat it and curse it, but we can't escape it, not even by dying. [p. 147]

Bean's official history tell us that in the early hours of 21 February, under cover of rifle-grenadiers and trench mortars, the attack was successfully carried out; 300 metres of trench was captured, with 17 Australian casualties. The role that Lynch gave Nulla and his mates – to keep the Allied attackers supplied with bombs – was a crucial one on that night, for no artillery bombardment was used in the attack.

The success of the operation depended in large part on ensuring the attackers had a constant supply of bombs. The call for 'Bombs!' was urgent and frantic.

The Australians used the Mills grenade, which weighed 680 grams and could be thrown about 30 metres, compared to the lighter German 'egg grenade', which weighed far less and had a range of 50 metres. During this attack, though, the Australians fired Mills grenades with cup attachments on the front of their rifles, which meant they could fire them up to 150 metres. The type of trench mortar used in this attack was the Stokes mortar, basically a metal tube supported by two legs and fixed to a base plate. When a mortar bomb was dropped into the tube, it struck a firing pin at the base that triggered a charge and propelled the bomb from the tube towards the enemy. A Stokes mortar could fire as many as 22 bombs a minute, up to a kilometre away. Each mortar bomb weighed around 4.5 kilograms.

Nulla and his mates climb over the block into the part of the trench that the Australians have just stormed, after mortars and grenades have been rained down upon it. There are many Germans lying dead or wounded on the trench floor; others are surrendering, yelling '*Kamerad*!' – meaning comrade or companion.

Once the attack is over, Nulla and Jacko are given the job of carting heavy loads of bombs to the newly won trench position. Their hands are full when they spot movement behind a blanket covering a dugout. Nulla assumes it's one of the Australians searching for Fritz souvenirs, but the blanket is suddenly flung aside and a German comes charging for the unarmed Jacko with his bayonet. Nulla is unarmed too but has the sense to fling one of his bags of bombs into the German's face, just in time, as Jacko has frozen in fear and shock. Then Jacko not only snaps out of his immobility but pitches into a violent, frenzied attack on the German soldier, repeatedly kicking him hard in the face and neck.

The dry battalion history can describe how the Australian frontline was transformed by attacks or retreats, but it cannot show us the shattering transformations that individual men went through during those operations. Lynch, the survivor of many military operations, understood the changes men go through when their lives are under threat, when the rules of ordinary civilisation have broken down:

> Jacko is no longer an Australian schoolboy. He's gone back fifty thousand years. No joy, aim or ambition in life but to smash that face into a gory pulp . . . I know the fellow has gone out to it and Jacko hopes he's killed him, but he doesn't kick again. Civilisation regains control; the caveman's paroxysm of blood-lust gives way to the sportsman's code that won't kick a man when he's out to it. [pp. 160–1]

In Stormy Trench, the 45th Battalion came under counter-attack from the Germans, described in 'The Carrying Party' as a harrowing episode of shelling. That is where Lynch ended the story of the attack on Stormy Trench, but in fact the following night, according to Bean, the Australians resumed their attack and captured another 150 metres of trench, a German trench mortar and 32 prisoners (in addition to the 23 they had captured the first night).[3] The battalion history reports:

> The captured trench was then consolidated by a party under Captain Schadel, who, when out in no-man's-land, dispersed with his revolver a German patrol. The attacking party had three men wounded, but besides the capture of the prisoners, they killed and wounded many Germans. One of the prisoners, a German cadet officer and ex-Oxford student, who spoke excellent English, indignantly complained to battalion headquarters that one Australian in the attacking party had jumped on him and rudely said, 'Tick Tick' meaning he should hand over his watch.[4]

The practice of souveniring items from German prisoners – known by the men as 'ratting' – is highlighted by Lynch in 'The Carrying Party', so perhaps the operation in Stormy Trench was a particularly fruitful one in that regard. When things are quiet, the men compare 'watches, iron crosses, field glasses and a few pistols and trench daggers' [p. 163].

The Australians were renowned amongst the other forces for stripping German prisoners of anything they could pocket, including wallets, buttons, medals and insignia. And in an army famous for its ratting, one of the most famous ratters was a 45th Battalion man, Private John 'Barney' Hines. The 'Souvenir King', as he became known, was born in Liverpool,

England, in 1873. At the age of 14 he ran away to enlist in the British army, but was taken home by his mother. He is supposed to have spent time in the Royal Navy and seen action in the Boxer Rebellion in China (1900) and the Boer War (1899–1902) before he arrived in Australia just before the outbreak of the First World War.

Initially, when he tried to join the AIF he was already in his forties and was rejected, but he persisted and finally joined in August 1915. He was discharged as medically unfit in early 1916 but joined up again in May 1916 and was one of the 150 men of the fourth reinforcement with Lynch on the HMAT *Wiltshire*; there is no doubt that Private Lynch would have known Barney Hines, if not personally then certainly through reputation.

Though he was an effective fighter on the line, Hines is better known for his ratting and for causing trouble off the battlefield. In early December 1916, about six weeks after arriving in England, he took himself off to Bethnal Green in London for over a month and was punished by losing two months' pay. By late 1918, he had racked up a number of Absent Without Leave charges, one for Drunkenness and another for forging entries in his paybook.

His ratting was legendary. One tale (possibly a tall one) even went that he came by a grandfather clock, but men from his own unit blew it up because they became a target of enemy shelling every time it chimed. He became widely known as a result of a photograph that was taken after the fighting at Polygon Wood, in September 1917, of Hines surrounded by bounty he had collected from conquered Germans. The story goes that copies of this picture were passed around in the trenches, the Germans found one on an Australian prisoner and from there it found its way into the hands of the Kaiser himself, who declared Hines a 'barbarian' and put a reward on his head – dead or alive. The photo is one of the famous and enduring images of the war. (Today, if you pass through Pozières and stop off at Le Tommy Café de Souvenir, you will even find Hines's image on the place mats on the tables and on postcards.) Hines was wounded twice and returned to Australia in early 1919, where he became a post-war celebrity. In his sixties, he volunteered for the Second World War, but was turned down.

The AIF was under the control of the British Commander-in-Chief, Douglas Haig, but in 1917 the incoming British Prime Minister, David Lloyd George, endorsed France's strategic plans for the coming year, even offering to put Haig, and therefore the Dominion forces, under the direct control of the new French commander, General Nivelle, who had been successful in the counter-offensives at Verdun. The Allies' strategy was focused on the Western Front; the aim was to break through the German defences, flood into the gap and overrun the Germans' rear. This would rely on a heavy concentration of French infantry, which meant the British would have to extend their front and mount a series of attacks to divert the enemy's attention. The Australians were to play a key role in these diversionary plans in the coming spring.

In Germany, as in England, France and Australia, the early hopes of a quick victory had long passed. British efforts to cut off imports into Germany were beginning to bite and food rationing and a shortage of raw materials such as coal had started to affect daily life and war production. German casualties, especially after the Somme and Verdun battles, had become unsustainable. Field Marshal Paul von Hindenburg and General Erich Ludendorff, had taken control of the war effort in 1916 and reappraised Germany's military strategy.

In February 1917, the Germans' big hope was their U-boat campaign, with their renewed focus on unrestricted submarine warfare, by which any ship believed to be associated with the Allies – whether it was a naval, passenger or merchant ship – was a target for German torpedoes. Their aim was to starve Britain into submission; they believed that a successful submarine blockade would create economic and social difficulties that would force Britain to sue for peace. On land, they would take a more defensive position and hold out as long as possible for the submarine victory. England began to experience increased shipping losses in the Atlantic and around the coast of Britain, with a concentration of sinkings along the south coast and around Ireland.

On the Eastern Front, Germany feared they would have to fight off an offensive, but after months of turmoil, official ineptitude, widespread starvation and enormous casualties, it appeared that the abdication of the Tsar – who in 1915 had disastrously taken over the command of the military – was imminent. The burgeoning socialist revolutionary movement was having a negative impact on the morale of the troops and desertions exceeded two million men, with some sources putting this figure as upward of three million. Russian armies had suffered enormous casualties with over two million men dying in 1915 and a similar number in 1916. The soldiers were undernourished, weapons and ammunition were in poor supply, and transport and communications were totally disorganised. Strikes and riots broke out over shortages of food and the troops, particularly in Petrograd, refused to suppress them, placing increased pressure on the Tsar to abdicate. This in turn led to a breakdown in the military command and offensive action by Russian forces on the Eastern Front virtually ceased.

On the Western Front, the Allies and the Germans were in a stalemate, locked in a war of attrition in which each side's greatest hope was to hammer away at the manpower, materials, equipment and morale of the other until they were so weakened that they could be overrun. Initially, Ludendorff and Hindenburg would have preferred to attack at the sides of the British salients – those parts of the frontline that projected out from the rest of the line. But they believed that the British were too strong and they did not wish to commit their reserves for an offensive, especially when the Allies were likely to mount offensives north and south of the Somme in the spring. The Germans particularly feared that the Allies would strike at the German salient north of the Somme.

Unlike the British, who still believed in the strategy of

attrition, the Germans had learnt their lesson at Verdun and decided that there would be no more wearing-out offensives. They would go on the defensive and let the Allies bleed instead. Unknown to the Allies, since September 1916 they had been constructing a shorter, far stronger frontline 20 kilometres in the rear. Rather than placing their troops all along an extended trench system, the Germans would adopt a practice of 'defence in depth', a system of defences several layers deep that enabled men to retreat if they came under attack and reserves to flood forward, so that a counter-attack could be mounted.

The brainchild of von Hindenburg and Ludendorff, the Germans called this new line the Siegfried Stellung Line, but the Allies dubbed it the Hindenburg Line. It extended 125 kilometres from Arras, through the high ground at Mont St Quentin and on to Soissons in the southeast, and contracted the frontline by 40 kilometres, allowing the Germans to withdraw 13 divisions as reserves.

The Hindenburg Line consisted of three zones: a 500-metre-deep 'outpost zone' that was to be thinly manned, intended to break up or provide warning of an attack; a second line 2.5 kilometres deep called the 'battle zone' comprising prefabricated concrete blockhouses, also known as pillboxes, that were used as machine-gun emplacements and could act as minor fortresses if the British attacked, with thick wire entanglements and deep underground shelters; and a third zone known as the 'rear zone' with a depth of 5.5 kilometres, where reserves would be stationed so they could be rushed to any point of breakthrough. Before the Allies got to the new outpost zone, they would have to make their way through a 15-kilometre-deep zone in which the Germans had destroyed or booby-trapped all the roads, bridges, railways, communication lines, houses and any shelter at all for advancing troops.

Withdrawing to this new defensive line would bring some major benefits. Immediately, the Germans could abandon some of the dangerous salients in the line and hold more men in reserve at the rear. Equally important, British and French plans for the spring offensive would be dislocated and delayed, giving more time for the submarine offensive to achieve results.

When the German prisoners taken by the 45th Battalion in Stormy Trench were interrogated they did not give away that a big troop movement was about to happen. This, and continued activity along the German line, meant that the Allies went on believing that the enemy were still holding the line in strength. Who would anticipate or expect such a major withdrawal?

All appeared normal through the daylight hours of 23 February, the day after the 45th Battalion's attacks on Stormy Trench. But as night closed in over the battlefield, patrols started to return with reports that the German positions were unusually quiet. Patrols from other divisions returned with similar intelligence: the German front, which had been very active the day before, was suddenly still. There was no fire from known machine-gun positions and the flares being thrown into the sky were coming from the rear rather than frontline positions. Reports came in that British patrols further to the west had also found German positions abandoned. It was all very strange.

Gradually it dawned on the stunned Allies that a major German withdrawal and redeployment was taking place that would not only shorten and straighten, and so strengthen, the German line, but also severely dislocate British and French offensive plans for the coming spring and summer. 'I am afraid it is a very clever thing the Germans have done,' declared the AIF's Major General White.[5]

Though the withdrawal is briefly mentioned in the 45th Battalion's history, no mention is made in *Somme Mud*. One wonders how this major German redeployment was seen and understood by the privates in the field. Did they realise the significance of what was happening, or was it kept from them or not fully explained? There was a lack of communication at the highest levels in the early days of the German withdrawal, so perhaps it is no wonder that Lynch did not show Nulla grasping the significance of this new strategic situation.

The 45th Battalion was sent to the rear to rest after the Stormy Trench stunt, but other Australian units now found themselves advancing across no-man's-land or open country without opposition. They had been geared up to attack the German salient at Bapaume, tackle the Maze, storm the Butte de Warlencourt, but now they were able to take those positions with only minor German resistance. Charles Bean makes an interesting observation that it was difficult for the

Allies to go from fighting a stalemated war, confined to trenches and narrow fronts, to moving in the open, across large distances and in semi-open warfare. It would have been frightening and stressful to say the least, for the Germans had destroyed their trenches, dugouts and earthworks as they retreated and in their place left booby traps and mines. On 25 March, about eight days after the Australians entered Bapaume, there was a huge explosion in the Bapaume Town Hall, the result of a mine hidden by the Germans, and twenty-four men were killed. Soon after, a dugout being used as an officers' headquarters exploded, burying two signal clerks, and from then on, men and officers were banned from occupying dugouts and houses.

For the remaining two years of the war, the breaching of the Hindenburg Line would become the primary aim and occupation of the AIF.

# TEN

# Mixing
# it at
# Messines

In the days that followed the taking of Stormy Trench in late February 1917, the men of the 45th Battalion were relieved and moved back to Mametz camp, about 12 kilometres to the rear. From there, the battalion moved to Bécourt, just to the east of Albert, for training, and then on 23 March they moved out to Shelter Wood, near Fricourt. Private Lynch did not join them in Fricourt, though, for according to his personal medical records, he had a severe case of trench foot and was admitted to hospital in Rouen on 22 March 1917. He was transferred to the 4th Division hospital at Étaples on 14 April and did not return to his unit until 28 April. It is curious that Lynch was hospitalised for trench foot at this time rather than while in the frontline, and it raises questions such as whether Lynch was in fact with his battalion behind the line or elsewhere; if he had suffered the beginnings of trench foot in silence, until he could put off treatment no longer; or whether he in fact developed it during training at Mametz or Bécourt. We will never know.

While Lynch received treatment for the agonising condition, his battalion footslogged north along the famous Albert to Bapaume road, past the old British frontline at La Boiselle, on past the moonscape of Pozières, up over the rise at the windmill and down the long slope and on to Le Sars. On 28 March, they reached a tented camp at Le Barque, where the battalion was awarded 37 decorations for bravery in the fighting at Stormy Trench.

The battalion pushed on towards the frontline through the remains of Bapaume, where troops were assembling for attacks on the outpost villages. The Germans had brought artillery forward into these villages and the Allies would have to take them before they could tackle the formidable Hindenburg Line about 10 kilometres away. The small fortified village of Noreuil had been captured by the Australian 13th Brigade, but ahead lay the real obstacles, where breakthroughs were planned by British High Command: Arras and Bullecourt. The attack on Bullecourt was to be made by the 62nd British Division and the Australian 4th Division, with Lynch's 45th Battalion held back in reserve.

The first assault was scheduled for 10 April, to be spearheaded by something the Australian troops had never seen in action before: tanks. These were to advance first, crushing the wire and firing on the enemy's frontline, the Allied troops following on behind them. The Australians had taken up their positions ready for the early morning attack, but the British tanks were delayed by a heavy snowstorm and could not get into position; exhausted and demoralised, the men were forced to return to their frontline and ready themselves to mount the attack the following day, at 4.30 a.m. Again many of the tanks failed to arrive on time – one even went in the wrong direction and ended up with its nose stuck in the bank of a sunken road. Despite this, the Australians crossed their start line and moved across the flat, featureless ground, following the few tanks that were operational. The 46th and 48th battalions crossed the first belt of German barbed wire that had been broken by the British artillery and rushed on. By 5.50 a.m., the 46th had captured their first objective, the old German frontline trench, and by 6.20 a.m., the 48th Battalion were at their objective, the old German reserve trench.

Things started to go wrong. A savage German counter-attack drove both battalions back to their original start line, leaving many men dead and wounded behind them. Communications were poor, the tanks were all but useless and Allied artillery failed to support the attack, which had been dismally and hastily planned by General Gough of the British High Command. On that awful day, the 12th Brigade, having committed three battalions or around 3,000 men, had casualties of 30 officers and 900 men. The 4th Brigade, which had also sent in 3,000 men, had nearly 2,400 casualties. And all in just ten hours. Though it was not on the scale of the disastrous first day of the Somme offensive on 1 July 1916, the disaster at Bullecourt was to become a prime example of British battlefield blundering and incompetence and was used as a vivid example in officer training schools for the rest of the war of how *not* to plan an attack.

Fortunately for Lynch's 45th Battalion, they were not called forward to join the butcher's picnic. From Fricourt they had marched to Noreuil, where they took over the old front-line, established a line of advanced posts and patrolled to prevent further German counter-attacks. The 45th Battalion was kept busy bringing in the dead and wounded. Though Edward Lynch was in hospital at this time, he did place Nulla at Bullecourt, presumably basing his account on the battalion history and perhaps the stories told to him by his mates when he rejoined his unit.

Nulla observes remarkable heroism, such as Longun's mate from the 13th Battalion who jovially apologises for being unable to shake hands – because his hands are the only thing holding in his bowels, the result of a bullet wound to the abdomen. There is the man who fights off seven Germans with a trench spade and is shot through each knee but who will not be taken out on a stretcher because he thinks his mate needs it more. There is the 'young lad of seventeen who had his knee slit clean open' [pp. 176–7] yet makes a desperate stand, throwing grenades at the Germans at close range so fast he doesn't have time to pull the pins out.

Nulla is quick to also point out the bravery of the German gunners. When they find one chained to his gun, Nulla discounts the story going around that the Germans are now chaining their gunners to their machine-guns, and believes the German when he says that he chained himself to it, fearing that his 'nerves might break'. Nulla has seen too many brave Germans die while working their machine-guns and concludes: 'Some of the bravest men we've ever bumped have been Fritz gunners: we know that to our sorrow.' [p. 177]

Two days after the failed Bullecourt attack, the men of the 45th Battalion moved back to Bapaume, where they entrained and returned to their old camp at Shelter Wood near Fricourt, before going into more comfortable billets at Bresle, on the outskirts of Albert. Although the frontline had moved forward, removing the threat of German long-range artillery bombardment, their 'rest' time behind the line was far from a holiday camp. A solid round of training started immediately and officers and NCOs were sent to various courses. Select men were also sent to Britain to undertake officer training while others were sent for periods of six months to the divisional training camps on the Salisbury Plain to train the new arrivals from Australia.

While the battalion is at Bresle, Lynch provides Nulla – and the reader – with a bit of light relief in the form of an unauthorised visit to some local towns to sample cognac and other delicacies, and he and his mate Snow are punished with a night in the clink, loss of wages and a week confined to barracks. Lynch's personal records do not indicate that he was ever charged Absent Without Leave while in France, though of course that proves only that he was never caught, not that he never took a break away from his battalion. Indeed, the Australians had been renowned for high rates of men going Absent Without Leave since the fighting at Pozières in 1916.

Unlike the British army, which executed around 350 men during the First World War, the Australian army never enforced the death penalty.

Since the announcement by Germany of unrestricted submarine warfare, the Allies had set their sights on the Belgian ports of Oostende and Zeebrugge on the North Sea, which were important German U-boat bases. Because of shipping losses, particularly the deaths of American civilians on passenger ships such as the *Lusitania*, the United States had declared war on Germany on 6 April; soon after, Congress adopted conscription. In Russia, the revolution had begun. In the Middle East, the British had occupied Baghdad and the first battle of Gaza was under way. The French army was on the offensive on the River Aisne, to the south of the Somme.

The British, and thus Australian, focus turned northward, to the German frontline in Belgium. Their goal was to eliminate the salient in the line east of Ypres and force the Germans from the high ground at Passchendaele. But first they needed to capture the German line along the ridge that extended from Wytschaete, some 8 kilometres south of Ypres, to Messines, 2 kilometres further south. The Messines–Wytschaete Ridge gave the Germans the high ground, enabling them to observe the Allies, so its capture was crucial to the Allies' plans for the coming offensive against Passchendaele.

The German defences along the salient were laid out according to Ludendorff's plan, with the forward positions only lightly defended, often by machine-gun crews stationed in shell-holes and supported by concrete blockhouses. Waiting in the rear were mobile units ready to counter-attack if the Allies broke through the line. The Allied response to this set-up was to plan an initial artillery barrage to destroy the enemy's barbed wire and machine-gun nests, then to target the Germans' rear assembly areas. They would also target German artillery batteries and lines of communication, to cut off supplies to the frontline and prevent the movement of reserves into forward areas.

By now, spring had replaced winter, improving the comfort of the troops. Leaves began to return to the trees, the hedges and wildflowers were in bloom, and the roads had turned from mud to dust. With the arrival of spring rose the spirit of the men who began to look back on the winter campaign as a hideous dream. On 12 May 1917, after an inspection by General Birdwood and a one-month rest at Bresle, the 45th Battalion, which Lynch had rejoined about two weeks before, entrained for Bailleul, on the border of France and Belgium, ready for their next big test: Messines and the Ypres salient.

In the week before the attack, which was to take place on 7 June, the 45th Battalion was concentrated near Neuve-Église, in Belgium, about 5 kilometres from the German line. Here the men prepared for the coming attack, the officers and NCOs reconnoitred the approaches to the frontline and the whole battalion had the battle plans explained to them with the aid of a large relief model specially built for the purpose. The map was marked out on the ground and raised platforms were constructed so the men could look down on it, understand the terrain and have the battle plan outlined for them. Unlike other armies, the AIF made every effort to explain to soldiers of all ranks the details of an attack and the objectives to be taken, so that individual initiative could contribute to the outcome of the battle. At Messines, this was going to prove necessary.

The map was set up near a farm called Petit Pont, to the southwest of Messines and on the other side of Ploegsteert Wood. The farm is still there today, but the exact site of the map is something of a mystery. I studied a photograph taken the day before the attack, of men standing on the platforms surveying the map; on the right of the photograph a straight road can be seen. When I was in Belgium I tried to locate this road at Petit Pont, but to no avail.

In command of the battle was Field Marshal Sir Herbert Plumer, a favourite of the men. He had started planning the assault on the Messines–Wytschaete ridge two years before and was very thorough in his preparations. The British had built 23 deep mine shafts stretching 21 kilometres under the German frontlines along the ridge, having started construction in August 1915. These shafts were dug to a depth of 30 metres and opened out into galleries extending 1.6 kilometres directly under the German frontline. Before the attack, these galleries would be packed with 400 tons of the explosive ammonal, ready for detonation. Twelve mines were concentrated at the apex of the salient near Messines village.

The Germans knew shafts had been dug along the Messines–Wytschaete ridge and had even blown some camouflets – that is, they had detonated explosive charges in an effort to undermine shafts and cause them to collapse. As a result, one of the galleries was cut off for three months and only re-opened four days before the Messines offensive. This type of success led them to believe the shafts had been abandoned by the Allies, and that the British offensive on the Messines Ridge was unlikely or perhaps even impossible. They did know the British were still actively digging at Hill 60, but a German officer stated that his men 'had them beaten',[1] according to Bean. But the Germans had conducted counter-mining operations only near the surface, and as Bean dryly concludes, 'The capacity of the British miners was disastrously underrated,'[2] and along the whole front the Germans were cleverly deceived and totally ignorant of the British mining.

At 3.10 a.m. on 7 June 1917, 19 mines were fired (four were not detonated), creating a phenomenal series of massive explosions. Lynch perhaps observed this just as his character Nulla does, walking to a nearby hill especially to watch it happen, like a spectator. First the Allies' big guns fire on the German line and 'like the slamming of the door of Doom, a terrific roar goes up'. Moments later, there is an 'appalling roar, drowning even our guns' firing, as the sound of nineteen great mines going up bursts upon our ears. The ground rumbles, shivers and vibrates under us.' [p. 183]

Immediately, nearly 2,300 guns fired on the enemy's

frontline and their artillery in the rear. The attacking battalions moved forward into the thick dust thrown up by the mines and the artillery. Massive numbers of Germans were killed by the explosions – an estimated 10,000 men – and the Allies easily dealt with the rest, who were so badly shaken that they surrendered in droves. Bean explained:

> Elsewhere, after firing a few scattered shots, the Germans surrendered as the troops approached. Men went along the trenches bombing the shelters, whose occupants then came out, some of them cringing like beaten animals. They 'made many fruitless attempts to embrace us' reported Lieutenant Garrard of the 40th. 'I have never seen men so demoralised.'[3]

The night before the 45th went into the attack at Messines, the battalion was quartered in Kortypyp Camp near Neuve-Église. In *Somme Mud*, Nulla tells us that the camp was shelled with shrapnel, which ripped through the roof and walls of their huts. This area had previously been heavily shelled with gas, which lay in trenches and hollows in the forested area, protected from the winds that would otherwise have dispersed it. It is here that Nulla and his mates are fed a breakfast of stew tainted with gas, which leaves them heaving and vomiting. This gas, he explains, 'has been drawn up out of the grass by the morning mist that rose with the sun' [p. 184].

We are also told by Nulla that on that morning, he and Snow 'tramp off a good mile and climb a big hill where we settle down to watch [the mines being detonated]' [p. 182], but this is doubtful. They would have needed to be back very early to be ready for breakfast and it is unlikely they would have seen the explosion as clearly as they describe at three in the morning. Besides, Kortypyp Camp was behind Hill 63 and about 6 kilometres from Messines.

Early on the morning of 7 June, the battalion left Kortypyp Camp and marched to Stinking Farm, west of Messines. On their way, they are horrified by the sight of three green, bloated corpses, gunners killed by gas. This would have been a common scene in the area. Today, you can still follow the track that Lynch would have taken to the front, and that he describes Nulla taking. The farms where the men sheltered are still there, probably still in the same families who owned them then. The countryside is rolling and green, heavy with crops, and the roads, once deep in mud and lined with smashed wagons and horses, are today sealed and easily accessible. Stinking Farm is still where it was at the time, rebuilt with large barns and machinery sheds and an attractive farmhouse, all enclosed by corn planted right up to the sides of the buildings. Across the crops, the high ground that is the Messines ridge can be clearly seen, dominated from this angle by the stark white New Zealand Memorial and the Irish Peace Tower.

The 45th Battalion moved forward from Stinking Farm to what had been no-man's-land before the series of explosions. They were told that in the previous seven hours, all major objectives had been taken with minimal casualties, the Allied line had advanced to their objectives and the Germans had suffered massive casualties. Ahead of the 45th, the New

Zealand Division had attacked up this same hill and through the village of Messines, establishing a new line on the other side of the crest of the ridge. To the north, the British had advanced their line through the village of Wytschaete and as far as St Eloi.

As the men of the 45th began their ascent of the Messines Ridge, the bodies of New Zealanders would have lain strewn where they'd fallen. Today on this slope is the white New Zealand Memorial and, just beneath it, the remains of two German blockhouses that would have impeded the New Zealanders' advance up the hillside. These would have lain shattered, the bodies of their dead German defenders nearby or still inside. Unlike today, the slope would have been bare of trees or grass, instead cratered and desolate from the severe Allied shelling prior to the attack.

The 45th came under enemy shelling as they made their way to the crest of the ridge, and in *Somme Mud* this is when another of Nulla's mates is wounded – Snow, who must be left behind for the stretcher-bearers. They make their way through the 'crumbled rubble heap of Messines' on past the first line of New Zealand outposts and hurry towards the tape that has been laid to show where they are to jump off for the attack, along with the 47th, 49th and 52nd battalions. Lynch describes a surreal moment of beauty captured amidst the dust and smoke of artillery fire: 'We've topped the Ridge and see below a sweep of beautiful country stretching for miles away into the distance' [p. 187]. This brings him within sight not only of the German line nears Huns' Walk and the defensive

Oosttaverne Line, but also the German artillery far off to the north and east near Warneton.

Now the 45th Battalion came under German artillery and enfilading fire and casualties rose sharply. They reached their start line in plenty of time to carry out the attack at 1.10 p.m., only to be told it had been postponed for two hours – two hours in which they had no choice but to 'lie out in the open in full view of Fritz', in Nulla's words. 'Criminal mismanagement somewhere, but what can we do?' he asks. General Plumer had ordered the postponement to allow other British units involved in the attack to catch up and in order to synchronise with an Allied attack to their north. Due to communication problems, the men found themselves under fire from the Australian and British artillery as well, and suffered heavy casualties. Finally, the battalion moved off to their first objective, Oxygen Trench.

The battalion history states that the two-hour delay:

Made all the difference between an easy victory and a hard fought success, as it gave the enemy time to recover from his demoralised condition to meet the attack of the 4th Division, and to bring up fresh troops for his strong counter-attacks.[4]

Nevertheless the 45th, with the aid of their mates from the 47th Battalion and a tank, succeeded in taking Oxygen Trench. The next objective was Owl Trench. On the way to their goal, the Australians came under heavy machine-gun fire from German concrete blockhouses that afforded the enemy protection from all but the heaviest of shelling. It was the first time the Australians had faced this new German tactic – well-sited blockhouses, protecting each other by inter-locking fire – which was to become characteristic of all the battles in Flanders.

Two companies, A and B, of the 45th captured Oxygen and Owl Trench and with it 120 prisoners and two machine-guns, but Edward Lynch's D Company, along with C Company, suffered severe casualties and were forced to retire to their jumping-off line. Meanwhile, A and B companies were subjected to savage German counter-attacks and then mistakenly shelled by Australian artillery. Being attacked from the front and the flanks and shelled from the rear, they too withdrew to their start line of six hours before. For all their effort and through no fault of their own, they were back where they had started.

During the night, the decimated 45th Battalion was reorganised by senior officers and reinforced with two companies of the 48th Battalion. In *Somme Mud*, we see evidence of this in Nulla and his mate Longun being sent to find German bombs, as the battalion is running short on grenades.

At 8.30 the following morning, exhausted and hungry, the 45th again attacked and this time captured both Owl Trench and Owl Support. As expected, the Germans counter-attacked but the Allies drove them off. Yet their casualties mounted as they came under enemy shelling.

Several more days and nights of fighting ensued as the men of the 45th fought their way into parts of the trench still held by the Germans and came under sustained enemy fire, which continued to thin out the battalion. In *Somme Mud*, this fighting takes Nulla's last mate, Longun, who has 'a horrible gash up his face' [p. 208] and is sent to a rear dressing station for treatment.

The war has finally got to Nulla. When asked if he heard the dying screams of one of his fellows, Nulla observes, 'No, I didn't hear him scream. We don't any longer notice screams. We're used to them.' He is so numb and resigned that he does not even feel relief when he hears the 45th is soon to be replaced in the frontline. So many men must have experienced something akin to this feeling, which has shades of guilt at being a survivor.

> The news of relief awakes no enthusiasm and very little hope.
> We're past caring and almost past hope. So many of our mates
> have gone west and we find it hard to realise that we are
> somehow to be saved where so many have fallen. [p. 210]

The men of the 45th Battalion were now totally exhausted. Some actually fell asleep while they dug their trench and had to be shaken awake. At night, fighting patrols moved eastward, attacking towards Gapaard, where they encountered more German concrete blockhouses. These strongpoints had withstood the Allies' shelling and so the attacking platoons immediately began taking casualties from enemy machine-gun fire. Two German blockhouses remained holding up the 45th's advance down the trench and able to enfilade them.

On the afternoon of 10 June, the CO of the 45th Battalion, Colonel Herring, telephoned Lieutenant Thomas McIntyre and told him that the two blockhouses holding up the advance must be taken. McIntyre had already led three attacks on the strongpoints and knew Herring's order was his death warrant, but he responded with, 'All right, sir; if it is to be taken, it will be taken' and so at 10 p.m., he led his men into the fateful attack.[5]

Lieutenant McIntyre is without doubt the officer Lynch refers to in *Somme Mud* who leads his few remaining men on this futile attack, only hours before they were to be relieved and sent back from the frontline. Nulla doesn't hold it against the lieutenant, who with a 'break in the voice . . . told us of the attack. It's not his doing. Already he has led three separate bombing attacks . . . His responsibility has been heavy.' He continues, 'We know how he regrets the order that must send many of the few survivors to their deaths, but he is powerless to do other than lead us to the slaughter.' [p. 211]

Lieutenant Thomas Alexandria McIntyre (not 'Alexander' as the Battalion records suggest) was from the New South Wales south coast town of Berry, where he worked before the war as a carpenter. He enlisted on 21 September 1914 and went to Gallipoli with the 13th Battalion, returning to Egypt after the December evacuation. There he became part of the new 45th Battalion and sailed with his mates for Marseilles on the *Kinfauns Castle*, arriving in early June 1916. He was then a sergeant, but was promoted to second lieutenant in July 1916 and to lieutenant in February 1917. The battalion history applauds his 'splendid' work during the fighting at Owl Trench. Sadly, as Nulla recounts, McIntyre was killed during the attack on 10 June, when he fell along with a sergeant only 5 metres from the German blockhouse. The attack was a failure.

After the action at Owl Support, Lieutenant McIntyre was reported 'missing believed wounded', but four days later he was confirmed killed in action, at the age of 30. There is a reference to his death in the Red Cross Society Wounded and Missing Enquiry Bureau Records, by Private Matthew Gilmore, who was in 13 Platoon (Lynch was in 14 Platoon).

I was informed that Lieut. McIntyre was killed. He was in charge of a party who went out at night to storm and bomb a German strongpoint. I was wounded and upon making enquiries was informed that Lieut. McIntyre did not return with the party but those who did appeared to have no doubt as to what had happened to him.[6]

Private Leslie Dollisson provided the Red Cross with another eyewitness report:

I was with Lieut. McIntyre on June 10th at Messines. We were on a bombing party and the Lieut. was in charge. It was about 11 o'clock at night. I was in one shell hole and the Lieut. with Sgt. Lamborne was in another about 20 yards away. A shell or bomb exploded nearer to the Lieut. and the Sgt. than to us. Sgt. Lamborne sang out that he was wounded and I went and helped him back to the trench. He said the shell or bomb exploded within five yards of the Lieut. and killed him instantly. Sgt. Lamborne seemed pretty badly wounded. I left him with the stretcher bearers in the trench and heard afterwards that he did not get to the dressing station.[7]

In 'Mixing it at Messines', Nulla is badly wounded in the back while advancing and spends a terrifying night in a shell-hole in no-man's-land near the German blockhouse. A photograph of one of the two smashed blockhouses is in the Australian War Memorial's photograph collection and, surprisingly, one of these blockhouses still exists today near Messines on the line of the old Owl Support trench.

Private Lynch did receive an injury like Nulla's. According to his personal medical record dated 30 June 1917 he had a 'bullet wound – back' along with 'bomb fragments', which put him in hospital for some time. However, Lynch gives Nulla this injury on the night of the attack on the blockhouse, though he received his own back injury on 30 June, 20 days later.

In many ways there could be no more fitting conclusion to a chapter of unremitting threat and violence than Nulla, the last of his mates still standing, finally succumbing to a wound and being taken from the field of battle.

Indeed, Lynch was very lucky not to have been wounded at Messines. Four days after entering the line, the few remaining soldiers of the 45th Battalion were relieved and sent back to La Plus Douve Farm, about 3 kilometres behind the line, and from there were marched to the rear, to La Crèche. In those four days, of all the 20 battalions plus machine-gun and light mortar units who took part in the battle of Messines, the 45th took the most casualties: 16 officers and 552 other ranks. It was a shattered force that marched back to La Crèche and on to Morbecque, where it met up with the 'nucleus' that had been left behind for such an eventuality. What a sad and shocking sight they must have been, those few men who returned that day.

For the British, the attack on the Messines–Wytschaete salient was very welcome news and a brilliant success, the best operation up to that point in the war. Though the attack had not taken the German guns, the success of the mining operation, the counter-battery fire, the resupply to the front and the work of the flying corps had all added to an impressive British victory. For the first time, the Australian troops had faith in the British High Command, although they had taken half of the estimated 26,000 casualties of the battle. For the Germans, it had been costly in men and territory and as General von Kuhl later said, 'One of the worst tragedies in the world war'.[8]

Australian horse-drawn transports returning from the frontline beyond Bapaume for supplies. In the background is the Butte de Warlencourt, the scene of fierce fighting. *Courtesy of Australian War Memorial (E00432)*

The Albert–Bapaume road near the village of Le Sars today. The Butte is the site of a memorial and is now a tourist attraction. *Copyright Will Davies*

The Dernancourt railway bridge after its recapture. It was the site of heavy fighting on 5 April 1918. *Courtesy of Australian War Memorial (E03798)*

The railway bridge today. The town of Dernancourt is just visible in the background. *Copyright Will Davies*

The shattered, sunken road known as Fritz's Folly was very familiar to Private Lynch and the men of the 45th Battalion. *Courtesy of Australian War Memorial (E00502)*

The same road today, on the outskirts of Gueudecourt village, is bounded on one side by a thicket of trees and on the other by open fields. *Copyright Will Davies*

The White Gate crossroads, where Major General Holmes was mortally wounded by a German shell while accompanying the New South Wales Premier on a tour of the area in July 1917. *Courtesy of Australian War Memorial (E04537)*

The crossroads today, with farm buildings and well-cultivated fields beyond. *Copyright Will Davies*

Australians coming out of the line for a rest, passing through the ruined village of Vaulx, near Bapaume, in April 1917. *Courtesy of Australian War Memorial (E00589)*

The same corner on the sloping road into Vaulx. *Copyright Will Davies*

Signal headquarters on the outskirts of Vaulx. A despatch rider is seen leaving for the forward units with a basket containing carrier pigeons for distribution among the fighting troops. *Courtesy of Australian War Memorial (E00647)*

A private house occupies the site of the signal headquarters and the battalion cookhouse along the Vaulx–Beugny road today. *Copyright Will Davies*

The Town Hall in the Grand Place at Bapaume, photographed on 19 March 1917 just before the building was blown up by a German delayed-action mine. *Courtesy of Australian War Memorial (E00390)*

The rebuilt Bapaume Town Hall occupies the same position in the main square as it did in 1917. *Copyright Will Davies*

Vaire-sur-Corbie, France, 1918. Australian soldiers rest at the ferry landing on the bank of the River Somme. Note 'Circular Quay' is painted on the wall, a reference to the ferry terminal in Sydney. *Courtesy of Australian War Memorial (E04795)*

The ferryman's landing and house at Vaire-sur-Corbie have long since been replaced by a bridge across the Somme. *Copyright Will Davies*

# ELEVEN

# A Quiet Innings

In June and July 1917, a series of German air raids on London brought the war closer to the British public and provoked a new wave of anti-German feeling. The British royal family, so closely related to the German royal family, changed their name from Saxe-Coburg-Gotha to Windsor, while the Battenbergs changed their name to Mountbatten.

Shipping losses in the Atlantic also increased with over 100 ships sunk in May 1917 alone, following the German declaration of an unrestricted U-boat offensive against neutral merchant shipping. Though this was seen by Germany as initially successful, it could neither be sustained nor reach the levels required to strangle Britain's war effort. In response, the Royal Navy introduced a system of convoys, with slow freighters and transports sailing in groups, protected by warships. Losses soon decreased.

When America entered the war in April 1917, it had only a small standing army that was not prepared for battle or equipped for what lay ahead in Europe. Mobilisation and recruitment were sluggish to begin with but by late June, after President Wilson introduced stiff penalties for men avoiding the draft, enlistment reached nearly ten million men. On 27 June, the first US troops landed in France under the command of a veteran of the Mexican and Philippine wars, Major General 'Black Jack' Pershing. Their arrival was witnessed by huge crowds who cheered their coming ashore. They were the first of 180,000 Americans who would land in Europe by the end of the year.

In Russia, Vladimir Lenin had been living in exile in Zurich, but in April, with the support of the Germans, he was returned home secretly by train. It was hoped he might foment revolution, create social chaos and possibly even lead revolutionary Russia to sign a separate peace, eliminating the German Eastern Front in the process. The Russian army was in disarray and unable to take any offensive action. Due to poor transportation, bad planning and the desertion of two million men, the summer campaign, planned to begin on 1 May, had not eventuated. By mid-July, the offensive against the Austro-Hungarians was over and the Russian army in headlong retreat.

In Australia, Billy Hughes had swept back into government in May 1917, having formed a coalition between the Liberal and National parties. Recruitment remained slow. The war had taken many sportsmen, so in Rugby Union and cricket there were no first-grade competitions. Nor were there any Australian Rules competitions in South Australia or Western

Australia. Rugby League continued, however, in Sydney and Brisbane, with Balmain winning the Sydney premiership and Valley winning in Brisbane that year. In Victoria, the VFL continued, with Collingwood going on to win the premiership. The Melbourne Cup was also run in November that year (won by Westcourt) and the Stawell Gift – a 100-yard dash for men that is still an annual event today – took place. Nothing, it seems, could keep the Victorians from their sport.

This was also the year that saw the drawing of the first Golden Casket Lottery in Queensland, with the profits going to patriotic war funds. These funds were first raised during the Boer War and resumed at the beginning of hostilities in 1914. Money raised went to a range of organisations, individual towns and countries, and most notably for the relief and comfort of Australian troops and their families. By the end of the war, patriotic funds paid the largest share of separation payments to families, repatriation costs and the education of soldiers' children.

In Melbourne, the National Council of Women voted to express their sympathy to the war-ravaged women of Europe, especially those who were the victims of war crimes. In Adelaide, the state parliament voted to close Lutheran schools because of their German connections. In Maitland in New South Wales, crowds turned out for the funeral of the 21-year-old champion boxer Les Darcy, who had caused controversy by failing to enlist. Denied a passport to travel to the US to take a shot at the world title, he stowed away on a boat and went to New York. When America got swept up in its own war fervour, to avoid any more criticism he joined the US army. Given a couple of weeks' leave to train for the world title, he died of a blood infection due to an infected tooth.

It was about this time that the term 'Digger' became popular with AIF and New Zealand units. There are a number of possible explanations for the term, one being that it comes from New Zealand's 'gum-diggers', workers who dug up fossilised kauri gum used in the manufacture of linoleum and varnish. Others claim it originated with the battalions with a high number of men who had worked before the war as miners, who were known as 'diggers'. Whatever the source, the term quickly spread through the Anzacs as a term of endearment.

In *Somme Mud*, after lying unconscious and wounded for a night in a shell-hole, Nulla discovers that men of the 48th Battalion now hold the German pillbox he nearly lost his life for. He rues the bad luck of the 45th's attacking party, for it turns out that the Germans had been scheduled to retreat only hours after their unsuccessful attack. The Germans, quietly and without disturbance, withdrew to the defensive Warneton Line – named for the village east of Messines – nearly 2 kilometres in the rear, but when they saw that the British were not going to fully exploit their advantage, they halted and waited for the renewed British attack. Just as had been the case when the Germans withdrew south of Bapaume, the Allied advance was hesitant and cautious. Patrols moved forward and set up posts in what had been until recently German-held territory, establishing a new frontline to the east of Wambeke and north to Joye Farm. By 14 June, the battle of Messines had come to an end.

The 45th Battalion had fought hard along the Messines Ridge. As Nulla aptly puts it, 'The battalion had gone into the stunt as the strongest in the brigade and come out the weakest'. The AIF had suffered over 6,800 casualties, an enormous casualty rate for about five days in the line. The battalion history notes:

> For their fine work at Messines, the following honours were awarded to members of the battalion: Distinguished Service Order (DSO) 1, Military Cross 4, Distinguished Conduct Medal 4 and Military Medal 20.[1]

They lost many officers at Messines, including Gallipoli veteran Second Lieutenant William Whitley Gocher. A Sydney boy, from Newtown, he was 22 years old when he was among the first rush of men to enlist in October 1914. He served with the 13th Battalion at Gallipoli and was transferred to the 45th Battalion in March 1916. He sailed from Egypt with the battalion on the *Kinfauns Castle*, but was sick during the voyage and put off in Malta, where he was admitted to hospital. Yet Gocher felt well enough to break out of hospital, 'remaining absent until apprehended' more than three hours later, for which he received detention. A note in his personal file states:

5.8.16, 168 hours detention. On 2.8.16 for breaking out of hospital when a patient about 7pm and remaining absent until apprehended by garrison piquet at 10.20pm.

William Gocher distinguished himself on the field of battle. In August 1916, during the fighting around Pozières, he was promoted to sergeant and the following month was awarded the Military Medal. In February 1917, he was an instructor at a live grenade practice session at which a rifle grenade accidentally exploded, injuring a number of men, including Gocher, who was wounded in the face. In March 1917, he received a bar to his Military Medal and the following month was promoted to second lieutenant. Upon returning to his battalion after receiving his commission, he was killed in action at Messines on 7 June 1917. In July 1920, his identity disc was returned to his mother, who sent the following reply to the army:

> Dear Sir,
> I received my son's disc and wish to thank you for your kind attention. Poor fellow must have been riddled by the state of the disc.[2]

William Gocher is buried in Messines Ridge Military Cemetery, Belgium, one of dozens of cemeteries in the area.

Today, Messines still shows signs of the terrible struggle. Of the 19 mines blown on 7 June, a number of craters remain, mostly filled with water. Of these, the Spanbroekmolen crater, known as the 'Pool of Peace', is the best known and most easily visited. There are also a number of surviving pillboxes and German strongpoints including the one where Nulla was wounded on the night raid of 10 June and where Lieutenant McIntyre was killed. Below the village and the ridgeline is the Irish Peace Tower, dedicated to all Irishmen whatever their political, religious or cultural tradition, who died in the First World War, especially those of the three Irish Divisions. A short distance away is the New Zealand Memorial, with its poignant inscription, 'From the uttermost ends of the Earth', and just below it, two German pillboxes taken by the New Zealanders early in the battle. Six kilometres further south is the large circular Ploegsteert Memorial at Berks Cemetery Extension at Hyde Park Corner on the edge of Ploegsteert Wood, to the 11,000 servicemen of the United Kingdom and South Africa who died in this sector.

Upon regaining consciousness, our narrator Nulla makes his way back alone over the shattered Messines Ridge, littered with the bodies of Australian and German dead, and on down to his battalion trenches at La Plus Douve Farm. Arriving on 12 June, he finds that he has been reported 'missing, believed killed' in the attack on the pillbox on 10 June and that his family would have been notified of this by telegram. Fearing the reaction at home, Nulla quickly sends a telegram to say he is still alive, mentioning that he 'borrowed a few francs and sent a cable to my people telling them I was quite okay on the 12th June as I knew they would receive an official advice that I had been reported "missing, believed killed on 10 June 1917".'

But could he have done this? The notification of his death was not instant and would have taken time to be processed, a signal sent to Australia and a telegram prepared for the family, or, alternatively, a minister or priest organised to deliver the sad news. There were no postal or telegraphic services available, no corner post office at the front, and even in the unlikely event a private soldier had access to such a service, he would probably not be able to afford a telegram to Australia. And what of the censor?

There is, however, every chance that Edward Lynch did walk back independently on the morning of 11 June, as the battalion was shattered and had been relieved at three o'clock that morning, moving back to their subsidiary line near La Plus Douve Farm. It was here that the extent of the battalion's casualties would have been fully realised as a roll call would have been undertaken and a list made of men who were still missing, or were known to have been killed.

The injured Nulla marches off with the remnants of his battalion to the French village of La Crèche, about 10 kilometres by road west of Ploegsteert Wood, and this is borne out by the 45th Battalion history. What a sad and shocking sight they must have been, those few men who returned that day. As Nulla says: 'It was a sore and sorry battalion that marched towards La Crèche that night. Our mates back on Messines Ridge were ever on our minds.' And he cites the words they sang:

*Take me back to dear old Aussie,*
*Put me on a boat for Woolloomooloo;*
*Take me over there, drop me anywhere,*
*Sydney, Melbourne, Adelaide, well I don't care;*
*I just want to see my best girl,*
*Cuddling up again we soon shall be;*
*Oh! France it is a failure,*
*Take me back to Australia,*
*Aussie is the place for me.* [p. 217]

At this point in the story, Nulla presents himself on sick parade and is sent to a military hospital at Steenwerck, France, for 11 days. Meanwhile, the remnants of the 45th Battalion march on to Morbecque, rest for a few days, enjoy hot baths and are issued fresh clothes. They were joined by the 'nucleus' of the battalion who had been kept out of the attack, a common practice within Australian units so that should the battalion suffer heavy casualties, a core of officers and battle-hardened men would remain to form the core of the newly reinforced battalion.

When Nulla is discharged from hospital, 'physically fit with seven open wounds covered with adhesive tape', he sets out to find his battalion, chasing it around the countryside as it moves from village to village. Along the way he meets an old French couple who provide him with a meal and a bed for the night. They have lost three sons in the war and this would have been typical for French families at the time. Throughout France today are village memorials much like you find in any Australian country town, bearing long lists of local boys who died in the Great War – sad reminders for travellers whose minds are perhaps on their own countrymen rather than the millions of Frenchmen who also died directly defending their country.

On 25 June 1917, Nulla finally catches up with his battalion at Le Doulieu, but this was the period in which Edward Lynch was wounded, according to his personal records. It is difficult to understand how, because the battalion at this time was well behind the line, perhaps 20 kilometres from the fighting. One possibility is that these wounds were received at Owl Trench on 10 June, were still unhealed and were recorded as being inflicted on 25 June. It is something of a mystery.

While at Le Doulieu, the 45th Battalion was called upon to send a small group of men to join a ceremonial parade at Bailleul, just to the north. The battalion history states that it 'was represented at an Army ceremonial parade at Bailleul in honour of the Duke of Connaught'.[3] Nulla's spin is slightly different:

> The battalion is to send a party of men in to Bailleul tomorrow to some big showy parade before the Duke of Connaught, a cobber of the king. Only the big men are being chosen. 'The big strappin' Anzacs' we jokingly call them. [p. 219]

I wonder, however, just how 'big' these men were, as the average height of men in the AIF at the time seems to have been 5 feet 6 inches (168 centimetres). Private Lynch was only

5 feet 4 inches (162 centimetres) and of other selected men I have researched in an attempt to find the true identity of his mates, the tallest was 5 feet 7 inches (170 centimetres).

From here the battalion moved to 'Hyde Park Corner' in the catacombs, a massive underground complex of tunnels under Hill 63, just to the north of Ploegsteert Wood. It was damp and prone to flooding, but it was equipped with gas-proof doors and electric light and was capable of housing hundreds of men in comfort and safety.

Ploegsteert Wood and the area around Hill 63 is now covered by trees but, like many French and Belgian forests, still shows the shallow craters and scars of the war, over 90 years later. Today the entrance to the catacombs is on private land but there is a steep, muddy public path to the top of Hill 63, with a view of the village of Messines and the shallow valley and open hillside up which the Australians, the New Zealanders and the British battalions attacked the town.

Soon after the 45th's arrival, on 2 July, Major General W. Holmes, who had commanded the 4th Division through both the disaster of Bullecourt and the success at Messines, escorted the Premier of New South Wales, William A. Holman, on a tour of inspection at Ploegsteert Wood. Holmes's usual practice was to take the most direct route, however dangerous, but this day, with the Premier in his care, he took what was usually a safe track behind Hill 63. A German salvo, probably fired from long distance at this obscure grid reference, mortally wounded the general in the chest and lungs. The Premier escaped injury, but General Holmes died while being carried to the nearest medical post at Kandahar Farm. He was the highest-ranked Australian to lose his life on the Western Front during the war. Around the same time, Captain Harold Charles Howden of the 45th Battalion, who had earned a Military Cross and bar, was killed. He had risen from a private at Gallipoli to second in command of his battalion. Having just returned from Aldershot in England, he was killed while eating breakfast with other officers when the Germans shelled the wood.

The deaths of high-ranking officers, especially of the division's commander, Major General Holmes, were serious losses for the AIF but Lynch makes no mention of them in *Somme Mud* – for this is more a story of men, not officers. Nulla's immediate concern is for his mates. At the catacombs he meets up again with Longun, also back from hospital, and reflects on the mates that he travelled to France with in the fourth reinforcement: Longun, Dark, Snow, the Prof, Farmer and Yacob. These six characters may have been among the 150 men who embarked on the HMAT *Wiltshire* with Lynch. He left us very few clues to their real identities.

We are told that Longun is 'Six feet two of long leisurely bullock-driver from the black soil of the outback.' [p. 220] On the Embarkation Roll, 31 men listed rural occupations, but if we narrow down the list by focusing on north-western New South Wales, the 'black soil' area, two men stand out as possibilities: Joseph Claude Keys, a station hand from Gunnedah, and Michael Emanuel John Wartley, a farm labourer of Gilgandra.

Joseph Keys' service number (2203) was only four different from Lynch's (2207). Longun is considered the best-educated and the leader of the gang of mates, and Keys was 30 years old, certainly much older than Lynch, who was just 18. Keys, a bullock driver who became a driver in the army, enlisted in Bathurst, so may have been known to Lynch. However, he was only 5 feet 7 inches (170 centimetres), much shorter than the 6 feet 2 inches (188 centimetres) that we are told Longun is. After the war Keys returned to Australia on a different ship to Lynch, while in *Somme Mud* the mates travel home together.

Michael Emanuel John Wartley (service number 2297) was born at Boggabri and came from Gilgandra where his girlfriend, Miss Maud Evison, received his pay. His next of kin, his mother, lived in Narrabri. He was in Lynch's D Company, but several factors make him a less likely candidate for the character of Longun. He too was only 5 feet 7 inches (170 centimetres) tall, was aged only 22 at the time of his enlistment, and was captured by the Germans in early 1918 and not repatriated until May 1919. He returned to Australia on the *Medic*, a different ship to Lynch. There is an interesting entry in Wartley's personal file stating that he 'deserted' between 8.30 a.m. on 26 September 1917 and 6.35 p.m. the following day. He was court-martialled and given a sentence of five years, which it seems he did not serve.

Of the character Darky we are given few clues other than 'Wiry, wild and witty. As hard boiled as you make 'em. A fellow who'd been everywhere and done everything and perhaps everyone worth doing.' His identity remains a mystery.

Yacob, we are told, is a Russian Jew who deserted his ship, but only one man on the *Wiltshire*, Frederick Bradley (service number 2142), was listed as a seaman. Bradley was from Birkenhead, Cheshire, and his religion was Church of England, so we can safely assume it was not him. He spent most of his time in the 13th Battalion, was captured at Riencourt, near Bullecourt, in June 1917 and was repatriated to England in late December 1918. There were no Russian names on the embarkation list – in fact, very few non-Anglo Saxon names at all – and no men listed their religion as Jewish.

Although we are told Yacob 'stopped a bullet in the shin during a hop-over in front of Gueudecourt . . . and we have no idea where he is' [p. 222], we have no way of researching this further nor any clues within the manuscript that can help us identify this man.

Next we have Snow. All we know about him is that he has a lot of sisters and gets 'decent tucker and more knitted socks and scarves' than he has 'feet or neck for' [p. 221]. There are no clues that might identify him, but being nicknamed 'Snow', he was probably very blond.

Going by his nickname, Farmer was probably a farmer or worked on the land. 'A slow podgy old cove', he may have been older than the average man. Of the 31 men in rural occupations, three were over 30 years of age. Of these, George

Ernest Mills (service number 2210), a dairyman aged 42 years old, might be our man. His service number was just three away from Private Lynch's and though he signed up at St Peters, Sydney, he also went through the Bathurst Army Depot. But in *Somme Mud*, Farmer has already collected a sniper's bullet while burying a man and is 'over in England at Dartford Hospital' in mid-1917 [p. 222]. This seems to rule out George Ernest Mills, who was transferred to the 13th Battalion and was wounded on 7 October 1917 when the 45th battalion were at Halifax Camp west of Ypres. All we know from his file is that he returned to his battalion on 10 December 1917 after three months' recuperation.

And then there is the Prof. Nulla tells us he was a high school teacher and 'very learned, book wise, but in other ways he was a dope' [p. 221]. In Lynch's reinforcement there was only one man listed as a teacher: Archibald White McKenzie (service number 2276), who was a public school teacher, aged 32, single and whose father was an Inspector of Schools. According to the Embarkation Roll he too enlisted at Bathurst, but perhaps most telling is the fact that he was sent to the 12th Brigade Training Centre at Codford as a clerk, as he was medically unfit to remain in France, a detail that Lynch includes in 'A Quiet Innings'.

Finally, Nulla has a special mention for one mate who joined the group later, on the Somme, but whom they had immediately looked upon as one of their crowd. 'Messines got poor little Jacko for keeps,' he laments.

On 7 August the 45th Battalion moved up to Lumm Farm, just to the east of the Messines–Wytschaete road, and for a week strengthened the reserve line trenches and carried ammunition and supplies to the frontline, another 2 kilometres to the east. On the night of 14 August the battalion moved into the frontline. They would remain there until 22 August and during those eight days a number of German raiding parties would hit their section of the line. On each occasion, they drove the Germans back. This battalion report of 21 August is typical of the period:

> At daybreak an enemy raiding party approached one of our posts, but was dispersed by sharp Lewis gun and rifle fire and grenades, suffering considerable casualties. A patrol under Captain Schadel went out for identification and captured a complete machine-gun (Nordenfeldt 655) which had been abandoned by the raiders.[4]

This stint in the line is an 'exceptionally quiet innings'. Nevertheless, five or six men are killed and about 30 wounded, because 'even in a quiet innings the wickets fall and players get their despatch to the pavilion, their innings ended' [p. 229].

# TWELVE

# Passing it on at Passchendaele

In the first half of 1917, there had been deep murmuring in the ranks of the French army, leading to a series of spontaneous acts of collective disobedience. General Nivelle, who was the French commander-in-chief, had failed to provide solid leadership or to advance the protracted war and, within a short time, just over half of the French divisions, especially those who had returned to rest areas behind the lines, refused to return to the front. This amounted to mutiny, but dealing with it was difficult. In the end there were an estimated 30 executions – a mild response given the magnitude and potential effect of this dangerous situation.

To address the problem, in May the French government replaced Nivelle with the popular General Pétain and French soldiers were provided with better conditions, billets and food, and longer leave. Though their soldiers returned, the French army reverted to the defensive, focusing on holding the line. The Italians also failed to take the offensive. The Allies had no likely support in the east, either, as Russia's provisional government, after the abdication of the Tsar in March 1917, had its mind on consolidating its power and eliminating opposition rather than continuing the war against Germany. Should the Russians make a separate peace, nearly 60 German divisions now on the Eastern Front could be diverted to the Western Front, a daunting possibility for the Allies.

With unreliable and reluctant allies, Britain's General Haig was forced to take the initiative again. The success of the British at the battle of Messines, even though it had cost 17,000 Allied casualties, opened the way for the next phase of the great offensive, which became known as the Third Battle of Ypres, or simply Passchendaele, the town that was the last objective of the 14-week series of battles.

Eliminating the salient and advancing the line at Messines Ridge had been a welcome victory for the Allies, but the hope remained for a major breakout, ideally one that would carry them to the Channel coast, and so in early October 1917, the British renewed their attacks on the Ypres sector in the expectation of capturing the high ground to the northeast of the town. There was, however, fear in military and political circles that ambitious large-scale offensives such as that in 1916 on the Somme were recipes for disaster and that small-scale operations – known as 'bite and hold' – that achieved limited gains, were more effective. The successful Canadian attack on Vimy Ridge, France, in April 1917 had confirmed this strategy, as had the success at Messines.

But now Haig planned another great offensive, this time to straighten the Ypres salient, take the high ground along the Passchendaele Ridge and push through to the Belgian coast.

The offensive was to be launched from the Allied-held Belgian town of Ypres. Dominated by the cathedral built in the thirteenth century and by the enormous Cloth Hall completed in 1304, Ypres had been an important centre for the weaving of wool and the trading of fabrics. Because of its commercial importance it was encircled by a defensive wall and these ramparts were to offer protection to the Allied armies for the remainder of the war. At the northeastern edge of the town was the Menin Gate, featuring two prominent lion statues, which now stand at the entrance to the Australian War Memorial in Canberra; to the southwest was the Lille Gate.

Ypres had been close to the frontline since the start of the war. In late 1914, the town formed part of the British defensive line and just survived a concerted German attack. Then in April 1915, the Germans used gas – for the first time in the Western Front – near Ypres and nearly took the town, but it survived and remained in Allied hands. During this period, enemy shelling had reduced the city to ruins and destroyed both the cathedral and the Cloth Hall.

From then until the offensives of late 1917, known in history as the 'Third Battle of Ypres', a stalemate existed along the front, with neither side able to make or hold gains, although limited localised offensives were mounted by each side. However, the Germans held the high ground to the east, and taking this from them was a key goal of the Allied offensive in 1917.

After Messines, General Haig had put General Sir Hubert Gough in charge of the area instead of General Plumer, who had carried out the successful Messines attack. The battle began on 31 July 1917. The operational plan was ambitious and even after a heavy artillery bombardment, advances were limited. And then came the rains, turning the battlefields to mud. Gough's failure to capture the first objectives before the Passchendaele Ridge soon had him replaced by Plumer, a man more cautious and careful in advancing and more methodical and professional in preparations. Having shown his concern for his men and a high degree of planning, he was also popular with the Australians, something most British senior staff could not claim, if indeed they cared.

The Australians entered the Third Battle of Ypres on 20 September, when the 1st and 2nd divisions were used in an attack to the southeast of Ypres along the Menin Road, and by late September had switched their attack to the east of Ypres near Zonnebeke. At 5.30 a.m. on 26 September, the Australian 4th and 5th divisions were part of a large Allied force that attacked along a 10-kilometre front that stretched from south of the Menin Road to north of Zonnebeke. The Australian front was 2,500 metres and ran through Polygon Wood, with its main objective a mound of high ground that had once been the butt of the local rifle range.

Today the wood is thick, with well-established trees, but at the time it was shattered and desolate after a period of pro-longed artillery barrage. Although the Australians took their objectives, they suffered heavy casualties, particularly the 5th Division, who after the war sited their divisional memorial on this hard-fought-over high ground.

After taking terrible casualties at Messines, the 45th Battalion had spent late August and the first weeks of September rebuilding the battalion, absorbing reinforcements and carrying out vigorous training and exercises. At Cuhem in the Bomy area, southwest of Aire, the battalion history records:

> The billets were not good but, although it was the first time Australians had been billeted in this locality, the diggers soon made friends with the hospitable French people.[1]

Not Private Lynch, though. His medical record states he was wounded on 20 August, when the battalion was in the frontline at Wambeke, northeast of Messines village, and taken to the rear and shipped to England on the 23rd. Like Nulla, who is wounded in the foot in this chapter, Lynch's medical record notes 'GSW foot', meaning 'gunshot wound, foot'. Lynch chose to put his narrator at Passchendaele and, given the historical and geographical accuracy of his account, it seems that he turned to the official battalion history for details and perhaps to photographs of the battlefields.

The battalion was given a number of inspections by

General Plumer, General Birdwood and the new divisional commander, Major General Sinclair-Maclagan. Men were presented with their decorations and no doubt congratulated on their fine work at Messines.

But Nulla knows what these inspections are really all about:

> Three inspections, plenty of reinforcements and an overdose of drill told us we were in for another stunt. A few inspections from the heads and it's a case of 'into the line' again. We know it only too well. It's not the first time we've seen the cooks inspecting the geese. [p. 230]

On 25 September, the 45th Battalion were brought up to be in the reserve line for an attack on Broodseinde Ridge. To get there, the men were forced on extended and exhausting route marches, sometimes 30 kilometres in a day, each weighed down with full packs, ammunition and a rifle. Although mechanised transport in the form of trucks, buses and trains was available, these long marches were made, both coming into and leaving the frontline, and this continued as the most common way of moving men for the rest of the war.

The road to the line took them through Ypres, past the ruined cathedral and the crumbling walls of the Cloth Hall, along the narrow streets, out through the Menin Gate and onto the Menin Road. Today, it is lined with commercial buildings and the once-feared Hellfire Corner that Nulla refers to – a vital crossroads that came under constant fire from the Germans on the high ground – is a sweeping landscaped roundabout. From here the road runs down a slight hill to Birr Cross Roads, easily missed except for the large Allied cemetery on the right. From there, the route to the front split off the Menin Road and became a corduroy track littered with smashed wagons, dead animals and the detritus of war.

Duckboards and corduroy roads were essential for moving men over the mud, but they were also death traps, as they were targets for German artillery, were easily seen and attacked from the air and there was often nowhere to escape off them. The area from Hellfire Corner to the frontline was under continual German observation and shelling. It is no wonder then that there were dead men and horses and wasted and destroyed war material and supplies strewn in the mud.

Reading these passages of Lynch's work, it is as if the unforgettable photographs of Australian photographer Frank Hurley have sprung to life. His photographs introduced the world to the hell of Passchendaele: stark, limbless trees, churned-up mud, lifeless bodies and Australian soldiers making their way over duckboard tracks that skirted water-filled shell-holes.

In August 1917, James Frances (Frank) Hurley had been appointed one of the AIF's official photographers and given the honorary rank of captain. Hurley had made a name for himself filming Ernest Shackleton's famous Antarctic expedition of 1914 to 1916, where he graphically captured the crushing of the expedition ship *Endurance* by pack ice and survived to present an exhibition in London. Sent by the AIF to Belgium, he took many graphic and horrifying photographs of the Broodseinde–Passchendaele fighting and photographed the 45th Battalion on Anzac Ridge, Garter Point, near Ypres.

If Hurley missed an event, he would sometimes get soldiers to re-stage it. For the sake of aesthetics and drama, he would mix images from different negatives to form a composite image. He was soon clashing with official historian Charles Bean, who criticised such methods. Due to the friction between the two men, Hurley threatened to resign, then was sent to Palestine to photograph the Light Horse.

Nulla mentions coming to the 'shell-torn ground of Bellewaerde Ridge' and today this is the site of a sprawling fun park. The men made their way to Westhoek Ridge and were kept busy in working parties, repairing the Westhoek to Zonnebeke road. Parties were also sent forward to reconnoitre possible routes to the Australian frontline positions they would shortly be required to take over. Moving forward, they occupied support-line positions at Garter Point on Anzac Ridge, relieving the Australian 50th Battalion just north of Polygon Wood. On 28 September, they took the right sector of the divisional front from the 13th and 15th battalions. Here they established four strongposts on the newly captured line and carried out 'vigorous patrolling'.

After four days in support of the 4th and 5th divisions' attack on Polygon Wood, the 45th were relieved and marched back to a communications trench dubbed The Great Wall of China, just a few hundred metres from the perilous Hellfire

Corner. The nearby Perth (China Wall) British Cemetery was probably a burial ground for men who died while in the medical lines at China Wall. Even though the battalion had been in the reserve line, they had suffered 17 men killed, two officers and 50 men wounded and one officer missing believed killed. From here they were bussed to Steenvoorde to join the nucleus who had been left behind.

While the 45th were at Garter Point on Anzac Ridge, the 1st, 2nd and 3rd Australian divisions, along with the New Zealanders, were preparing to push over the Broodseinde Ridge towards Passchendaele. The assault began on 4 October, the men having moved into position the previous night under constant drizzle. Just after 5 a.m., as they lay waiting on their start line for the advance, a deadly German artillery barrage fell upon them, inflicting heavy casualties. The Australian barrage in support of their attack opened up, but as the men rose out of the shell-holes in which they were waiting, they came under attack. Unknown to each other, the Germans and the Allies had planned attacks at exactly the same time. The two advancing lines of infantrymen suddenly found themselves in hand-to-hand fighting in no-man's-land.

The Allies took Broodseinde Ridge, but their casualties were far greater than they had expected. Further attacks were planned, but by 8 October the rain that had started just before the attack was torrential. Suddenly the offensive – reliant on men being in position, supplies coming forward and artillery advancing with the troops – became all but impossible. The ground turned into such a quagmire that in many places the frontline was indiscernible and battalion headquarters found it hard to locate their men and resupply and feed them. Progress was extremely difficult as men and transports had to skirt shell-holes full of water and meander across the shattered, muddy ground. As difficult as it was for infantry to move in such conditions, it was impossible for artillery batteries with horses and heavy gun carriages. Artillery was crucial to the advance but General Haig, oblivious to the mud and the conditions at the frontline, expected that they too could take their place in the attack. Passchendaele became synonymous with bottomless mud, rain, destruction and the insanity of command that resulted in enormous casualties for the Germans and the Allies.

The relief of the men in the 45th Battalion was short-lived, for after five days at Steenvoorde they were on the move, heading towards the front, as fighting on the ridgeline had slowed to a crawl and the battle was chewing up men daily. The battalion was not happy. As Nulla says early in the chapter, 'some of the men very decidedly voiced their opinions that the army heads had broken faith with our division'. The 4th Division had had the least rest as it had been rotating in and out of the line constantly, unlike the other four divisions of the AIF, which had had long periods in back areas. It was also weakest in numbers.

The fighting slowly moved forward through Zonnebeke to the Broodseinde Ridge just below Passchendaele. On 9 October, the 45th Battalion was sent forward on a forced march with a break of five minutes every hour. The narrow corduroy track was lit by exploding shells and German flares and congested by hundreds of men, including many wounded moving to the rear.

Uncertain of just where the frontline was, the battalion took up a defensive line along the Broodseinde Ridge just off the Zonnebeke to Passchendaele road in an area where a modern factory stands today. Looking at that modern factory with its metal walls, car parks and signage, it is all but impossible to believe this was part of the frontline and a place of such destruction and muddy desolation.

Cold, tired and wet, Nulla and his mates take their positions, load their rifles, snap on their bayonets and wait for first light. However, before dawn they must first establish contact with the posts next to them. Nulla and a sergeant crawl out into the mud to find themselves in a shattered trench near a narrow-gauge railway line, a length of track having been flung into the trench by shellfire. This was the remains of the Roulers to Ypres railway and the embankment and cuttings still exist today. The disused remnant of this railway crosses the road about 50 metres from the factory site and no more than 20 metres from the line of outposts that Lynch found himself in. This low railway cutting features in a famous Frank Hurley photograph and shows exhausted, wounded and dead Australians lying in the muddy ground.

As we know from his personal record, Lynch did not experience first-hand the action he wrote about, but was already in England recovering from his wounds. It is fascinating to see how he skilfully translated the 45th Battalion history into Nulla's unique and characteristic voice. In the battalion history we read:

Active patrolling was carried out and in one patrol . . . all the members were wounded, but managed to get back to our lines. Three prisoners were captured by a patrol under Sgt Payne and another patrol . . . captured two Germans . . . [2]

In *Somme Mud*, we read:

Suddenly rifles crash in front. An enemy machine-gun is sputtering savagely in the darkness. We grab our rifles and stand to anxiously. Gradually the racket quietens down. Our first patrol is out and back again. Word comes along that our patrol almost walked into an enemy post and were fired upon. The patrol had run for it and got back in, but every man was wounded . . . [p. 235]

And soon after:

Night drags slowly on. We hear that a patrol has captured three Fritz. An hour or so later word comes through that another patrol has landed two more prisoners. The boys are doing good work tonight. [p. 236]

The attack by the 2nd Division on 9 October failed, so on 12 October the Australian 47th and 48th battalions, in conjunction with the 3rd Division, attacked the Germans in the village of Passchendaele, on top of the Passchendaele Ridge. Carrying parties were sent from the 45th Battalion to take up rifle ammunition for the attack. Readers of *Somme Mud* see the action from the point of view of Nulla, who is working as a runner, delivering messages between his frontline position and the battalion headquarters.

The men involved in the attack faced heavy fire, and in 'Passing it on at Passchendaele', very soon we see the wounded streaming back, toppling into the shallow post where Nulla is awaiting further orders. These men carry smashed arms; they limp back with bloodshot eyes and, as Nulla says, 'tortured faces'. He joins with other able-bodied men to bind up the wounds, noting, 'Our teeth and lips are brown with iodine stains from biting through the tops of iodine bottles' [p. 240]. Word comes through that the first and then the second objective for the attack have been taken, as captured Germans stream back, forced to carry Australian wounded but glad to be out of the fight.

With another runner, Nulla is sent to deliver a message to the rear, when they are caught in a terrific barrage. Blown off his feet by a shell burst, he finds himself in a trench, lying awkwardly on the hard wooden duckboards and in great pain. Given that Lynch himself sustained a serious gunshot wound to the foot, there is little doubt that his account of Nulla's experiences authentically reflects his personal experience.

Indeed, what he describes is typical of many thousands of men wounded in the First World War.

Nulla is quickly helped, given water and assisted by the stretcher-bearers who come to his aid. They find it hard, however, to cut his laces and get his boot off until they realise he has used insulated telephone wire for bootlaces. With his boot off, they dress the wound and bandage it up. A stretcher cannot be used in the narrow trench, so they put him on the back of a strong stretcher-bearer to take him to the rear.

With shells exploding all around him, he is carried along, his mangled foot painfully banging against the side of the trench. At a relay station he is transferred to a stretcher and is subjected to a terrifying journey, held aloft, exposed as bullets whistle past. When the stretcher party is bombed by a German plane, Nulla manages to get off the stretcher and run for cover until the plane passes. The stretcher-bearers then carry him through the night and place him in a motor ambulance. Though it is a more comfortable ride with a mattress and blankets, the corrugations of the log roads increased wounded men's pain and suffering. And being in a clearly marked Red Cross vehicle did not guarantee protection. Ambulances came to grief, breaking through the corduroy roads or skidding into the mud and tipping over – or, as in Nulla's case, driving through enemy shelling.

Nulla arrives at a large Casualty Clearing Station. The doctors at Regimental Aid Posts and battalion headquarters could only provide basic medical help, such as stopping bleeding and ensuring wounds were sterilised and bandaged.

At the Casualty Clearing Centre, a man's wounds could finally be given more than cursory attention. Men were bathed and cleaned up before being operated on in a more sterile environment. Then they were each given one of the 'row upon row of beds, clean beds' that entice Nulla.

> Just the sight of a bed with snowy sheets seems to fly one into another world, a world removed from mud and slush, from bursting shells and tangled wire, from belching guns and circling flares. [p. 250]

Here too was a comforting sight to the wounded: female Australian nurses, who had been with the soldiers overseas from the very beginning of Australia's involvement in the war. Nurses had been part of the first convoy that left in October 1914, had arrived in Marseilles and travelled in mid-April 1916 to base hospitals in Étaples, Le Havre, Rouen and other places in northern France. Nurses were paid seven shillings a day, a shilling more than a private soldier, and sisters were paid nine shillings and sixpence a day. A total of 2,139 served with the Australian Army Nursing Service during the course of the war. Australian nurses also served in England with the Queen Alexandra Imperial Military Nursing Service, while others served in Salonika, in present-day Greece, and India.

Like all wounded men, Nulla is taken from the Casualty Clearing Station by slow train to the coast, in his case to Le Havre via Rouen, to be placed aboard a steamer for the short trip across the Channel to a large military hospital. Men with lesser wounds would have been sent to the hospitals at Étaples just south of Boulogne or to other rear areas to recover and convalesce.

On the wharf in England, men were helped from the ships by conscientious objectors. Lynch does not recoil from showing the lack of respect Nulla and the men have for those who refused to serve:

> They are perhaps doing their bit on home service, but never-theless we somehow despise them. Able-bodied men lurking at home when hundreds of army nurses and other women's units are often under shellfire across the Channel. [p. 254]

For a time, the war was over for both Edward Lynch, and his character Nulla. Lynch's wounds were to keep him out of the war for nine months, between late August 1917 and May 1918, when his personal record says he returned to his unit. For the rest of his life he would carry not only the physical and mental scars of his injuries, but also four pieces of shrapnel that were left in his body because they were considered too difficult to extract. They were still there when the family buried him in 1980.

Meanwhile, on the frontline at Passchendaele, in the face of heavy fire, the Australians could not hold the ground they had taken. The conditions remained bad, with men trying to fight through a morass of mud. Casualties climbed to an alarming level and eventually they had to fall back. Exhausted, their numbers severely depleted, they could do no more. Passchendaele would live on in Australia's memory as a deplorable, muddy nightmare, epitomised in row upon row of graves in the Tyne Cot cemetery.

# THIRTEEN

# Digging
# in at
# Dernancourt

While Private Lynch convalesced in England, the Great War
ground on. At Passchendaele, Canadian troops took over
from the Australians and by mid-November 1917 they had
taken the village, bringing to an end the Allied offensive
General Haig had begun in July. In all of this time, the
Allies had advanced only 8 kilometres yet had suffered
310,000 men killed, wounded or captured, while German
casualties numbered a further 260,000 men. Haig had
continued the offensive all those months, even when the rain
had set in and turned the battlefield to bottomless mud, the
Germans had assailed the troops with mustard gas, and any
hope of a breakthrough to the coast had faded. This brought
him widespread criticism and the loss of support within his
army – in particular a loss in confidence from his stalwart
Commander-in-Chief, Sir William Robertson, the Chief of
the Imperial General Staff.

On other fronts, the Italians had suffered high casualties in a severe defeat at the battle of Caporetto, north of Trieste, in what is now Slovenia, during October and November 1917. They were driven back by the German and Austro-Hungarian armies and had 300,000 men taken as prisoners of war; the rest retreated south, towards Venice.

In Palestine, taking the city of Gaza, a major Turkish position, had long been the Allies' goal, but attacks in March and April 1917 had failed. Late in October, the Third Battle of Gaza was launched by the British commander of the Egyptian Expeditionary Force, General Sir Edmund Allenby, and this attack utilised a new strategy. This time, Gaza was bombarded in order to trick the Turks into believing another attack was about to be launched, drawing Turkish forces to defend the city. Meanwhile, the Australian 4th Light Horse Brigade, in a famous charge at the Turkish guns, captured Beersheba, at the far eastern end of the Turkish defensive line. Once Beersheba had fallen, the Allies were able to overcome the Turks and take Gaza on 7 November. In December, Allenby entered Jerusalem and early the following year, Jericho fell to the Light Horse.

In France, in October 1917 the mysterious exotic dancer Mata Hari was executed by firing squad for spying. It was claimed she had passed secrets to German officers, but today her guilt seems doubtful. Her style of dancing was provocative and she appeared on stage wearing little clothing. She had a scandalously erotic lifestyle, being separated from her husband but keeping many lovers, including military officers. A mystique surrounded her: she purported to be a Javanese princess whose name was the Indonesian word for 'sun', but her background had been entirely fabricated. She was really Gertrud Margarete Zelle, the daughter of a Dutch hatter. It was probably these factors that led not only to her great popularity with the public but also doomed her to a death sentence. In the context of French disasters on the battlefield and the fact that her accuser, Georges Ladoux, was himself later convicted as a double agent, it seems she was simply a scapegoat in a larger espionage war between the French and the Germans.

On 27 October, American troops fired their opening shots in the war and in early November, the first Americans were killed. Later the same month, the American 'Rainbow Division', representing every state in the Union, arrived in France under Colonel Douglas MacArthur, someone we would hear a lot more about during the Second World War. It was the beginning of a massive American troop build-up and by the end of hostilities more than two million Americans would have joined the war in Europe, seriously tipping the balance in favour of the Allies in the last half of 1918.

On 20 November 1917, the Allies launched an attack on the French town of Cambrai, about 80 kilometres northeast of Amiens. Up to that point, tanks had been used in limited numbers and with disappointing results, but the Allies hoped that a new strategy of tanks attacking en masse would finally prove their worth. A total of 476 tanks, accompanied by infantry, cavalry and gunners, advanced at dawn across a 10-kilometre front and for the first time in the war, the Allies breached all three defensive layers of the Hindenburg Line. But stubborn German resistance, mechanical failure of tanks and bad co-ordination between tanks and supporting infantry thwarted the advance. The Germans counter-attacked using short bombardments, low-flying aircraft and new shock troops known as storm-troopers and by 7 December they had regained all of the ground won by the British offensive. However, the battle had shown that tanks, when massed, could effectively break through the strongest of trench defences. The lessons from Cambrai would influence planning for the rest of the war.

A bold new style of warfare had been introduced by the Germans in April of 1917, when they began bombing England during daylight hours. Utilising heavy bombers known as Gothas, they attacked from bases in Belgium, with London their main target; hundreds of civilians were killed. As anti-aircraft defences around the capital improved, the Germans reverted to night attacks and 19 raids were recorded between September 1917 and May 1918. The Germans also sent over Zeppelins and in a raid in October 1917, eight Zeppelins attacked London, four of which were shot down on their return over France. Paris too was bombed and in a raid in February 1918, 45 people were killed.

In Russia, on 7 November 1917, the Bolsheviks under Lenin occupied strategic buildings in the capital, Petrograd, including the Winter Palace, which was the seat of the Provisional Government. The Bolsheviks seized control and, soon after, Lenin offered Germany an armistice and peace talks began. But the Bolsheviks were slow to agree to peace terms and the Germans recommenced hostilities in February 1918. The next month, the Russians were forced to sign a humiliating treaty at Brest-Litovsk, giving up control of many areas including the Ukraine, which was a crucial acquisition for starved Germany, as it gave them access to the Ukrainians' grain harvest.

In London, the government was already planning ahead and trying to decide the question of how the Ottoman Empire, which included Palestine, should be divided up following an Allied victory in the war. In November 1917, the British Foreign Secretary, Arthur Balfour, supported a proposal by the Chairman of the British Zionist Federation, Lord Rothschild, for the establishment of a Jewish homeland in Palestine. It came to be known as the 'Balfour Declaration'. In England, as in Germany, rationing was biting. Meat, butter and margarine were rationed in London and the adjacent Home Counties. The German air raids and the February 1918 sinking of the British hospital ship *Glenart Castle* by a U-boat in the Bristol Channel kept the British people focused and fearful.

In January 1918, US President Woodrow Wilson put forward a 14-point peace plan designed to prevent future war, settle international disputes and provide national self-determination and collective security. At the end of hostilities, those 14 points would become the basis for the Treaty of Versailles.

In Australia, Billy Hughes, who had failed once with his

conscription referendum, again ignited the debate and took it to the people. In late November 1917, he arrived in Warwick in southern Queensland as part of his campaign for the second conscription rally. While addressing the crowd, he was pelted with eggs and asked that the police arrest the egg-thrower, only to be informed by the policeman that he obeyed the laws of Queensland first and had no right to arrest the demonstrator. Aware he had neither protection nor a legal right to request it, Hughes established what became the Australian Federal Police – and all because someone threw an egg at him.

In December 1917, Hughes held a second conscription plebiscite, which again failed to produce his hoped-for 'Yes' vote. He resigned as prime minister, only to be recommissioned by the governor-general. Meanwhile, Australians suspected of being pro-German were being rounded up. One man interned at this time was the Prussian-born Sydney brewer Edmund Resch, snatched from his home in Darling Point where, it was believed by the police, he had watched and reported on Allied shipping movements on Sydney Harbour. German nationals, even German descendants, were interned, as there remained a strong fear of spies and saboteurs continuing their work. German place names were changed, especially in South Australia, where a large German community lived in the Barossa Valley. In New South Wales, Germantown was renamed Holbrook and in central South Australia, Herrgott Springs became Marree.

Since the expansion of the Australian and New Zealand forces in Egypt after the evacuation of Gallipoli, they had been fighting in two separate formations, known as I Anzac Corps and II Anzac Corps. Although their composition varied, particulary in 1917, the first comprised the 1st, 2nd, 4th and 5th Australian divisions, under General Birdwood's command. The second was made up of the Australian 3rd Division plus the New Zealanders, and it came under General Sir Alexander Godley's command. Birdwood and Godley were both British, as were many of the other officers of I Anzac and II Anzac.

From the beginning of the war there had been murmurings that Australians should fight as a national army and now the failure of the British command structure and the unreliability of British troops emphasised the urgency for a unified Australian corps in the minds of military and political leaders. The Australian soldiers had little time for the British army, had long distrusted the British High Command and held scant regard for the average British soldier, whom they viewed as generally weak, skinny, sallow and undernourished. When it came to a stoush, most dismissed the Tommies as unreliable, second-rate soldiers who could not be relied on to hold the line and fight. Some were compared unfavourably with the Chinese Labour Corps. General Monash confided his feelings about English troops in a letter dated 4 April 1918 to his wife in Melbourne: 'Some of these Tommy Divisions are the absolute limit, and not worth the money it costs to put them in uniform . . . bad troops, bad staffs, bad commanders.'[1]

Not that the Australians were particularly liked by the British Tommy. One is quoted as saying 'I hate the Aussies as do all British Tommies.' From the High Command down, the Australians were seen as ill-disciplined, boisterous, arrogant and conceited. They were famous for 'ratting' prisoners, lacked manners, were seen as looters and thieves and when they were on leave in England they were always up to mischief. There were ten times the number of Australians in military prisons compared to English soldiers, and the number of Absent Without Leave cases in the AIF far exceeded any other army.[2] Fortunately for the Australians, they were not shot for this offence, which could easily be classed as desertion from the front but in Australian terms was seen as time-out to go to the pub.

The absence of the death penalty for Australian troops, enshrined in the Defence Act, annoyed the British High Command. They saw serious discipline problems in the AIF and wished to make an example of the Australian men; they also found it difficult applying one set of rules to their troops and another to the Australians. Even the New Zealand Division allowed the death penalty, and executed five men during the course of the war. In Rawlinson's Fourth Army, of 182 cases of Absence Without Leave, 130 were Australians. In the Fifth Army, the police reported that of 43 prisoners who escaped from detention, 30 were Australians. The early threat of being sent home to Australia in disgrace no longer worked and men in many cases preferred gaol to the risks of the frontline.

Pleas from British field commanders to introduce the death penalty in the AIF fell on deaf ears in Australia. Public feeling was strongly against such a step. These men were, after all, volunteers who had travelled to a distant war not of their making. Opposition to the death penalty came down to a sense of common justice and the need to encourage volunteers. Punishment for being AWL was field imprisonment, with nine in 1,000 Australians imprisoned, compared to one per 1,000 British troops and less than two per 1,000 Canadians, New Zealanders and South Africans.

But one thing the Australians could do was fight and, in large measure, this made up for their lack of discipline, their disrespect and their general contempt for the English.

By mid-1917, the idea of a separate Australian army under Australian command was being openly espoused by newspaperman Keith Murdoch (father of Rupert Murdoch), who was highly influential and acted as an intermediary between the British and Australian prime ministers, Lloyd George and Billy Hughes. Murdoch implored Hughes to embrace the Australian soldiers' desire to form a unified Australian corps led by Australian officers and, in doing so, bring I Anzac and II Anzac together (and without General Sir Alexander Godley) under one corps. This would, it was hoped, bring due recognition and a sense of identity to the Australian divisions, which had previously been considered and referred to in communiqués as 'British' troops.

And so, on 1 January 1918, the five Australian divisions were united for the first time and called the Australian Army Corps, under the overall command of Lieutenant General William Birdwood. From May 1918, this was commanded by

Major General John Monash, a Victorian engineer who became the first Australian to command the five Australian Divisions and was to take responsibility for the massive repatriation of Australian troops back to Australia after the armistice. The New Zealanders and two British divisions that had been fighting with II Anzac were renamed XXII Corps.

After Passchendaele, in late November 1917, the 45th Battalion marched 110 kilometres over eight days – a massive distance to walk by today's standards – to St Quentin-la-Motte, 3 kilometres from the English Channel. Just nine days later, the battalion moved to Péronne, on the Somme. There the men spent a miserable month, cold and housed in poor accommodation. They did not even celebrate Christmas as they were constantly on alert, being the only reserve battalion in that part of the line. The men had the opportunity to vote in the second conscription plebiscite but few men took any interest as, according to the battalion history, they were 'fatalists'.

On 8 January 1918, the battalion entrained at Péronne and moved north to Hollebeke, in Belgium, arriving there on 11 January. It was another cold winter with heavy snow; whenever the snow thawed, mud and slush made the frontline trenches very uncomfortable. Fortunately, enemy shelling caused few casualties and although the battalion was rotated in and out of the line, they had little activity.

The Allied commanders were all too aware of the situation in Russia and Italy and knew that a German offensive was likely in the coming spring. The focus turned to building defensive lines and preparing for the attack. Once the peace treaty between Germany and the Bolsheviks had been signed, in March 1918, the war on the Eastern Front ceased. The Germans quickly moved an estimated 44 divisions to the Western Front and on 21 March 1918, General Ludendorff launched 'Operation Michael' with the hope of splitting the French and British armies along the line of the Amiens to Péronne road, driving them back to the Channel and capturing Paris. Suddenly, after all the stalemate and the attrition, the war had taken on a new urgency. The Allies found themselves in deep trouble.

The offensive was devastating and the Germans quickly ripped a gaping hole in the British front and forced them back toward Amiens. The Allies' fear was that if the Germans captured the railhead of Amiens, it would seriously, perhaps catastrophically, disrupt Allied railway communication for much of Northern France and Belgium. With the British falling back and totally demoralised, the Australian 3rd and 4th divisions were rushed south to strengthen the front that extended north and south of the Somme, from west of Albert near Dernancourt to south of Villers-Bretonneux.

Concern was spreading in the British and French High Commands, and tension was growing between General Haig and the French General Pétain as to where to place reserve troops and what defensive line to hold. The objective of the Allies was clarified at a meeting of political and military leaders at Doullens on 26 March, where the newly appointed supreme commander of the Allied forces, General Foch, declared, 'We must fight in front of Amiens, we must fight where we are now. As we have not been able to stop the Germans on the Somme, we must not now retire a single inch.'[3]

The 45th was among the battalions sent to plug the gaps in the British line and stem the German onslaught. As part of a unified Australian Corps, they had a new pride and enthusiasm for the war ahead. The Australians were eager for a fight and welcomed the German offensive as a chance to give the enemy a good hiding. Now the Australians were in defensive positions and the Germans were in the open and running at their guns, not the reverse, as had been the case for so long and would be again in the near future.

After a hot meal – and carrying all the ammunition they could – the battalion set out from Méteren at 10 p.m. on 25 March 1918, four days after the start of the German offensive. By seven the next morning, they had marched 17 miles (about 27 kilometres) – an amazing distance to cover in just nine hours. As the battalion history records:

> This march through the night was a memorable one as the route was only a few kilometres from the fluctuating line, and owing to the presence of the enemy, it was necessary to have advanced and flank guards for the protection of the main body.[4]

By this time, the German advance had pushed 40 kilometres into the Allied front. The Allies had lost all the hard-won ground they had taken in the previous 18 months. Now places such as Bapaume, Pozières, Gueudecourt and Stormy Trench were behind German lines. Nulla is, as he says, 'back with the old battalion again after half a year in English hospitals and various base depots and feeling good'. While Nulla may have been back, Private Lynch was still recuperating and convalescing in England, so bad were his wounds. It would be another three months before he was fit enough to return to the rigour of the frontline in France.

The 45th were rushed to Dernancourt along roads thick with French refugees fleeing before the German advance. The civilians put their faith in the Australians. A group of refugees from Hébuterne, about 12 kilometres north of Pozières, trundling west before the German advance, are reported to have stopped when they saw the Australian troops and said, *'Pas nécessaire maintenant – vous les tiendrez'*, meaning 'It's not necessary now – you'll hold them.'[5] For their part, the Australian soldiers were confident they could live up to the local people's expectations. One was heard to tell a village woman about to join the flood of refugees: *'Fini retreat Madame – beaucoup Australiens ici!'*, meaning 'No more retreat Madame – many Australians here.'[6]

On a hillside overlooking the village of Dernancourt the 45th Battalion dug in, working all night in preparation for the anticipated dawn attack by the Germans, while below them the 47th and 48th battalions were defending a railway embankment. With a front so long and few available men, the Australians' defensive line was very thin, in places only secured by a small sentry party. One such party was Sergeant Stan McDougall and two men of the 47th Battalion, who were sent out to keep watch near a level crossing along the railway line to the north of Dernancourt. In the half light of dawn, as a low mist swirled around, Sergeant McDougall heard the distinctive slap of bayonet scabbards on the thighs of marching troops not 100 metres away. He quickly warned his men, then suddenly found himself confronted by Germans advancing on a wide front.

Immediately, German bombs burst among the small group of Australians, seriously wounding two Lewis gunners who had just opened up on the advancing line of enemy. McDougall grabbed the Lewis gun and, charging, killed two German machine-gun crews and scattered the attack. He then ran along the edge of the embankment, where he found himself looking down onto a party of 20 Germans crouched in potholes and shell-holes. He turned the Lewis gun on them, hosing their position with fire, and they fled. Seeing about 50 Germans who had just crossed the railway line, he began to fire on them, but by now his hands were badly blistered from the barrel casing, which had become hot. His mate Sergeant Lawrence, a station overseer from Cloncurry in Queensland, came to his aid, holding the gun so that McDougall could fire it with his uninjured hand. McDougall then charged the Germans with a rifle and bayonet, driving them off. For this he was awarded the Victoria Cross. Just eight days later, he won a Military Medal close to the same position.

By the morning of 28 March, the Germans had taken Albert, about 4 kilometres northeast of Dernancourt, and were attacking along the railway line that ran from Albert to Amiens. The Germans attacked the Australian positions on the reverse side of the railway embankment just outside the village and were driven off. During that day, nine further German attacks were made. They were not successful but, owing to the number of casualties, the 45th Battalion's B Company moved into the frontline to relieve the exhausted men of the 47th. The Germans meanwhile moved troops into Dernancourt, ready to break out of the village and storm across the railway line to attack the Australians on the hillside to the north and northwest.

On 29 March, the 45th took over the frontline extending nearly a kilometre north of Dernancourt. In *Somme Mud*, on 1 April, Nulla recounts that the Australians have been waving at two women in the village. The women have been waving back and pointing to indicate that the Germans are in one of the houses, but when the Australians signal for them to make their escape, they don't attempt to, as the Germans would see them. This incident is also reported by C. E. W. Bean in his chapter on Dernancourt, but he mentions one old Frenchwoman rather than two. He quotes Captain Adams of the 45th Battalion, who reported that on 31 March:

She . . . pointed behind her as though the Germans were in her house. We waved to her to come over, but she shook her head. She also appeared to be using very unladylike language, probably using insulting words.[7]

Meanwhile, Australian snipers accounted for one German officer and 20 other ranks and on the following day, 25 Germans.

On 2 April, the 45th Battalion was relieved; but for the nine days at Dernancourt they had two of their officers and 21 other ranks had been killed and one officer and 60 other ranks wounded.

They were not out of the line for long. Information from a captured German revealed that a major attack was to be launched at Dernancourt, so the battalion moved back, taking up a position on the hillside to the northwest that overlooked the railway line and beyond it the village. In *Somme Mud*, the opening of the German attack is a strange, surreal, almost dreamlike sequence. From afar comes the sound of marching music, the unmistakable yet unbelievable sound of a German military band. And sure enough, as the morning mist clears, the sun glints off their brass instruments. They are leading a battalion of soldiers, with officers on horses and a line of horse-drawn transports in the rear. As the Australians open fire and the Germans fall wounded or run for Dernancourt, Nulla notices, 'Something bright lies shining on the road – band instruments' [p. 267].

There is no mention of these events in Bean's official histories nor in the history of the 45th Battalion, so Lynch's account is hard to verify. It is worth remembering that at this time Lynch was still away from his battalion recuperating from his injuries and also that, according to Bean, visibility was low due to heavy fog.

On the morning of 5 April, the much-anticipated major German attack was launched. The units holding the railway embankment were forced to retreat, and hundreds of German infantry streamed over the embankment and through a railway arch, penetrating the Australian position and capturing some of the high ground. The Australian frontline was pushed back to Pioneer Trench, on the slope. The German attack at Dernancourt was later described by Bean in the official history as 'the strongest ever met by Australian troops . . . and one of the most difficult to resist'.[8] It had involved three German divisions against two Australian brigades – a ratio of about six men to one in favour of the German attackers.

The 45th Battalion were brought forward to Pioneer Trench and late in the day they, along with the 47th and 49th, counter-attacked. This counter-attack is the one so memorably described by Lynch in *Somme Mud*, where the men keep 'that perfect parade-ground formation . . . despite flying bullets and falling mates' [p. 274]. Nulla goes on to muse, 'Yet they say the Australians lack discipline – the biggest lie of jealous lying criticism.' The battalion history clearly describes the attack:

The counter stroke was made with great dash, the platoons and companies keeping excellent formation and maintaining touch with the units on the flanks. As they advanced, they suffered severely from the enemy's machine-gun fire, but they kept steadily on until about a hundred yards from their objective when they charged with fixed bayonets. After some hand to hand fighting the enemy retreated in disorder, leaving behind prisoners and machine-guns. The superior fighting qualities of the Australians had told and the ridge was again in our possession.[9]

They succeeded in pushing the Germans part of the way back down the slope, but did not attempt to go all the way and recapture the railway. As for the Australian counter-attack, Bean judged it to be 'one of the finest ever carried out by Australian troops'.[10] Although the fighting caused heavy losses, the Australians did succeed in preventing the Germans from commanding the high ground to the west of Albert, which seriously curtailed German operations in the area.

The 45th withdrew from the frontline, spent a few days in support, then undertook a long and tiring march to Bussy-lès-Daours, about 12 kilometres east of Amiens. Though exhausted, not a man fell out on this long march. Arriving at their billets, they were welcomed, according to the battalion history, by the battalion band and a well-earned hot meal. In the fighting at Dernancourt, in just 14 days the 45th Battalion had suffered total casualties of 16 officers and 237 men, including seven officers and 46 other ranks killed.

Dernancourt slumbers in a low valley, bounded on one side by the railway line and on the other by the River Ancre.

Looking down from the hillside on the northwest where the 45th Battalion were positioned, the view today is of a long line of rooftops above the railway embankment, dominated by the spire of the church. Behind, the rolling hills are broken in places by small wooded areas. Tree-lined roads dissect the golden yellow wheat fields. The area could almost be mistaken for southern New South Wales, around Yass, or further west at Binalong, except for the absence of gum trees and the odd hillside scoured by erosion. The railway line still passes close to the village, the railway underpass still remains and the embankment defended so gallantly by the men of the Australian 4th Division is much as it was in 1918, though an old wooden bridge the Australians fought hard to defend but had to retreat from has been replaced. Near the railway underpass is the Dernancourt town cemetery, in the same place it was during the fighting in early 1918, and now, beside it, the Dernancourt Communal Cemetery Extension, where 418 Australians are buried.

Here lie the bodies of a number of men from the 45th Battalion, including Scottish-born Lieutenant James Sutter Terras, who was killed in action on the first day of the German attack. He was a married 33-year-old schoolmaster who embarked on the HMAT *Ceramic* in November 1916 as part of the sixth reinforcement to the 45th Battalion. (His name appears on the war memorial in the north Sydney suburb of Hornsby.) In a letter to his wife from the officer in charge of Base Records, it stated, 'Your husband . . . was shot through the head and chest by a sniper and is buried at Albert, France', adding, 'It is the policy of the Department to forward all information received in connection with deaths of members of the Australian Imperial Force.'[11]

Also buried there is Private Arthur David Wells (army service number 4328), another British-born Australian from Sussex. He was single and stated his trade as a stonemason, but was killed at 34. An initial report notes that he was wounded and believed captured, however his personal file states he was 'Missing believed to be a POW'. There were still enquiries and official letters going out to his family in late September 1918 and a Commission of Inquiry was launched to inquire into his fate. There is a note in his file that he could not be traced as a POW in Germany and it was only after Australians captured at Dernancourt were released and gave statements to the Red Cross after the war, that the circumstances of his death could be cleared up.

In November, the family finally received a letter stating that 'we deeply regret having to inform you that he is now officially reported as Killed in Action on the 5th or 6th April 1918'.[12] It is interesting to note the trouble both the AIF and the Red Cross went to in trying to ascertain how individuals died and to report these findings to the next of kin. Although information travelled slowly by today's standards, it was a detailed and efficient system.

# FOURTEEN

# Around
# Villers-Bret

It was just after first light as I made my way along the towpath. The hoot of a nightjar broke the stillness of the dawn as the mist rose, curling in wisps from the river Somme. A fish broke the surface, gulping at insects and churning the placid green water in its wake before disappearing into the murky depths. Far off, the hum of traffic on the Amiens to St Quentin road was all that broke the dawn silence. So still, I thought; in early 1918 it was not this peaceful.

The German counter-attack of March was the last great gamble of the German army against the British section of the front. Both sides were exhausted, having fought each other to a standstill, and if one side was to win, it would be from the last ounce of strength, perhaps 'the last man and the last shilling'[1] as Andrew Fisher (the leader of the Labor Opposition in 1914) had said, that would do it. For the

Germans, they now had the Eastern Front divisions, but their army was war-weary, hungry, low on men and the recruits to the front were very young and inexperienced.

German supplies of raw material were exhausted and the British naval blockade was starving the German population. The Allies too were exhausted, but the influx of American troops was a great morale booster and would quickly change the balance of the war.

While the 4th Division had been holding the Germans at Dernancourt (and also at Hébuterne, about 20 kilometres to the north), the 3rd Division had dug in on the heights at Sailly-le-Sec on the high ground above the Somme and the nearby Somme canal, about 9 kilometres southwest of Dernancourt. Here they held back the German advance in April with daring acts of 'peaceful penetration'.[2] These trench raids kept the front active and enabled the Australians to secure prisoners for interrogation, collect valuable intelligence and capture enemy machine-gun posts. Peaceful penetration stunts were carried out by small groups of men and the bold, cocky strategy worked, helping to garner information about the Germans' plans while striking fear in the hearts of the German frontline troops.

One such example was an audacious daylight raid undertaken on the German trenches by the Intelligence Officer of the 17th Battalion, Lieutenant A. W. Irvine. During the struggle over the small village of Morlancourt, Irvine noticed that the warm sun had sent most of his men to sleep. Even the sentry was half asleep. Realising the Germans would also likely be drowsy, he led a raiding party on the nearby German lines, killed four of the enemy and captured another 22, returning without casualties ten minutes later.

Each of the five Australian divisions has its own battlefield memorial and, after the war, the men of the 3rd Division decided they would place theirs on the well-fought-over ground around Sailly-le-Sec instead of the heights at Messines, the site of their first major battle after they were formed in February 1916. Today, this memorial sits at the crossroads of the Bray to Corbie road and the road from Sailly-le-Sec and is easily found by travellers.

The villages along the Somme in this area are especially pretty. In spring, they are decked in flowers that spill over walls and soften the landscape. There is a dreamy, rural feel about the places where Australian soldiers once raided orchards and swam in the Somme. It is a good place for a quiet holiday, as a base for a visit to the battlefields or to reflect on Australian history along the Somme valley. Driving from Corbie to Bray, the most scenic route follows the river through the villages of Vaux-sur-Somme, Sailly-Laurette and Chipilly, but if you go along the ridgeline you will pass the 3rd Division Memorial and the crash site of the Red Baron, German flying ace Baron Manfred von Richthofen, who was shot down by the Australians on 21 April 1918.

While the 3rd Division was holding the open country between Sailly-le-Sec and Morlancourt, the Germans diverted their advance and began their attack on Villers-Bretonneux. The town, southwest of Sailly-le-Sec, was important to the

Allies' defence of Paris. From the ridgeline at Villers-Bretonneux, the Germans could see the cathedral at Amiens about 18 kilometres to the west, and the city spread out, a tempting target. Amiens was a railway town, vital for Allied resupply, so the town's rail infrastructure attracted German shelling.

The Germans' first assault on Villers-Bretonneux came on 28 March 1918, but they were held back by the British 1st Cavalry Division. On 4 April, after an intense artillery barrage, 15 German divisions mounted a massive attack against the cavalry and the Australian 33rd Battalion. With the support of the Lancers (a British cavalry unit), the 33rd and 34th Australian battalions counter-attacked to the southeast of Villers-Bretonneux, through Lancer Wood and into the open fields beyond. They were halted by German machine-guns, but the 34th Battalion swept through the ragged line and attacked the Germans with bayonets. An eyewitness, Private John Hardie of the 33rd, who was a farmer from Grong Grong near Junee in New South Wales, later wrote:

> The enemy screamed and howled for mercy, but all he got was the bayonet, that is, those that didn't run away. Our lads didn't fire a shot, but used the bayonet something awful . . . they passed over our wounded and dying coming up and it roused their blood.[3]

While the frontline fighting around Villers-Bretonneux continued, Nulla and the 45th were marched out of

Dernancourt to a rest area at Bussy-lès-Daours on the Somme, just outside Amiens. This was only about 7 kilometres from the fighting. After a brief rest, they moved to Cardonnette, another 7 kilometres north. Apart from the recent fighting, like most of the Australian divisions they had been out of the line for months; training, rebuilding their battalions and getting ready for their next contact with the enemy. And now feeling part of the Australian Corps, in theory under Australian control through General Monash, there was fresh pride and enthusiasm for the war ahead and a new keenness to come to grips with the enemy.

After a lull, the Germans heavily shelled Villers-Bretonneux, drenching it in gas on 17 and 18 April 1918, causing nearly 1,000 Australian casualties on those two days alone. But the big German attack came a week later, when defence of the area had been handed back to the British while the Australian battalions regrouped. At 3.45 a.m. on 24 April, they laid down a heavy bombardment along the whole front, across the village, the nearby woods and the surrounding roads and strategic strongpoints. The attack was assisted by a heavy fog, made all the worse by smoke and gas shells. Suddenly, out of the mist came German tanks, heavy lumbering monsters weighing 30 tons, bristling with machine-guns and each crewed by 18 men.

The appearance of the tanks created instant panic in the English defenders, who had no suitable anti-tank weapons to use against them. The German attack also included storm-troopers armed with light machine-guns and flamethrowers.

They quickly pushed back the British, leaving many dead and wounded. For the rest of the day, the Germans continued their attack.

When news of the German assault and the capture of the town reached Allied High Command, they immediately ordered an Australian counter-attack the next day, which happened to be the third anniversary of the landing at Anzac Cove. There was very little time for the Australian command to plan the operation, brief the platoon commanders, organise the attacking battalions and get them to their start lines.

After a brief rain shower early in the night and with the full moon covered by dark clouds, the men of the 13th Brigade marched for their start line, about 3 kilometres southwest of Villers-Bretonneux, with the town of Cachy to their right and L'Abbé Wood to their left. They had been instructed to skirt the wood on their left because, they were told, it was free of the enemy, having been cleared and secured by British troops earlier in the day. Their objective was Monument Wood, named for a monument commemorating an 1870 battle during the Franco-Prussian War. There they were to meet up with the 15th Brigade, who would have skirted around the other side of the village; thus the two brigades would surround the Germans and drive them out.

The 13th Brigade formed up, ready to move off at 10 p.m. Captain Billy Harburn, a West Australian of the 51st Battalion, was quite emphatic with his men about the need to press on and reach their objective by 11 p.m.: 'The Monument is your goal and nothing is to stop your getting there. Kill every bloody German you see, we don't want any prisoners, and God Bless you.'[4]

As the Australians started to move forward, the Germans were quick to react. Flares lit the sky and machine-guns raked the lines of advancing men. Lieutenant Clifford Sadlier was leading a platoon of Captain Harburn's men, on the left flank, closest to L'Abbé Wood. Sadlier had reassured the men not to worry about any noises coming from the wood, as it would only be English troops cleaning up the last of the enemy. What the Allies didn't realise was that enemy troops were in fact holding the southern and south-western edges of the wood. Thirty-nine of Sadlier's 42 men were hit by German fire. In response, Sadlier led a party of men, including Seargeant Stokes, who was leading the platoon next to his, into the wood to wipe out the Germans. Sadlier was soon shot in the thigh but continued to charge on through the darkness, firing wildly as he attacked the German machine-guns. Wounded again, he was taken to the rear, but Stokes led the dwindling number of uninjured men, subduing the last remaining German guns and eliminating the threat to the Australian advance. Both Sadlier and Stokes were recommended for the Victoria Cross, but it was only awarded to Sadlier as it was said he was the leader and responsible for this gallant action. Sergeant Stokes was awarded the Distinguished Conduct Medal.

On the other side of Villers-Bretonneux, Brigadier General 'Pompey' Elliott's boys – the 15th Brigade – were forming up for their attack on a line stretching from near Hill 104 to the line of the Hamel road. The men had to march 3 kilometres up from the flats near the river to the start line, but because of the darkness and gas that had settled in the hollows of the landscape, there was a delay getting all the battalions in place. Finally, at midnight, two hours after the scheduled 'zero hour', the men began their advance. When a German flare fell near a group of men, the order was given to charge. Artillery had been bombarding Villers-Bretonneux and with the flames from a large house acting as a landmark in the darkness, the men charged forward, yelling at the top of their voices. Bean later wrote that the 'men had thrown off the restraints of civilised intercourse and were what the bayonet instructors of all armies aimed at producing . . . primitive, savage men'.[5]

It was a terrible time for the German defenders. 'With a ferocious roar and the cry of "Into the bastards, boys," we were down on them before the Boche realised what had happened . . . They screamed for mercy . . . and old scores were wiped out two or three times over,'[6] wrote Sergeant Fynch of the 59th Battalion, a Victorian plasterer who was to die in the fighting at Le Hamel in early July 1918. Colonel Watson, Elliott's special intelligence officer, said that men later reported 'they had not had such a feast with their bayonets before',[7] and the next day the ground over which the attack surged was littered with the bodies of butchered Germans. Early on in the counter-attack, few Germans survived as prisoners, but when 'the men tired of killing, prisoners came back by droves',[8] Bean commented.

By 3.30 a.m. on 25 April, the Australians had nearly

encircled Villers-Bretonneux and, although they had not retaken the old British frontline, they had regained in five hours the ground lost by the British the previous day. Neither the 13th nor the 14th had quite reached their objectives, which would have completely cut off the town, but they were so close that it now looked promising that the Germans could be pushed out of Villers-Bretonneux and the nearby woods.

To that end, the British mopped up Germans who were cut off in the town, taking many prisoners, while other British units attacked across almost a kilometre-wide frontage towards Hangard Wood south of Villers-Bretonneux. A German counter-attack was delayed and finally cancelled when the morning fog lifted, enabling British artillery to shell their forming-up areas and the troops sent to strengthen their line.

The 45th Battalion meanwhile was at Querrieu, 10 kilometres northwest of Villers-Bretonneux. Plans were in hand for a sports meeting to celebrate the third anniversary of the landing, but according to the unit war diary of the 45th Battalion, 'In view of the uncertainty of the battalion's movements, the gathering was postponed indefinitely.'[9]

The following two days, 26 and 27 April, Australians of the 4th and 12th brigades of the 4th Division moved into Villers-Bretonneux and took over from the exhausted men of the 13th and 15th brigades while Nulla and his mates took over from the 50th Battalion to the south of the town. Here it became the most southerly Allied unit in the British frontline, an honour that was noted in the battalion history, with the 8th

Zouave Regiment from the famous Moroccan Division of the French army on its left flank. However, the main fight was over and Villers-Bretonneux would not see Germans in town for another 22 years, when advancing Wehrmacht units would storm down the same Roman road and this time make it to Amiens.

Nulla is sent into Villers-Bretonneux after the battle, on a trip to collect war material, and it is through his eyes we see a town that was heavily damaged and continually shelled long after it was captured. It was strewn with the bodies of dead Germans and Allied troops and its cellars were often full of gas and very dangerous. However, the town had good pickings for the looters, including food and wine left by the townsfolk, plus a woollen mill where clothing of all types lay stored, ready for shipment. This was naturally made use of by the troops and included, as Nulla says:

> Shelves and shelves of socks and singlets, cardigans and jerseys . . . thousands of good knitted scarves too . . . I get loaded up . . . for the boys and even the officer has a bag of it. [p. 286]

He goes on about the good day of pilfering:

> It's dusk now and we're making back to the line loaded with bags of socks and singlets, wine, timber, corrugated iron, heavy planks and iron rails.

While in Villers-Bretonneux, the Australians found 15 wounded Germans (in *Somme Mud* Nulla tells us there were eight but the War Diary states 15) who had been hiding for five days in a cellar in the town since its capture. This was a dangerous period for these German troops as the German shelling of the town with both high explosives and gas was relentless and buildings were being demolished everywhere. To be trapped in a cellar would have been a frightening option for these Germans, so their final release and their ultimate capture was possibly something of a godsend.

On 4 May, the men of the 45th were relieved at 1.30 a.m. by men of the Australian 51st Battalion and came out of the frontline at Villers-Bretonneux. They marched back to Blangy-Tronville, arriving at 3.30 a.m. By 6 a.m. the cookers had arrived and after breakfast the rest of the day was spent bathing and resting.

We know little of Lynch in the period he was away from his battalion, except what we can glean from his personal file. It shows that on 20 April 1918, just days before the glorious Australian attack at Villers-Bretonneux, he was getting into trouble at Codford, one of the towns near the 4th Division training area outside Salisbury in England. He was charged with 'Conduct to the prejudice of good order and military discipline in that he at Codford on the 14.4.18 tampered with goods and property of the public'. It is hard to know what his actual offence was, but his file states that he was to forfeit four days' pay.

On 28 April, Private Lynch travelled from Codford to

Folkestone and thence to France. The next entry in his personal file notes his arrival at the British and Australian base at Étaples on 30 April. He remained there until he rejoined his battalion at Villers-Bretonneux on 17 May and soon he was back in the frontline, for by 20 May they had returned for their 'second innings' on the frontline at Villers-Bretonneux. Though the crucial battle had been won, the enemy was still active and causing Australian casualties. Although the town of Villers-Bretonneux was secured, the area in the immediate vicinity was still in German hands. This included the south-eastern side of Monument Wood, which remained a hostile front for some time.

The highly effective counter-attack at Villers-Bretonneux had added greatly to the reputation of the AIF as a supreme fighting unit. Even the British responded favourably, with Brigadier General George Grogan stating the attack was 'perhaps the greatest individual feat of the war'. Australian troops were praised as 'about the finest in the world' and described as displaying 'such magnificent moral [sic].'[10] The Australian staff, from Monash down, showed great pride in their men, even crediting the success to the troops rather than to the staff's organisation and foresight. Brigadier 'Pompey' Elliot, whose men had undertaken the gallant charge on 25 April, called it 'a soldier's fight, pure and simple'.[11]

Villers-Bretonneux is now much like any other small French town, except for all the reminders of Australia. After the war, the town took on a very special significance to Australians, especially to Victorians, as it was that state's battalions that made up the 15th Brigade. With money collected by schoolchildren in Victoria, a new school was built, known to this day as the 'Victoria School'. Its top floor houses a sizeable and well-endowed museum of Australian military equipment and photographs. Some of the town's streets, shops and cafés have Australian names and there is an Australian flag flying from the town hall. In 1984, Villers-Bretonneux became a sister town to Robinvale, a small Victorian town on the banks of the Murray River.

On the road north, on what was the strategic Hill 104, stands the Australian National Memorial. This was built in the mid-1930s and dedicated by King George VI in July 1938. It contains the names of nearly 11,000 Australians killed in France with no known grave. On Anzac Day 2008, the first full official Dawn Service was held there and it is hoped that this will become an annual service in years to come. The memorial overlooks a large cemetery containing more than 2,100 graves, beautifully maintained by the Commonwealth War Graves Commission. Buried in the cemetery are 779 Australians, many of whom fell during the fighting for the town, but also others who were re-interred here from temporary burial sites in the Somme area.

Villers-Bretonneux is the starting and ending point for Australian visitors to the Somme battlefields and the focus of Australian commemorations in France. One of the stops on many Australians' visits used to be the Red Chateau, the ruins of the big house that had been on fire in the early hours of 25 April, which the 15th Brigade had used as a landmark. Following the capture of Villers-Bretonneux, the chateau was the headquarters for the 45th Battalion and after the war this wonderful building was used by the Australian Graves Registration Unit. The beautiful shell of the Red Chateau was demolished in 2004 – to make way for a supermarket. Its senseless destruction has been roundly condemned and there was widespread disappointment within Australia that the building was not protected by the local council or offered to Australia as an important site of historical interest.

Nevertheless, there are still reminders of the events of 1918. It is amazing for Australians to find a collective remembrance to their sacrifice so long ago, to see a sign in the schoolyard in letters a metre high: 'DO NOT FORGET AUSTRALIA' and, as is found in other parts of the Somme: 'Never Forget Australia' or the French '*Nous n'oublions pas l'Australie*' (We do not forget Australia). Given the huge British effort in the Great War, why is there not some recognition of the enormous English sacrifice in saving France?

The demolition of the Red Chateau perhaps removed the last major edifice that linked Australian troops to the town, but there is of course the Adelaide Cemetery on the road to Amiens. It is the final resting place of 522 Australians and was where the Unknown Soldier had lain until he was taken for re-interment at the Australian War Memorial in 1993. Today the gravesite – plot III, row M, grave 13 – has a headstone that reads:

*The remains of an Unknown Australian Soldier lay in this grave for 75 years. On 2nd November 1993 they were exhumed and now rest in the Tomb of the Unknown Australian Soldier at the Australian War Memorial in Canberra.*

# FIFTEEN

# Hammering at Hamel

The success of the counter-attack at Villers-Bretonneux not only halted the German advance towards Amiens, but drove the Germans back to a new line to the west of the tiny village of Le Hamel, 6 kilometres to the northeast of Villers-Bretonneux. To the north lay the river Somme and to the south the old Roman road between Péronne and Amiens. To the east, on the outskirts of Villers-Bretonneux along the N29, stands one of the few remaining demarcation stones placed after the war to mark the furthest extent of the German advance into France in the Great War. This stone is a significant and popular stop-off for Australian battlefield visitors.

Though Lynch's 45th Battalion had seen little action during two periods in and around Villers-Bretonneux, 13 of their men had been killed and a further 52 wounded, of which three were officers. As Nulla puts it, 'Just the rats of war forever gnawing precious lives away.' After their second period in the line of eight days, the men were sent to Rivery, today a suburb of Amiens, where they were able to rest, get clean clothes and prepare themselves for their next stint in the line. At Rivery, men of the 47th Battalion joined the 45th. Almost four years into the war and with a dwindling supply of recruits coming from Australia, there were not enough reinforcements to keep the battalions of the 12th Brigade up to full strength, so the 47th was disbanded and the men spread among the three other battalions. The move was opposed by the men of the 47th, who naturally wished to retain their battalion as a serving unit, but the redistribution of men was inevitable. It was beginning to happen across all brigades of the AIF.

As the 45th Battalion history states:

It was a sad fate for so fine a corps as the 47th to lose its identity, but it had already happened to other Australian battalions for the same reason. In order to ascertain which battalion of the brigade the officers and other ranks of the 47th Bn. wished to go to, a ballot was taken. It was a gratifying indication of the popularity of the 45th Bn. to find that 75% of the 47th voted to transfer to the 45th.[1]

It was summer and the men were able to swim in the river Somme, the canals and the waterways that pass quietly through this area. They were able to enjoy the countryside, particularly the orchards of ripe fruit. The men also wandered the streets of Amiens, a city dominated by its beautiful medieval cathedral. The battalion history describes it thus:

This famous city . . . was almost deserted. It resembled a city of the dead for there were thousands of empty houses and closed shops and not a living soul to be seen.[2]

A few bistros bravely stayed open and the men no doubt enjoyed those, and perhaps other earthly pleasures that the ruined city could offer.

Amiens was regularly shelled by German railway guns, large, heavy long-range guns mounted on railway rolling stock. One of these, the 'Amiens Gun', was located on the railway line at Wiencourt, about 25 kilometres to the east of Amiens, and was capable of firing twelve 28-centimetre shells an hour, each weighing 302 kilograms, to a maximum distance of 31 kilometres. It would be captured by men of the 31st Battalion on 8 August and, after some argument as to who could actually lay claim to its capture and ultimate fate, is today displayed in the grounds of the Australian War Memorial in Canberra. Another of the guns that fired on Amiens was to be captured in Arcy Wood near Proyart after being destroyed by the retreating Germans on 8 August. With a calibre of 35.6 centimetres, it was the largest gun to fire on the city and had done so since May 1918.

The Germans also bombed Amiens from the air day and night, starting many fires. The main target was the railway station and the adjoining rail junction and yards, which were the end of the railway line for Allied troops going to the front and for supplies including the new Mark V tanks. The city suffered widespread damage and even the cathedral, although protected by sandbags, did not escape unharmed.

In early June, the 45th Battalion was split in half and two companies were sent to the south side of the Somme, near Daours, and the other two companies, including Private Lynch's D Company, went to occupy the support trenches between Villers-Bretonneux and Corbie, about 7 kilometres north of Villers-Bretonneux. But they were soon moved into the frontline near Vaire-sur-Corbie, a beautiful little village on the banks of the river. This was the site of the ferry crossing immortalised in a well-known photograph from the war, where Australians had painted 'Circular Quay' in large letters across the wall of the ferryman's cottage. The house has long ago been demolished and replaced by a bridge which crosses the Somme at the same point.

While the battalion was in the line at Vaire-sur-Corbie, they were joined by officers and NCOs from the American 33rd Division, which had arrived in the back areas during May. An Australian had written in his diary that the Americans were 'very big men – some tremendous men among them', while General Haig noted that the Americans were 'fine big men; reminded me of tall Australians'.[3] Vast numbers of Americans were arriving at the front, and although well equipped, they were generally not well trained or ready for the fighting that lay ahead of them. Bean says that when they arrived the Americans were 'as yet too crudely trained to count for much more than cannon-fodder in fighting'. Yet their bearing and their keenness impressed the Australians, especially the fact that they did not brag. Bean quotes an Australian soldier who, probably stirring, asked a newly arrived American on the Somme, 'Are you going to win the war for us?' to which the American quickly answered, 'Well, we hope we'll fight like the Australians.'[4]

To assist the Americans to get acclimatised to the war in France and prepare them for battle, they were sent to Allied units to spend time in frontline positions and participate in training. According to the 45th Battalion history, 'The outstanding features of these attachments of the Americans were their ignorance of modern warfare and their keenness to remedy this defect.'[5] The Americans were popular with the Australians, who were keen to pass on their battle experience and to make them welcome in their camps and in their offensive operations.

The Australian 2nd Division were driving the Germans eastward on the north bank of the Somme at Sailly-Le-Sec and Morlancourt, to the northeast. This meant that the German artillery to the south of the Somme around Le Hamel could enfilade their flank. To eliminate this threat, various options were discussed for advancing the Allied frontline that ran southwest from the river to the Roman road east of Villers-Bretonneux. There was lengthy consultation between the Australian command, General Rawlinson and the British High Command. The Australians believed that a complete Australian division would be needed to make the attack on a front of nearly 6 kilometres to capture the village of Le Hamel and the heights above the town known by the Germans as the *Wolfsberg*. They feared that should the attack fail, a whole Australian division might well be wiped out.

Then something happened to change the logistics of the attack: the arrival at the front of the new model of British tanks, the Mark V. The commander of the British Tank Corps, Brigadier General Hugh Elles, had long espoused the value of the tank as an offensive weapon to support the infantry, but he realised that suitable tactics needed to be developed to maximise the operational capabilities of the tank when working with the infantry. Although artillery could knock out a tank, the Germans did not have an effective infantry counter measure to the British tanks, and the German tanks that had appeared at Villers-Bretonneux were unreliable, heavy and cumbersome. Elles' message was to take advantage of the situation, as once the Germans armed themselves with a tank of equal worth to the new British model, the opportunity would be lost.

The Australians had little faith in tanks after their disas- trous involvement at Bullecourt in April 1917 when the AIF was badly let down by them. If they were to be used at Le Hamel, the British would first have to convince General Monash and his chief-of-staff, Brigadier General Blamey. As an incentive, they offered Monash two battalions of tanks – a total of 72. With Monash behind the idea, now the Australian officers and men would need a lot of convincing and a better understanding of how tanks operated, their strengths and weaknesses and how they could be used in an offensive operation. So, late in June they received demonstrations of the tanks' capabilities and were sent to practise – and picnic –

with the tank crews at Vaux-en-Amiénois, in a quiet valley northwest of Amiens. The men were able to climb over the tanks and even drive them; some chalked their pet names on the sides.

In the chapter titled 'Hammering at Hamel', Nulla notes that the officers believe the attack has been planned for 4 July, American Independence Day, for symbolic reasons. Indeed General Rawlinson did choose that date for the attack because it was the first time American troops would be fighting with the Australians. The Allies would attack on a front stretching 5,500 metres from the Somme in the north to near the Roman road at Lamotte-Warfusée in the south. There were three main areas that would need to be captured in the attack, before the Allies could make it to their objective, the ridge east of Le Hamel and the German positions on the *Wolfsberg*. First, the village of Le Hamel, second, the defensive trench system known as Pear Trench and further east to Kidney Trench and, finally, the German positions in Hamel and Vaire Woods.

Monash's planning was meticulous and detailed. Armed with Mark V tanks, a further four carrier tanks, a squadron of big Handley Page bombers, 326 light field artillery pieces, plus 313 pieces of heavy artillery, he had the hardware necessary for a successful attack. Most importantly, Monash also had the authority to plan his own attack using his own Australian Corps plus the Americans – the first time in the war this had happened. Monash was anxious about further losses to his already under-strength corps and his planning for the attack reflected his concern for preventing casualties and ensuring the welfare of the men.

From the start of the planning, Monash maintained the highest secrecy. He was careful to restrict unnecessary movement until after dark and to thoroughly camouflage artillery positions and stores dumps brought up for the attack. Each night, preparations continued; by day, conferences were held with all participating units, including the flying corps, to work through likely problems. Despite the high level of secrecy, gradually word leaked out to the men that a major offensive was planned.

Knowing that the infantry would be exposed to snipers on the open ground behind Vaire Wood, prior to the attack Monash directed a battery of 9.2-inch howitzers to shell the area to make holes for the infantry to lie in.

> The battery has been firing in a desultory way at odd times in order to avoid arousing suspicion. We have had these shell holes mapped and the infantry know where they are.[6]

Annotated aerial photographs were issued to NCOs and a 'message map' was provided to each man, an innovation at the time. This was a small map of the battlefield with form messages printed on the back that could be filled in to save time and ensure accuracy should a message need to be sent to a commander during the attack.

In another first, the Allies planned to drop ammunition from the air. This was made possible by the invention of a special parachute by Wing Commander L. J. Wackett, who would go on to design a locally built training aircraft in Australia during the Second World War. His parachute allowed the delivery of small arms ammunition to machine-gun detachments on the frontline; all they needed to do was signal to the planes by laying out a special large 'V' on the ground using white cloth.

Monash secured four carrier tanks to dump large loads of supplies at four pre-determined points on the battlefield, which would save 1,200 men from doing that dangerous and strenuous work. The plan was that the locations of wounded men would be marked with rifles stuck into the ground with special white tape attached, eliminating the Diggers' fears that they might be run over by a tank while lying wounded in the waist-high crops in the fields. The tanks would look for the white tapes and collect the wounded men on their way back to the Allied lines.

On the morning before the attack, word came that the commander-in-chief of the American forces, General Pershing, had ordered that American troops not take part in the attack because they had not had enough training yet. First the message came through that six of the American companies must be withdrawn. This caused a major disruption to Monash's carefully laid plans and it was an enormous disappointment to the American officers and men. Then, later in the day, came the word that Pershing required the remaining four companies to be pulled from the attack too. Monash and Rawlinson opposed Pershing's decision and Monash ruled that the attack would have to be cancelled if those four American companies were taken out. Some Americans planned to dress as Australians and join the attack anyway, but in the end, Haig agreed with Monash and Rawlinson that it was too late to pull out the Americans without jeopardising the attack. He wrote in his diary: 'The first essential is to improve our position east of Amiens as soon as possible. The attack must therefore be launched as prepared'.[7] So, for the first time, American soldiers fought alongside Australians.

Zero hour was 3.10 a.m. on 4 July 1918. In the hours before, the wire in front of the Australian line had been cut and tapes marking the start line had been laid out. The tanks had moved up from the rear; to ensure the element of surprise in the attack, the sound of their engines was covered by that of Allied aircraft flying low along the German front, bombing the town of Le Hamel and the valleys behind it. At 3.02 a.m., the Allies started their nightly shelling, which they had been doing for an hour at this time each day for the last two weeks. The Germans expected it and dealt with it by putting on their gas masks and going back to sleep.

In *Somme Mud*, Nulla is acting as the OC's runner and joins him on high ground – or in Nulla's more colourful turn of phrase, 'the OC's gallery seats' – to watch the attack. The site Lynch was referring to is possibly the heights on the north side of the Somme just east of Corbie and about 6 kilometres behind Hamel and the northern end of the attack. (The 45th were being held in reserve, at La Neuville, just west of Corbie.) Nulla sees the tremendous barrage, which included gas shells and shells designed to create a smoke screen, crash along the German frontline and upon their artillery in the rear. What military planners had realised by this stage of the war was that in an attack it was vital to not only capture the first few lines of enemy trenches, but also take out the enemy's artillery, because otherwise it could quickly range effective fire on the captured trenches. Added to the Allies' artillery barrage was a machine-gun barrage, fired skywards at a steep angle to rain down bullets upon the German line. At the same time, in the words of the official history:

> Along nearly the whole line the infantry at once rose and, lighting their cigarettes and with rifles slung, as if on a march, moved up to the line of shells which in four minutes would make its first jump.[8]

The troops were to follow the Allied barrage, which had been carefully calculated so that the shells would fall just ahead of them as they advanced, exploding within 30 metres of the leading men. The theory was that by 'hugging' the barrage, the attacking troops could get right up to the German defensive line and take the trenches or pillboxes before the Germans were able to set up their machine-guns. Detailed planning went into producing 'barrage maps' that co-ordinated the artillery. The light artillery's shells were to land just ahead of the advancing Australians and the shells of the heavier guns were to fall onto the German rear. At predetermined intervals that allowed the men to advance, the guns would 'jump' or lift, their shells now falling perhaps another 100 metres deeper into the enemy's territory. Each type of gun was to lift at the same time in a carefully orchestrated way.

However, due to the secrecy of the Hamel operation, the Allied artillery were forced to rely on map co-ordinates as they were not given the chance to register the range of their guns. Due to this, some Australians and Americans were killed when shells fell short and into their advancing ranks.

Heavy German machine-gun fire came from Pear Trench, but the Queenslanders of the 15th Battalion, 'whose own losses had been heavy, killed right and left in both the trench and the sunken road'.[9] One, a 25-year-old private from Atherton in far north Queensland, Henry Dalziel, drew his revolver and, rushing the German machine-gun, shot two gunners and captured the post. During this action, his trigger finger had been shot away so Dalziel was ordered back to the rear for medical treatment, but he stayed with the attack as the men moved forward to their next objective. He was again ordered to the rear to seek medical assistance, but instead stayed on to help with the distribution of ammunition dropped by British aircraft. While doing so, he was shot in the head and finally received medical treatment. Dalziel was awarded the Victoria Cross for his actions that day and later attained the rank of sergeant.

To the south, the 16th Battalion attacked their objective: Vaire and Hamel woods, and the kidney-shaped trench that lay at the top of the slope leading to the woods. The front wave of the battalion made it through the wire, but then a machine-gun began firing, killing a company commander and his sergeant major and wiping out a team of Lewis gunners. Lance Corporal Thomas Axford, a 24-year-old labourer from Coolgardie, Western Australia, is described in the official history:

> [Axford] at once rushed to the front, threw his bombs among
> the machine-gun crew, and jumped into the trench, killing ten
> Germans and capturing six. He then threw the machine-gun
> on to the parapet and called for the platoon to come on, which
> it did.[10]

For this action, Axford was awarded the Victoria Cross, the second one earned in about 15 minutes.

The attack continued to surge forward into the woods. As hoped, many of the Germans still wore their gas masks, which made them easier to deal with. Men were advancing in line, firing their Lewis guns and rifles from the hip and driving the fleeing Germans into the barrage that was still falling ahead of them. Prisoners started trailing back and Bean notes that 'many were found to be very young and small'.[11] The Germans, like the Australians, were running out of men.

Later in the day, Victorians of the 14th Battalion who were digging a support trench were fired on by a group of Germans in a communication sap. When a tank was called in to deal with this position, the Germans waved a white flag above their parapet, so Lieutenant Rule went over with some men to take them prisoners. Halfway across, they were suddenly fired upon and a corporal was shot through the head. Furious, Rule ordered the Germans out of their dugout but it was found that the occupants were a 'crowd of young boys'.[12] After the war, Rule wrote the classic book *Jacka's Mob*, an account of the history of the 14th Battalion. In it he wrote:

> We could not kill children and these looked to be barely that. If you asked any of us how old they were, most of us would have said between fourteen and fifteen . . . With a boot to help them along they ran with their hands above their heads back to our lines.[13]

In the initial stages of the attack the tanks were delayed because the darkness, the smoke and dust had reduced visibility. But when the tanks had caught up with the infantry, they came into their own, quickly proving their worth and wiping out German strongpoints. German morale also suffered and often Germans simply surrendered on their approach. Large groups, as many as 50 men and their weapons, were captured.

As the Australians consolidated their new position and pushed forward, the tanks proved invaluable, especially the four carrier tanks, which now appeared with much-needed supplies. Twenty-one-year-old Colonel Douglas Marks, the commander of the 13th Battalion, was astonished when he found that in the area behind Vaire Wood, one tank had delivered 134 coils of barbed wire, 180 long- and 270 short-screw pickets, 45 sheets of corrugated iron, 50 petrol tins of water, 150 trench mortar bombs, 10,000 rounds of ammunition and

20 boxes of grenades. Never before had the Australians had supplies delivered during the advance of an attack with such speed and in such quantity. The value of using carrier tanks was considered one of the great lessons of the battle.

As the dawn light crept in across the battlefield, observers on the heights north of the Somme were able to report, '4.45. Tanks everywhere beyond Hamel. Beyond Vaire Wood.'[14] Aircraft from No. 3 Squadron, Australian Flying Corps, flew across the frontline positions tooting to the troops below, signalling for them to light small fires in shell-holes and trenches, out of sight of the Germans. These fires were then marked on a map which ten minutes later was dropped at the headquarters of the 4th Division.

By 5.30 a.m., most of the tanks had returned to the rear, widely acknowledged to have played a very important part in the operation. Only three of the 60 tanks had not reached their objective, all but five were back at their assembly points by 11 a.m. and these damaged tanks were recovered in the next two days. The tank crews' casualties were light, with only 13 men being put out of action. However, when the tanks returned to their staging area near Blangy-Tronville, eight men were killed when a German aircraft bombed their lines. The positive response of the officers to the tanks' performance at Le Hamel is mentioned in *Somme Mud* when an officer says:

'The tanks were great. They kept right on the barrage and each time a machine-gun nest held us up, we only had to

signal to a tank and it just waded in and shot up the gun
crew . . .' [p. 312]

As dawn broke, aircraft were able to deliver ammunition by
parachute. Each plane carried one box of small arms ammunition and the 12 planes involved averaged four trips each,
dropping ammunition under two brown parachutes wherever
they saw the 'V' sign displayed on the ground. In all, 93 boxes
of ammunition – some 111,600 rounds – were delivered in
this way, though some were carried by the wind and could not
safely be retrieved. Unfortunately, one aircraft was lost. There
were varying accounts of its fate, with one close observer
reporting that the parachute, thrown out at 1,200 feet, caught
in the wing. The pilot was seen to steady the aeroplane then
hand over control to his observer, climb out on the wing and
untangle the parachute. But 30 metres above the ground, as he
started to bring the plane safely down, something went wrong
and the plane crashed. Other observers said that the plane was
hit by a shell, but it is possible that both mishaps occurred.
Both pilot and observer were killed. Later a second ammunition carrier plane was shot down when more than 30 German
aircraft swarmed over the area, bombing and strafing ground
targets and directing German artillery onto the new Australian
frontline. The Germans tried delivering rations to their frontline
troops, without parachutes and, according to Bean, 'incidentally
delivered a few of these parcels to the Australian outposts'.[15]

Meanwhile, the Australians of the 43rd battalion had also
cleared the village of Hamel. Early in the fighting, Corporal B.

V. Schulz, a 25-year-old farmer from Willowie, South Australia, noticed on an aerial photograph the line of a buried German cable from the village to Notamel Wood to the north. He followed the cable to a house in the northern part of the village, where, with the aid of two German-speaking Americans, he asked to be allowed in.

Once inside, he captured a battalion commander and his staff at what proved to be a forward headquarters. In so doing, he denied the Germans any information about the Australian attack on the village. In fact it was two hours before the Germans realised that this position had been captured. Again tanks proved their worth. In the words of Lieutenant Colonel Drake Brockman, they proved 'particularly useful and efficient in the village.'[16] By 7 a.m., Hamel had been cleared.

A number of smaller operations had simultaneously taken place across the river to the north, as feints to draw German artillery away from the main focus of the attack. Near Sailly-Laurette, men of the 55th Battalion raised and lowered papier-mâché dummies, which occupied the German machine-gunners for half an hour. It was here that the most serious Australian casualties were taken in an area to the east of the village of Ville, where German resistance was stiff and where the open marshy ground gave little cover to the attacking troops. The Australians established their new line to the east of Le Hamel at their objective of the *Wolfsberg* and though the Germans counter-attacked, the line held. The day after Hamel fell, the 45th moved in to relieve the 42nd Battalion along the new frontline from the north of Hamel to the

Somme canal near Bouzencourt. They worked deepening the trenches begun by the 42nd Battalion and on connecting the disjointed line. Then, two nights later, C and D companies of the 45th advanced in an attack with the 46th Battalion and established a new line of posts which provided a better field of fire. Digging in fast, they erected wire under cover of rifle and machine-gun sections but the Germans, when they discovered their position, retaliated with a fierce gas bombardment resulting in a number of casualties.

Today, the trenches that were the objective of the successful Australian attack on 4 July 1918 are part of the Australian Corps Memorial Park. Still visible across the valley to the east are the short observation saps the Australians dug forward towards the German lines. For 80 years after the war, they remained virtually undiscovered, overgrown with brambles and privet, a narrow boat-shaped piece of ground crowning the hilltop that French farmers had ploughed around and somehow left undisturbed. Under the scrub and low brush, the trench still held the detritus of the time: old rusty cans, boots and unrecognisable pieces of iron.

Nearby in the furrows of the field, a shell lay menacingly along the line of the plough, turned up but not collected. And nearby lay another shallow trench system, the chalk beneath the surface easily visible and its zigzagging course still apparent. Since then, the land has been cleared and a memorial erected to the men of the five Australian infantry divisions. It was unveiled on 4 July 1998 to mark the 80th anniversary of the battle.

The men at Le Hamel had been allotted 90 minutes to reach their objective on the high ground east of the village. They reached it in 93 minutes, with about 1,400 casualties. It was an amazing feat.

The success of the battle of Hamel, particularly the innovation of co-ordinating tanks, artillery, infantry and aircraft, was studied afterwards by units of all the Allied armies. It would become the basis of the technique of Blitzkrieg introduced by the Germans in the Second World War – the co-ordination of various offensive units striking on a narrow front and driving through an enemy's frontline.

On the Sunday after the battle, the French Prime Minister, Georges Clemenceau, who had replaced Aristide Briand following General Nivelle's failed offensives, visited the headquarters of the 4th Division. Addressing the Australians at Bussy-lès-Daours, near Corbie, he spoke to them in English and said:

> When the Australians came to France, the French people expected a great deal of you . . . We knew that you would fight a real fight, but we did not know that from the very beginning you would astonish the whole continent . . . I shall go back tomorrow and say to my countrymen: 'I have seen the Australians. I have looked in their faces. I know that these men . . . will fight alongside of us again until the cause for which we are all fighting is safe for us and for our children.'[17]

# SIXTEEN

# Leap-frogging
# to Victory

The great German offensive of the spring of 1918 comprised a number of separate strategic initiatives. First there was the assault towards Amiens, which had originally been a more ambitious plan to roll up the whole Allied line to Arras to the northeast, but had been downscaled by the German commanders and then brought to a halt by the Australians at Villers-Bretonneux on 25 April. The Germans also launched an offensive in Flanders, Belgium, on 9 April, known as the Battle of the Lys, when they attacked south of Ypres and pushed northwest towards the city, but were stalled and finally halted by stout British defence on 29 April. Next, in May, General Ludendorff pushed southwest on the Chemin des Dames, a road along the ridgeline south of the river Aisne that led towards Paris. With his eye on the capital as the main objective, he advanced 65 kilometres in three days. But then he was met by the newly arrived Americans and strong French defences;

again, his offensive ground to a halt and was pushed back.

By July 1918, General Ludendorff's three major offensives had failed. Though initially he had overrun vast areas of France, he was now virtually back to where he had started in early March. He had failed to capture and retain any significant towns or strategically important ground or infrastructure, such as the railhead at Amiens, and the German army had suffered huge casualties and loss of *matériel* and stores, which, at this stage of the war could not be easily replaced.

When Hindenburg and Ludendorff had first arrived on the Western Front from the Eastern Front in 1916, they were shocked by the scale of the battles being fought, the immense artillery barrages conducted by both sides and the level of German casualties. Even then they realised they were losing the material war, the ability to match the Allies in artillery and ammunition. The Allies' naval blockade had cut off Germany from desperately important raw materials such as nitrates for explosive production, which were shipped from Chile. Tactically, the Germans were reliant on artillery to protect their frontline troops and shortages of shells became a serious problem the more they had to rely on defensive rather than offensive strategies. Although German scientists did develop a technique for making synthetic nitrates, this took time.

The problems that were facing Germany on the battlefield had their origins years before. Germany did not embrace total war – the commitment and devotion of all of a country's material and human resources to the war effort – to quite the same degree as the Allies. German women were not called into war production in anywhere near the numbers British women were. In fact, as the war drew on, increasing numbers of German men were withdrawn from the army to work in factories. By December 1917, nearly 2.1 million men had been released from the army for service in factories in Germany, and younger and younger men – many mere boys – were called up for military service.

The situation was very different in Britain. Though its material losses had been enormous in the retreat in March, the country was benefiting from America's war contribution, both in manpower and material. The German U-boat campaign had succeeded in sinking ships but had fallen far short of starving the island of food, raw materials and troops. With advances in anti-submarine technology such as depth charges, along with the addition of American destroyers and the use of the convoy system, the German submarine threat was being contained, allowing an influx of supplies from America. British industry had been able to massively increase its production levels since the beginning of the war.

Britain was also re-skilling and re-training the army and learning from the past: the lessons of the Somme and Arras were transforming military planning and tactics and improving their staff work. The army was being provided with new equipment, and weapon systems were being developed in the hope of breaking the stalemate. The new Mark V tanks were showing their value on the battlefield.

The reliability of artillery shells was improving after the early years in which a high percentage of the shells being produced were duds. British sound-ranging equipment could now locate, target and destroy German artillery with frightening precision. Artillery could be used effectively in creeping barrages, and machine-gunners standing shoulder to shoulder could rain bullets on German troop concentrations much like the English archers did to the French knights at Agincourt. Advances in British military technology combined with Britain's higher production rate dramatically increased the number of artillery pieces and machine-guns the Allies had at their disposal. Simply put, the Allies could now outgun the Germans.

What Britain understood was that this was a rich man's war. Superior technology and massive amounts of weapons and ammunition – which all came at a high cost – were needed if the war was to be won. The shell for the smallest and most common artillery piece used by the Allies, the 18-pound field gun, cost £4 per shell. This was a huge expenditure considering that towards the end of the war English troops received only three shillings per day. That means it cost nearly four times a British private's weekly wage for one shell for a gun that could fire 25 to 30 shells per minute. It is estimated that over 86 million 18-pound shells were fired during the Great War, which gives an indication of just how rich a nation needed to be.

By the middle of 1918, the French army had again become an effective fighting force. Esprit de corps was high and there was a burning sense of shame about the recent loss of French territory in the German spring offensive. French industry, which had been mainly concentrated in areas now behind German lines, had relocated in the south and established production to meet the enormous demands of the French army, especially after the losses at Verdun.

New tactics, increased amounts of equipment and the introduction of a command structure that worked all contributed to the vast Allied initiative, which was further aided by German offensive mistakes and their dwindling war economy. The balance was finally tipping.

In July 1918, preparations were under way for the next phase of the Allies' operations: a great offensive to be launched on 8 August. The Australian troops on the Somme were not idly waiting, though; this was the height of 'peaceful penetration', small-scale trench raids and audacious attacks on the German lines. It had become something of a sport for the Australians and they were never short of volunteers. Lieutenant E. J. Rule, writing after the war, said:

> Under cover of a barrage, they were to hop in, grab a few prisoners, kill all others they laid hands on and get out in fifteen minutes.[1]

The Germans came to fear these raids and one English-speaking prisoner is reported to have said: 'You bloody

Australians . . . when you are in the line you keep us on pins and needles; we never know when you are coming over.'[2]

On 6 July, as the Australians settled in to their new frontline at Le Hamel, a sergeant of the 20th Battalion, Walter Ernest Brown, who had just arrived at the line as part of an advance party of his battalion, was told of a German sniper nearby who was causing trouble. He headed off down the trench with the words that he would go see if he could 'have a pot at them himself'.[3] He looked out across the open ground and noticed a mound; soon a shot was fired, seemingly from that direction. Taking the initiative upon himself, he set down his rifle and ran towards the mound with two Mills bombs in his hands. Another shot was fired, so he stopped and threw a grenade at the mound, but not far enough – it exploded short of its target. He dropped to the ground and waited until all was quiet, then got up and ran towards the mound once more.

Brown found himself standing above a small, empty kidney-shaped trench with a machine-gun standing on the parados. He jumped down and ran to the entrance of a dugout at the end opposite him. As he reached it, a German emerged and Brown, with a swinging punch to his jaw, sent him flying back down the stair of the dugout. Suddenly, behind him, more Germans emerged from a dugout at the other end of the trench which he had not noticed until now. All he had was one grenade – and if he hurled it in the small trench, he would be in even deeper trouble, as he would have to face the ire of any survivors. So, he threatened them with it instead. Demoralised by the Australian rout two days before, and having been left without food and water and cut off from their own troops, they surrendered. Wielding his last remaining Mills bomb in his hand, he sent all the Germans in the trench – one officer and 12 men – across to the Australian lines.

Initially, Brown was unaware that his bold action was in any way noteworthy, except that the men in his trench growled at him because he had 'drawn the crabs'[4] (brought German shellfire upon them) and that his officer had reprimanded him with, 'What the devil have you been doing up there?' But word of his bravery quickly spread and Brown became famous in the AIF. General Monash was so impressed by the way Brown had taken advantage of the dislocation and low morale of the Germans following the Allied attack that he mentioned it in a circular he sent to the troops later that day. He urged officers, in the aftermath of future battles, to 'exploit our successes to the utmost by the incessant harassing of the enemy and the mopping up of small posts'.[5] The technique of peaceful penetration, developed and initiated by the men themselves, had attained a degree of official recognition.

Brown, who had already won the Distinguished Service Medal at Passchendaele, was awarded the Victoria Cross for his actions that day at Le Hamel. He enlisted again in the Second World War and died fighting the Japanese before the fall of Singapore.

The Germans in the frontline were vulnerable. They were poorly fed and perhaps further dispirited by the knowledge that their families back home were hungry too. In some places they were down to eating dead horses lying by the roadside; bands of German brigands were attacking supply trains heading for the front and pillaging stores. Many of the German reinforcements were very young, including some who were serving prison sentences and had been released early to go and fight. One of the German official military histories noted that a draft of men from Brandenburg who had been sent to the German line at Morlancourt, north of Dernancourt, on 29 June were 'extremely unreliable. Absent without leave, desertion, offences such as had never before been known, increased. These people were a cancer for the front.'[6]

As Allied commanders talked of a new offensive, they were quick to include the colonial divisions, especially the Canadians and the Australians, in their plans. Unlike British troops, they were not exhausted from the retreat in March and April; and they had succeeded as shock troops in previous offensives. The Canadians, in particular, were intact following the 1917 Ypres salient offensives. They had time to rebuild their four divisions and they had ample men in reserve. In the Australian Corps, reinforcements coming from Australia, the hospitals in England and the depots were down to a trickle, so three brigades had been reduced in size from four battalions per brigade to three. Though the Australian troops were stretched thin and battle-weary, they were said by their officers to have good morale – or as Nulla comments in this chapter, 'The men are keen and confident of success . . .'

The Australian and Canadian divisions would form the

vanguard of the offensive on 8 August, which would come to be known as the Battle of Amiens, and its success would depend upon them breaking through on a front spanning the area from the river Somme south to Villers-Bretonneux. They would be supported on the flanks by British and French divisions.

In the meantime, the Australian flanks north of the Somme needed securing, so on 30 July, a minor offensive was launched between Morlancourt and Sailly-le-Sec, straddling the Bray–Corbie Road. Attacking just after midnight, the Australian 5th Division surged through the German lines and took many prisoners. Finding only limited resistance, they quickly achieved their objective. In the official history, Bean notes:

> The rank and file were mostly young and obviously pleased to be captured, especially when the 'Diggers' after the first bloody fierceness of the assault gave them hot cocoa, biscuits and chocolate at the little YMCA canteen . . .[7]

Lieutenant Colonel McArthur of the 29th Battalion said of his men: 'They fight to kill if the enemy shows any resistance, but are extremely kind to prisoners when captured.'[8]

Great secrecy shrouded the preparation for the offensive on 8 August. Troops, supplies and equipment were moved at night; stores, ammunition dumps and artillery were carefully camouflaged; and aircraft flew over to check that they remained undiscovered by the enemy. Excuses were circulated for why divisions were being kept out of the line and diversions were put in place to deceive the enemy. When a number of Australian and British troops were captured in the days before the attack there were fears that they would give the enemy vital intelligence or clues, but these concerns were unfounded: the Germans remained in the dark about the impending offensive.

Late in the afternoon of 7 August 1918, Monash delivered a message which was read to his troops. In part it stated:

> For the first time in the history of this Corps all five Australian Divisions will tomorrow engage in the largest and most important battle operation ever undertaken by the Corps . . . Because of the completeness of our plans and dispositions, of the magnitude of the operations, of the number of troops employed, and of the depth to which we intend to overrun the enemy's positions, this battle will be one of the most memorable of the whole war . . . we shall inflict blows upon the enemy which will make him stagger, and will bring the end appreciably nearer. I entertain no sort of doubt that every Australian soldier will worthily rise to so great an occasion . . . for the sake of AUSTRALIA, the Empire, and our cause.[9]

As soon as darkness fell, the Australians, with the Canadians to the south and the British to the north, moved forward to their start lines; the white tapes laid out by intelligence officers to mark where the attacking battalions were to form up. The Australian 2nd, 3rd, 4th and 5th divisions were to take part on the first day of the offensive, with the 1st Division in reserve. By 3 a.m. on 8 August, nearly all battalions were in position, lying down and ready to move. Half an hour before the attack, the mist, which had settled across the area earlier in the night, was now so thick that it was feared aircraft could not be sent up to cover the noise of the approaching tanks and that the attacking battalions might lose direction and get lost. But fog or no fog, the attack must now go ahead.

Some of the men were guided through the fog to their jump-off point by petrol tins on poles with their battalion number cut out and a candle placed inside. Half an hour before the attack, at 3.50 a.m., north of the Somme came the reassuring sound of a British aircraft. Planes droned all along the German front to be attacked, hiding the noise of the tanks even from the Australians.

At precisely 4.20 a.m., 2,000 guns opened up on the German lines, 'almost with a single crash',[10] in Bean's words. Some of the troops had come under German shelling as they waited for the attack to begin and for them, especially, the sound of the Allied artillery was, according to Bean:

> . . . elating music. In some places the excited troops cheered the sound. Nearly every man lit a cigarette as all along the line the companies of the attacking brigades rose and moved forward.[11]

Advancing steadily, they encountered little resistance from German forward posts which immediately surrendered. The Allied barrage, the threatening advance of the tanks and the waves of infantry reduced pockets of resistance and lines of German prisoners were soon streaming back to the rear. The 17th and 18th battalions passed through the village of Warfusée, clearing Germans from buildings and bombing cellars and dugouts as they drove east along the line of the Amiens road.

At the time of the barrage, Lynch's 45th Battalion were waiting at their assembly point, as they were to take part in the second phase of the attack. Lynch's account echoes Bean's observations:

> Thousands of guns roar in an unending bark that seems to shake the very earth to its foundations. Our men are laughing and shouting, glad in the knowledge of how much easier our task will be as the result of this terrific bombardment. [p. 326]

The first phase of the attack was carried out by the 2nd Division to the east of Villers-Bretonneux and the 3rd Division from the east of Le Hamel and extending north to the Somme. Aided by the heavy artillery barrage and tanks, they advanced 2.75 kilometres, or 3,000 yards, to their objective, the 'Green Line'. The fog mixed with the smoke and dust of the barrage, obscuring the ground ahead. The attacking battalions soon fell out of formation, splitting into small groups led by whatever 'officer, NCO, or natural leader'[12] presented himself, according to Bean. Some men followed the tanks, but these didn't always lead in the right direction and numbers of tanks had been delayed by the low visibility. The men could not even see their own shells bursting, so the sound of the artillery falling on the German line became an important guide.

Despite the difficult conditions, they advanced steadily and encountered little resistance from German forward posts, though in the south the 2nd Division did meet with some pockets of strong defence until the tanks caught up with them and eliminated the threat. At one point, the Australians came to the aid of the Canadians, who also met some stiff resistance. The task of the 17th and 18th battalions was to go beyond the old Allied frontline to the Green Line beyond Warfusée, clearing Germans from buildings and bombing cellars and dugouts in the village as they drove east along the line of the Amiens road. They made their way through thick fog to the village, while other battalions still behind them on the road advanced along compass bearings, trying to confirm their reference points. In the fog, advancing battalions and tanks inevitably missed some German strongpoints, but the Australian fighters adapted quickly to the conditions. In the words of Captain J. B. Lane of the 18th Battalion, it came down to:

> . . . someone telling any one he met that there were some Germans down in some corner he had passed . . . collecting a few men and going round and grabbing the Germans, generally from the rear.[13]

The Allied barrage, the threatening advance of the tanks and the waves of infantry sent lines of German prisoners streaming back to the rear.

Like the other battalions, the 45th moved up to its allotted start line and at 5.30 a.m. advanced in artillery formation, with platoons in single file and scattered at irregular intervals across the line of their advance, to minimise casualties should they come under enemy shellfire. They crossed their old frontline, passed through what used to be no-man's-land and then what had been the German frontline.

At 8.20 a.m., four hours after the start of the attack, they reached the Green Line, where the troops of the 3rd Division had stopped and were digging in. In the second phase of the offensive, the 4th and 5th divisions were to 'leap-frog' the 2nd and 3rd and advance another 4,500 yards (just over 4 kilometres) to their objective, the 'Red Line'.

The A and B companies led the 45th Battalion's advance; C Company and D Company, to which Lynch (and his narrator, Nulla) belonged, were to follow behind mopping up the enemy, and behind them were the battalion's headquarters company, with pack animals in the rear.

By now, the Germans had grasped the extent of the attack. Though they had lost much of their forward artillery, they were able to lay down a barrage on the attacking formations advancing upon them in the clearing mist, concentrate their firepower and strengthen their defences. The 45th moved forward not only with German shells crashing around them, but also without the cover of the massive artillery barrage that had accompanied the first stage of the operation.

As had happened in the first wave of the attack, as the advancing troops surged forward they missed or bypassed some German strongpoints and the tanks, less effective in the fog and smoke, also missed German positions and lumbered past them. The German machine-guns needed to be put out of action, and in 'Leap-frogging to Victory' we find a classic example of how the Australians carried this out, one gun at a time. A small party of men, in this case Nulla, a handful of nervous new recruits and some seasoned men, would split off from the rest of their platoon and bravely rush the Germans at their post. It was a perilous job, as a young lad new to the fighting soon finds out when he is hit and, as Nulla says, 'pitches forward and I hear the soft sighing cough as the bullet-riddled body of the falling boy strikes the ground'. However, it was crucial to eliminate the machine-guns to avoid stalling the advance and to protect the men following on behind them.

The advancing companies skirted a number of woods, leaving them for the men of C and D companies to mop up and flush any remaining Germans out of the woods and trench systems, including dugouts. By 10.20 a.m., the battalion had reached their objective, the Red Line, and were digging in. As Nulla notes:

Our trench is taking shape under the hundreds of spades flashing in the morning sun, the men working in a lather of perspiration . . . Men are coming through from behind. We know these are the crow-eaters [South Australians], the 46th

Battalion men who are to 'leap-frog' us here on the Red Line and advance another thousand yards [about 915 metres] to the Blue Line. [p. 342]

In just two hours, the battalion had marched nearly 7 kilometres (about 4 miles), including an advance of over 4 kilometres and had captured 400 prisoners 'and an immense amount of war material',[14] according to the battalion history. This included 25 artillery pieces, eight *minenwerfers* and 18 machine-guns, probably a record for any Allied unit in one attack, especially given the battalion's low rate of casualties: four men killed and 44 wounded. In all, the attack was, in the words of the battalion historian, 'a magnificent success, one of the outstanding features being the splendid co-operation between the tanks and the infantry'.[15]

That night, the 45th Battalion advanced again to take over the frontline – the Blue Line that was earlier in the day captured by the Australian 46th and 48th battalions. They awaited the usual German counter-attack, but it did not come and the night passed quietly. The battalion, however, did enjoy a hot meal served by the battalion cookhouse which, knowing the importance of hot food to the men after a long and exhausting day, had also kept up with the advance. The following day, 9 August, the battalion remained in the line and Lieutenant C. M. Potts, MC, took a patrol nearly a kilometre ahead of the front to carry out a recce, returning with valuable information about the current disposition of the Germans and their defences.

That same day, a famous incident was playing out north of the river Somme. In the British sector, the advance had not progressed fast enough, exposing the Australian flank to the danger of enfilading fire from across the river. A company of the 2/10th London were seen sheltering half a mile from the village of Chipilly so at 6 p.m., Sergeants Hayes and Andrews were sent across with four men to investigate. They approached the Londoners and asked why the attack was not moving forward.

Their advance was being held up not so much by fire coming from the village but from the ridge and gullies on the other side. The British company's commander, Captain Berrell, advised the Australians not to advance on the village, but the six men spread out and rushed forward. They came under German machine-gun fire from the ridge, but made it safely through. Hayes and Andrews then led their own men and the British troops to advance past the village, attacking numerous German posts from their flanks. Having enabled the British advance to continue, the six Australians returned to their own company on the other side of the river at 10 p.m. With the aid of the Londoners, they had captured about 75 Germans and two machine-guns. The two sergeants were awarded the Distinguished Service Medal and the four privates each received the Military Medal for their brave work.

After the huge gains made on 8 August, over the following days the Allies continued to push their frontline forward, but by smaller increments and at greater cost. By 11 August the battle of Amiens was over and the AIF was digging in along the new line near Proyart. The 45th Battalion moved out of the frontline and went to Sailly-Laurette just to the north of the Somme near Corbie, to swim in the Somme canal and rest for a couple of days before returning to the line south-east of Harbonnières. The war was moving forward too fast now to slow the advance and every available man was needed in the line.

In four days, the Allied advance, spearheaded by the Australians and the Canadians, had moved the frontline forward by up to 10 kilometres in some places. The Australians had captured 8,000 prisoners and over 80 field guns, 40 trench mortars and 350 machine-guns. Surprisingly, there were far fewer casualties on both sides than would normally be expected in such a large offensive. Australian casualties were about 2,000 during the four-day period. Even the number of Germans killed and wounded was low; far greater was the number who surrendered, many without a fight. Short of experienced men and with morale low and an end to the war in sight, very few German regiments could be relied upon to stand and fight. Unlike in previous offensives, the Allies had not only taken the German support and reserve trenches but had also eliminated the German artillery, which in the past had smashed them with counter-bombardments.

The day after the battle ended, on 12 August 1918, 600 men formed a guard of honour along the gravel drive of the impressive Bertangles Chateau, the headquarters of General

Monash. Flanked by captured weapons, the men – 100 from each of the five Australian divisions plus 100 from the Royal Garrison Artillery – watched while their corps commander knelt before his king, George V, to be invested with the KCB. Sir John Monash would finish the war as one of the most successful and effective Allied commanders.

# SEVENTEEN

# Following
# Fritz

For the Allies, the battle of Amiens had been an unqualified success. For the Australians in particular, it had again proved their excellence as assault troops and further enhanced their reputation. But for the Germans, it was the beginning of the end. Ludendorff called 8 August 1918 'the black day for the German army'.[1]

In addition to their losses at Amiens, the Germans also suffered huge losses further south, in the Second Battle of the Marne. A major counter-attack begun on 18 July 1918 by British, American and French forces had by 3 August pushed the Germans back to where they had been before their spring offensive of March and, in the process, the Germans lost nearly 200,000 men in the battle. The full impact of American men and material, long feared by the German High Command, was now biting. The Germans' ability to mount offensive operations on the Western Front was at an end, and even an effective defence along the Hindenburg Line could not be relied upon.

In Russia, the seizure of power by the Bolsheviks had led to civil war, which saw the anti-Bolshevik White Army engage in intense fighting with the Bolshevik Red Army. With growing concern about the instability in Russia, the Americans and the British sent small military contingents there to aid the White Army and assist them in opening up a new Eastern Front against the Germans. After violent socialist-led strikes and subversive activities – including sabotage and murder – of the International Workers of the World, known as the 'Wobblies', President Wilson became fearful of the communist threat in the United States. He broke off diplomatic relations with the Bolshevik government on 15 August in what marked the start of a long period of mistrust between the two huge nations. In the far east of Russia, the Japanese put 70,000 troops ashore and occupied the port of Vladivostok.

A new threat arrived in Europe and on the Western Front in the summer of 1918: Spanish influenza. It had already caused millions of deaths in Asia, particularly in China and India, but now it hit Britain and the Continent. Just as Germany was suffering the impact of the Allied counter-offensive, the flu struck its forces and those of its allies, the Turks and Austro-Hungarians. The flu also hit British, French and Australian troops and had an often lethal effect on the civilian population. The disease was particularly deadly in areas where living conditions were poor, the diet was inadequate and the war had left people homeless and destitute, but even in the United States fatalities were immense. In August 1918, there was an outbreak in Australia, at the army camp at Broadmeadows near Melbourne, and fears quickly grew that the virulent disease, for which there was no cure or vaccine, would rapidly spread.

After the initial success of the offensive of early August 1918, German resistance increased, which slowed and finally halted the Allied advance. Now faced again with taking the Somme battlefields of 1916, the Allies paused to regroup while the Germans re-established themselves behind the vast and seemingly impregnable Hindenburg Line.

After the battle of Amiens, the 45th Battalion had been in rest areas, first near Corbie and then in the reserve line southeast of Harbonnières. The battalion then went to relieve the 3rd Battalion in the frontline near the town of Lihons, where they found themselves in old trenches from the Somme battles of 1916. These formed a dangerous maze and, as the German frontline was only 50 metres away, there was regular contact with the enemy. The Germans threw stick grenades and small egg grenades, while the Australians threw the heavier Mills bombs. Such bomb fights led to high casualty rates for both sides.

After fighting off numerous attempted attacks by the Germans and then on 19 August coming under heavy shelling (which was intended as retaliation against the Canadians to their right), the 45th were relieved by the 48th Battalion and went back into the reserve line near Harbonnières. Here they were put to work salvaging usable material from the rear battlefield areas, laying telephone lines and digging trenches. Waiting to be relieved by French troops after five days, they were subjected to a heavy gas bombardment, which resulted in some casualties. Finally, the battalion was relieved and travelled by bus to a rest area near Amiens, remaining there for nearly a fortnight.

From the outset of the battle of Amiens, the AIF had been in action across an extended front. They pushed east and northeast from Villers-Bretonneux, capturing towns and villages north and south of the Roman road between Péronne and Amiens, and also north to the Somme. Ahead of them was a great bend in the river and the Hindenburg Line, dominated by the heights and Mont St Quentin. Standing out from the surrounding countryside, it looked down upon the town of Péronne and the Somme, making it a valuable observation point and a vital element of the Germans' defence. It was heavily defended by the 2nd Prussian Guards Division, who had specific orders from Ludendorff to hold the strategically important high ground 'to the death'. If the Australians captured Mont St Quentin, the Germans would be forced from the Somme and have to retreat from this part of the Hindenburg Line. In Monash's eyes, the capture of Mont St Quentin was the ultimate test of his AIF.

Monash devised an attack plan, which was approved by the British High Command, involving the 2nd, 3rd and 5th Australian divisions. At 5 a.m. on 31 August 1918, a heavy artillery barrage descended upon the enemy front and the Australians charged up the hill into ferocious German machine-gun fire. Early in the battle, the Australians took the heights but were driven off. Over the next two days, the summit was savagely fought over, finally falling to the Australians, which opened the way for the capture of Peronne. The Germans abandoned the town and fell back to the Hindenburg Line, as the Allies hoped. Three Victoria Crosses were won by the Australians; and General Rawlinson – the commander of the Fourth British Army, to which the Australians were attached – called the action the 'finest single feat of the war'.[2]

While the 2nd, 3rd and 5th Divisions were fighting at Mont St Quentin and Péronne, the 1st and 4th divisions were resting in the rear. On 7 September, the battalion moved out by bus with the band playing and over the next two days marched to Stable Wood near Cartigny, southeast of Péronne, and from there towards the new frontline at Pœuilly in preparation for the next attack. The 1st and 4th divisions, which had not taken part in the attack at Mont St Quentin, were to retake the old British line and then advance further to take the outpost line, from which at a later date the Allies could break through the Hindenburg Line. Though the men of the 45th Battalion did not know it, the attack, to take place on 18 September 1918, would be their last action of the war, but sadly ten men would be killed, including four officers, and a further 63 men wounded. By then, the Allied offensive had been going on for six weeks. All along the frontline the Allies had maintained relentless pressure on the Germans, and French and American forces on the southern sector of the front had advanced as far as the forests of the Argonne.

In writing about the August advance in *Somme Mud*, Edward Lynch provides an interesting insight into the relationship between officers and their men at this time in the war. He evokes the men's anticipation of battle, the suspense and the dark fears and anxieties that lie beneath their outwardly 'calm and casual' exteriors. As each soldier's thoughts turn to his fate, formality and hierarchy, already comparatively loose in the Australian army, are broken down still further. This comes about when Nulla's mate Longun asks his platoon officer, a lieutenant by the name of Fred, about 'this Le Verguier joint'. Lynch states:

> Gone is the parade-ground 'Sir'. Men and officers are no longer separated by parade-ground discipline or the gulf of rank. That chasm has been bridged by the bond of mateship. Officers and men are united in a common test that will be carried through. Officers and men will fight and fall side by side in the mateship of men. The differences of rank, creed and calling have been swept aside by that splendid comradeship of men in battle. [p. 365]

The Australian fighting man as portrayed by Lynch is one who can think for himself and be relied upon to do what's right. When their platoon officer tells the men to fall in, as they are about to begin their advance, his 'words come not as a command, but more as a request'. This relationship between officers and their men would have been completely different in the British and certainly the German armies where discipline and blind obedience were rigorously enforced. Nulla goes on to say:

> Orders and commands are unnecessary now. Directions and guidance are necessary certainly, but our men will do their job as men. Each man is going into the attack a thinking individual and not merely just a cog in a driven wheel. [p. 365]

On the morning of the attack, the men rose early, had breakfast at 3.30 a.m. and moved off at 4.30 a.m. to their assembly positions. At 'zero hour' of 5.20 a.m., the 45th followed the attacking 48th Battalion at a distance, according to the battalion history, of 'some 600 yards' (550 metres) across a valley to the old British frontline on the next spur. Unlike on previous occasions, the Germans did not counterattack and most of the Allied casualties were from German shelling. The Germans kept shortening their artillery barrage to try to hit the advancing troops of the 48th Battalion but were always too late and so their shells fell on the 45th. As the 48th fought for the spur, taking numerous casualties, the 45th took shelter from the artillery barrage in a sunken road and in shell craters.

The infantry tactics are well described in *Somme Mud*, as is the taking of a farmhouse occupied by a dozen or so Germans. By providing heavy covering fire from a line of riflemen, six others charged the farmhouse, at which point the German occupants surrendered. This would have been a standard tactic and, although highly dangerous for those involved, proved very successful in quickly assaulting German strongpoints.

By 6.30 a.m. the 48th had gained their objective, the old British main line, and the 45th passed through to advance to their objective, the 'Red Line', the old British outpost line. This they reached by 9.20 a.m. and after digging in, sent out strong patrols to secure their front. In the stirring words of the official historian Bean:

> The forward parties of the 48th, completing their mopping up, were just sending their prisoners back over the spur when the 45th appeared on its summit, advancing in magnificent order.[3]

In this advance, the Germans generally put up little resistance and surrendered in large numbers. The battalion captured over 300 Germans in three hours. Nulla describes the surrendering Germans, who 'seldom attempt to dispute our progress' and who 'don't show any fight'. To him, they are 'cringing, crawling, cowardly fellows . . . Poor broken-spirited beggars, they've had the pluck knocked out of them.' But like those captured at Le Hamel, 'Many of them are just kids; poor, frightened, skinny little codgers of fifteen to seventeen . . . Clad in men's uniforms that flap over their under-nourished young bodies' [p. 372]. Little wonder they surrendered so readily and quickly chose a safer way out of the vast war they had little understanding of and no power or influence to change.

Nulla confides that he and the other men 'despise' a group of Germans who have just given up a concrete machine-gun emplacement, as they 'surrendered an almost impregnable position without firing a shot'. Such observations are echoed in the official histories of the war. Bean says this of the commander of the 16th Battalion, whose job was to clear the village of Le Verguier:

> If the German had had the fighting spirit of a louse, one
> battalion on the whole brigade front would have made it
> impossible to go forward; but he never fought an inch so far
> as we were concerned.[4]

Germans are running from the barrage, so he is 'continually dropping on one knee and firing, or just standing and blazing away at those running men'. Private Lynch possibly appears in a well-known photograph doing just this, at Ascension Farm. There are a number of photographs published in a booklet in the early 1920s of Lynch's D Company. They are believed to have been taken by Hubert Wilkins, one of Australia's official war photographers, who shot them over a half-hour period on the day of the battle.

Lynch had a copy of this booklet, which his family has kept. On a number of the photographs, someone – we assume Lynch – has drawn an 'x' above a man, presumably indicating that this is him. The negatives of these photographs are in the Australian War Memorial's collection, along with a detailed description, but none mentions Lynch. In one photo, nine men spread out in a line are advancing across a slight slope. Each man in the line has been named by the Australian War Memorial except for the last two men on the far right. In Lynch's personal collection, however, the man on the far right has been marked with an 'x'. Though we will never know, this is probably Private Lynch, as the man looks slightly shorter than the rest, even allowing for the sloping ground.

Another well-known photograph shows members of the company kneeling with rifles raised, sniping at retreating Germans. Again, someone, most probably Edward Lynch, has drawn an 'x' above a rifleman on the far left who is squatting and sniping, suggesting that this is him.

The 45th Battalion had reached the Red Line by 9.20 a.m. and begun digging in on the slope above Ascension Valley. Later in the day, in the final phase of the attack, the 46th Battalion carried the advance forward across the next valley and up to the crest of the hill, playing their part in taking the overall objective: the Hindenburg Outpost Line. The 45th Battalion remained in the old British outpost line, now the reserve, for three days, digging in and consolidating their position until they were relieved and returned to the rear. This time in the line was another great success for the 4th Division. They had entered the attack with only 3,000 men, but captured 2,500 Germans and killed and wounded hundreds more. In contrast, they suffered about 500 casualties. The 45th Battalion accounted for the capture of over 300 German prisoners, five artillery pieces and 15 machine-guns.

The most important outcome of the attack was that the

Hindenburg Outpost Line had now been captured and the way was open for the major attack, two weeks hence, on the formidable St Quentin Canal, the last remaining obstacle on the march towards Germany. By late September 1918, the Allies had virtually recovered all the ground lost in Operation Michael, the Germans' offensive in March, but there was both political and military pressure to continue the advance. Major offensives were planned on all fronts: the French and Americans were to attack near Reims, the British from Arras to the St Quentin Canal; and the Belgian, British and French armies north of Armentières to the English Channel. The end of the war was now just a matter of time.

# EIGHTEEN

## *'Fini la Guerre'*

By late September 1918, the men of the five Australian divisions were exhausted. The 1st and 4th divisions were out of the line and the general belief of the men was that this would be for some time. They knew they had done well, had once again shown their mettle and made Australia proud, but they felt they deserved a rest and a decent break from the line.

The other three Australian divisions were battle-weary too, but they still had some fighting ahead of them. On 29 September, the 3rd and 5th divisions, along with US troops, attacked a well-defended section of the Hindenburg Line near Bellicourt. They succeeded in breaking through the main part of the line, but the fighting was fierce and they failed to reach their ultimate objective: the third and final layer of the Hindenburg Line, known as the Beaurevoir Line. On 3 October, the 2nd Division pushed through and took it. Then, in the last AIF infantry action of the war, on 5 October 1918, the 2nd Division took the village of Montbrehain, which the

British had earlier taken but been unable to hold. With the capture of the village, the Hindenburg Line had been utterly smashed. The area was handed over to American troops and the last exhausted Australian battalions finally joined the other men at the rear.

While the boys of the Australian Corps rested behind the line and away from the fighting, the war was moving rapidly to a conclusion on a number of fronts and the other Allied forces were now out into open country. The Germans, unable to organise concentrated resistance against these steady, relentless offensives, were everywhere falling back. Ludendorff had no answers and later stated he had been 'stabbed in the back'[1] by the Kaiser, and betrayed by the socialists on the Home Front, who he felt failed to provide both moral and material support to his offensive.

Since 'the black day' of 8 August, Ludendorff had been trying to persuade the Kaiser and Chancellor that they should ask the Allies for an armistice. On 3 October, as the Australian 2nd Division was penetrating the last stage of the Hindenburg Line, the Chancellor did just that. The response came back from US President Woodrow Wilson that the Allies would not negotiate an armistice with a monarchy and monarchy-controlled military leadership, as they did not truly represent the German people. Germany would also have to surrender the territories it had invaded. In response, changes to the constitution were rushed through, limiting the role of the monarchy, and Ludendorff, such a public symbol of the military command, was dismissed. He would soon leave Germany for neutral Sweden.

Elsewhere, things were not looking good for Germany's allies. Empires and royal houses were crumbling and falling apart. After abdicating the year before, the Tsar, along with his wife and children, had been assassinated at Ekaterinburg in Siberia in July 1918 and civil war was still raging in Russia. But now other social and political forces, like Communism, were at work on the great monarchies of Europe, and the royal families and privileged classes were all soon to join the disintegration of the European monarchist orders. These included the kingdoms of Austria–Hungary, Bavaria, Montenegro and Saxony.

Bulgaria had also signed an armistice with the Allies on 30 September. The Austrians were in total disintegration, short of ammunition and supplies and plagued by mass desertions, with 350,000 men permanently absent by late September. In the Czech, Hungarian, Croatian and Bosnian armies, men simply laid down their arms and returned to their farms and their homes in cities and towns across Europe.

By the end of October 1918, the Austro-Hungarian army – and empire itself – was finished off by the Italian army at the battle of Vittoria Veneto, in northeast Italy, and by the Italian navy's capture of the port city of Trieste. On 28 October, Austria–Hungary sought a separate peace with the Allies, further eroding Germany's position. Over the next two days, German warship crews in the German seaport of Kiel staged a revolt after they were ordered to sea to fight the British. On the second day of the naval mutiny, 30 October, Turkey signed a separate armistice with the Allies. The German naval revolt quickly spread to the army, where there were widespread acts of disobedience. The German High Command ordered the withdrawal of troops across the Meuse but irrevocable damage had been done to morale. In Berlin there were food riots and people burnt pictures of the Kaiser. On 3 November, Austria–Hungary signed an armistice with the Allies and on 5 November, President Woodrow Wilson sent word to Germany that the Allied governments were now willing to negotiate a peace based on his 14 Points.

The German delegation sent to negotiate Germany's cease-fire terms was headed up by politician Matthias Erzberger. Erzberger had been vocal in the Reichstag in mid-1917 in calling for a negotiated peace and seemed the appropriate man – being a Catholic civilian politician rather than a member of the German royal family or military – to negotiate Germany's ceasefire terms. On 7 November, Erzberger and his delegation crossed the line to begin peace negotiations with Marshal Ferdinand Foch. But there would be no negotiations as such, for what the Allies sought was something far more demanding and harsh than a simple ceasefire: they wanted Germany's total and unconditional surrender.

On 8 November, the Germans were taken by train to a secret location: a railway siding in the forest at Compiègne, about 80 kilometres northeast of Paris. The train came to a stop and they were ushered into another train waiting on the next track, which acted as Foch's headquarters. There, in the stationary carriage, Foch handed over the Allies' armistice terms and gave the Germans 72 hours to consider them.

Unaware of just how close the end of the war was, Edward Lynch and his mates in the 45th Battalion were far away from the line in billets at Fluy, near Pissy, southwest of Amiens. By now they had been there for six weeks, playing sport, undergoing rigorous training, doing route marches and enjoying hot baths and clean clothes. They were well prepared for their next period in the line, but their departure kept being postponed by their commanders – a reflection of the uncertainty of the military situation.

With the armistice as yet unsigned, the Allies kept up the pressure on the German troops. It is said that only the cavalry could keep up with the German retreat; the Allied troops were advancing so fast it was difficult to provide them with food, ammunition and supplies. The British crossed the Scheldt River with little opposition and advanced on Mons and Ghent. The rapid advance was held up in some places, though, by delayed-action mines laid by the Germans. These were also to hold up the 1st and 4th Australian divisions as they returned to the line on 10 November. The devastating explosion caused by the mine left in Bapaume Town Hall by retreating Germans in March 1917 was still fresh in their minds, so they were very wary.

Meanwhile, in Germany, revolutionary changes were afoot. The Social Democratic Party demanded the end of the monarchy and there was a workers' uprising in Berlin. The Kaiser wavered on whether to give up the throne, but Prince Max of Baden, who had been chancellor since only October, announced the Kaiser's abdication, forcing his hand, and the next day the Kaiser's family, staff and a Prussian guard drove to the Netherlands and into exile. Prince Max himself resigned as chancellor in favour of the leader of the Social Democrats, Friedrich Ebert, who had been a saddlemaker and union activist up until not long before. On 9 November, the German Republic was proclaimed and Ebert's first act as chancellor was to accept the Allies' peace terms. The armistice was finally signed by both parties at 5 a.m. on 11 November in Foch's train carriage at Compiègne. Erzberger could do little to alter the conditions in Germany's favour and had scant input apart from correcting some factual details and making a short, emotional speech about the severity of the terms of surrender. The two sides agreed that the guns would fall silent at 11 a.m. on the 11th day of the 11th month, 1918. The war was finally over.

The conditions of the armistice were intended to remove any chance of Germany resuming the war. The Germans were to withdraw within 14 days from all captured and invaded territory and, within a further 16 days, to have withdrawn back 10 kilometres on the German side of the river Rhine – meaning that the Rhineland would be under Allied occupation. The many thousands of Allied prisoners of war were to be released, though German POWs were to remain in Allied captivity for a period to prevent them being re-formed into a fighting army. Germany was required to hand over 5,000 artillery pieces, 25,000 machine-guns, 3,000 trench mortars and 1,700 military aircraft. To prevent the movement of troops and supplies, Germany also had to hand over 5,000 locomotives, 150,000 railway wagons and 5,000 trucks. The German navy was stripped of ten battleships, six battle cruisers, eight light cruisers and 50 destroyers. German crews destroyed and sank many of these vessels in 1919, when it came time to hand them over at Scapa Flow in the Orkney Islands, off the Scottish coast. Nevertheless, the loss of all of these war materials and transportation was a huge blow to German pride and military preparedness.

In Australia and Britain, the news of the armistice was received with widespread joy and celebration. As church bells rang out, people poured into the streets, overjoyed that peace had come at last. Offices and factories closed and pubs did a roaring trade. In London, flags and bunting in red, white and blue sprouted everywhere; in Sydney, jubilant crowds poured into Martin Place. There was mass hysteria as people mobbed returned soldiers and carried them aloft, cheering and thanking them while others danced in the street or wound through the crowd in long, excited conga lines.

For Private Lynch and his mates in the 45th, however, the war felt far from over. The battalion history states:

In the first week of November, preparations were made for a move forward, but this move was postponed from day to day, and, on the morning of November 11th, the glad news of the Armistice came through.[2]

But did it? For the boys of the 45th, there seemed some confusion about the armistice. According to Lynch's account in '*Fini la Guerre*', on 10 November the men hear news of the Kaiser's abdication and 'rumours of peace are floating around, but we no longer worry over rumours these days'. On 11 November the men get word that they are heading to the front early the next day. Then the signallers intercept a message that an armistice has been signed, but the men hear that Foch 'won't entertain any peace proposals until the Allies have crossed the Rhine'. Even when their commanding officer announces that hostilities ceased at 11 a.m., ending the war, the men are doubtful. As Nulla says, 'Surely wars don't end like this.' Their uncertainty is compounded when the CO adds with a grin: 'I regret to announce that the message is unofficial.'

Today it seems amazing that the declaration of the end of the war would not be passed on to the Australian soldiers in a more official way. Yet, knowing the status of the Australian soldier in the Allied military hierarchy, Lynch's account seems entirely plausible. The private soldier in a colonial battalion far from home was at the lowest echelon of the power structure. Who in the British High Command would be worried about informing mere Australian privates that hostilities were over, that they had survived and could soon go home? And as a private, who would you believe? After all that the men had gone through, peace must have seemed almost inconceivable.

Though the guns fell silent at 11 a.m. on 11 November, Nulla and his mates are sent off for two hours of bayonet training. On the way, Farmer asks if there is anything in the peace rumours and one of his friends tells him, 'Yes, the war's over, all right. All over the flamin' place.' That night the French civilians are celebrating and getting drunk, but the men continue to debate whether the news is true. One can imagine the talk that night: the hope that yes, the war has ended; disbelief that it could be possible; and anticipation of the great disappointment they will feel if this turns out to be just another furphy. It is only exhaustion that closes down their discussion and they suffer another cold night without their blankets, which were sent ahead days ago for their oft-postponed trip to the frontline. They fall into 'a cold, broken sleep' still unsure whether the war is actually over.

Imagine how it would have been for Lynch's German equivalent that night: some poor private soldier, powerless, hungry, cold and now faced with defeat. He may have felt he had failed, that his effort was not enough and the Fatherland now lay in ruins because of his failure. Probably with no job to go to, he would have been looking into a bleak future. He would have heard about the rioting on the streets of Berlin and, given the situation in Russia, may have feared the effects socialist and communist agitators might have. The Kaiser was gone and Germany was now a 'republic' – an unfamiliar term that may have meant little to him. The German private would be returning to a rapidly changing and perhaps confusing political situation. He may have suspected his family were starving; that there was no coal for their fires nor bread for their table. Though he would no longer be facing death each day on the line, his fate probably looked grim, or at least uncertain.

Another cold morning dawns for Nulla and his mates. Reveille sounds at 4 a.m. – a noise anyone with military experience hates – and they drag themselves up from their uncomfortable bed on the floorboards, pack their equipment and march 'away from Pissy for the line again', perhaps for another stunt, another hop-over; perhaps death. But the rumours still linger and the discussions of the night before are still at the forefront of their minds – perhaps the war is over . . . if only. They march to Ailly-sur-Somme, just northwest of Amiens, and entrain to head east.

What finally convinces them that the war is over is the English-language newspaper that boys are selling on the railway platform. It is ironic that though they are the ones who have been risking their lives each day, they get confirmation of the armistice not from their superiors but from the media, the way today we might look to CNN or Fox News. Newspapers bought for a few pennies on some unknown and previously unheard of railway station carry the priceless words they have longed to hear: WAR ENDS.

The men are unimpressed about how they have been informed of the end of hostilities. They well know that the ceasefire details would have been received at division and brigade level, so why was it not officially passed on to them? They discuss the possibility that 'Perhaps they'd forgotten where we were,' to which the answer quickly comes, 'They'd have flamin' soon remembered if Fritz had broken through again.'

In contrast to the jubilation on the streets of Paris, London and 'the whole Allied world' that they read of in the papers, the reaction of Nulla and his mates is curiously subdued. They sit on the train digesting the news, making their way to the frontline they 'no longer dread'.

> We've convinced our innermost selves that the war is over, that we've seen it through, that we'll really again see our own people and our own homes that have seemed so hopelessly distant of late . . .
>
> Our men are as calm as ever. We, to whom the screeched 'Fini la guerre' of the newsboys really mean the most, are taking our release from all that war has meant very calmly and casually. [pp. 394–5]

They have dreamt of this day, but when it arrives their joy is perhaps complicated by other emotions. In the official history, Charles Bean observes:

> The 1st and 4th Australian Divisions were then arriving in the region about le Cateau. Neither there nor at the front was there any general demonstration – the sound of guns ceased; the gates of the future silently opened. Wonder, hope, grief, too deep and uncertain for speech, revolved for days in almost every man's mind . . .[3]

Edward Lynch, circa 1917. *Courtesy of family archive*

Lynch is seated on the left with soldiers from his battalion – probably his platoon – in 1917. It is possible that some of these men were the inspiration for the characters in *Somme Mud*. Sadly they remain unidentified. *Courtesy of family archive*

Troops of the 45th Battalion at Ascension Farm, sniping at retreating Germans on the far hillside in September 1918. The man kneeling on the far left is believed to be Lynch. *Courtesy of Australian War Memorial (E03260)*

Chatsbury School, 1922. *Courtesy of family archive*

The family home at Tumbarumba, 1926. *Courtesy of family archive*

Lynch at the home of his parents-in-law, Hurstville, 1922. *Courtesy of family archive*

Lynch's wife and children standing in front of the family's first car, circa 1933. *L–R*: Shirley, Ned, Yvonne, baby Greg and Richard. *Courtesy of family archive*

Lynch and his son Greg, snapped by a street photographer, Sydney, 1942. *Courtesy of family archive*

Lynch with his eldest son, Ned, off to the horse races, circa 1947. *Courtesy of family archive*

Lynch as an officer during the Second World War. *Courtesy of family archive*

Lynch just weeks before his death in September 1980. *Courtesy of family archive*

The 45th Battalion travelled on to Fresnoy-le-Grand, nearly 100 kilometres to the east of Amiens. Winter was coming on again and for a week, in cold conditions, they drilled, had inspections, washed and polished their equipment and practised ceremonial parades. They set out again on 22 November to be included in the triumphant Allied force that would cross the Rhine and enter Germany. But it wasn't to be: the Australian government decided that no Australian troops were to take part in the occupation, a great disappointment to many of the men, given the part they had played in the victory and the high casualties taken by all Australian divisions.

But the 45th Battalion continued east, stopping at numerous French towns on the way. In *Somme Mud*, when they are near Avesnes-sur-Helpe, they get 'all dolled up' to line the roadside with other Allied troops to be inspected by the King and Prince of Wales as they drive past. It is a freezing day with an icy wind blowing across snow-covered ground as they shuffle to line the roadside, battalion after battalion of Australian and English troops, waiting for two hours for the royals. Here we see once again the stark difference in attitude between the Australian and the British fighting men. The Australians try to get in a game of two-up; some sneak off to a nearby estaminet for a quick drink. The British on the other hand stand obediently at ease, causing Nulla and his mates to pass cheeky remarks about them, because 'the sight of this good soldier stuff generally gets our goat'. Finally, the Prince of Wales, who Nulla feels 'is a sort of cobber of ours, though we haven't told him so yet' and then the King, 'a little man, mostly beard and overcoat', glide by in big cars. The British troops loyally cheer the King; the Australians derisively cheer the cheering British. Nulla deadpans, 'Long live the King. Our crowd didn't shout and cheer, yet we somehow feel that the King didn't expect it.'

In the days after the signing of the armistice, Europe became a bubbling cauldron of political activity and turmoil, and would remain so for decades to come. Austria and Hungary became separate republics, as did Czechoslovakia, which had formerly been part of the Austro-Hungarian Empire. Poland, which had for over a century been split into three territories ruled by Russia, Prussia and Austria, declared its independent nationhood and expelled German troops from her soil. In Germany, the political power of the monarchies of Bavaria, Saxony and Württemberg came to an end with the abdications of their rulers. In the Balkans, where the war began, provinces formerly part of the Austro-Hungarian Empire joined with Serbia and Montenegro to form the Kingdom of Serbs, Croats and Slovenes (which would, in 1929, come to be known as Yugoslavia). As Allied warships entered the Dardanelles and anchored at Constantinople (present-day Istanbul), the government of Ahmed Isset Pasha fell; the curtain had fallen on the Ottoman Empire.

On 1 December, British, French and American forces moved into the Rhineland in accordance with the armistice and soon after they occupied three strategic bridgeheads: the

British at Cologne, the Americans at Coblenz and the French at Mainz. The Australians were on the move, too. Haig would not officially release the AIF from France and Belgium until February 1919, when it was anticipated that troops would not be needed for possible deployment, so the 45th Battalion went to Hastière-Lavaux in Belgium, on the left bank of the river Meuse, southwest of the major town of Dinant. Here their time was taken up with physical training, lectures, route marches and small arms training, or musketry. Each afternoon at two o'clock there was a 'recreational parade' that allowed the men to venture into the nearest town or have time to themselves. On Saturdays there was 'hat ironing', presumably in readiness for the church parade on Sunday. The weekly routine kept the men in a fighting state – fit, well practised and ready for a ceremonial parade at a moment's notice.

The French-speaking Belgians in this border area had suffered under the German occupation and though they had never met Australian troops before, they received them with great warmth and a special welcome. The 45th stayed in the town for over two months, from mid-December through Christmas and on into February 1919. When they departed for the Australian base area at Le Havre, in France, there was much sadness among the villagers. On 26 February 1919, the town's burgomaster wrote to the OC:

> The Australian troops left our locality some days ago and I beg you to accept the liveliest feelings of sympathy for the population which will always keep a good remembrance for the 45th.

We admire the Australians for their generous patriotism, which voluntarily brought them to our battlefields.

We love them for all their sufferings, and we send them our deepest gratitude for the active part they took in our deliverance.

We received and welcomed you according to our small means, we wanted our village to be hospitable agreeable [sic], so that after these anxious years, you might enjoy here a happy and calm life.

We are proud that we were destined to receive you and you may be sure that these two months during which you were staying here have tightened the bonds of friendship and gratitude which attach us to the brave sons of beautiful Australia.

To all we wish a happy return in their far away country. Please accept, Colonel, the expression of our kindest feelings.[4]

The Australian base at Le Havre had been quickly enlarged and modified to cope with the troops converging there from the battlefields of France and Belgium. Here the men handed in weapons and other equipment, were given medical checks, de-loused and provided with clean clothing and underwear. To keep them entertained, a sporting field was laid out, a theatre built and a newspaper published. Men spent their time playing two-up and enjoying the estaminets and local night spots and generally passing the days in a high state of boredom and anticipation. Some who had been away from Australia for nearly four years found this period of waiting wearisome and frustrating.

The British High Command and General Monash were keen to keep Australian troops moving away from the battle-fields towards home, so every effort was made to get men to the large holding bases on the Salisbury Plain, in England, as quickly and efficiently as possible. On 15 April 1919, Private Lynch bade farewell to France. It was a bittersweet occasion as the rain pelted down and the men headed west for England and home, leaving behind in the Somme mud so many 'fine mates who fell whilst we lived through it all', as Nulla says. This same kind of anguish overcame the men pulling out of Gallipoli during the evacuation in December 1915 – the great sadness of leaving the graves of their mates in a foreign land, so far from home. And so Private Lynch and the remaining men of the 45th Battalion AIF crossed the choppy English Channel. Behind them were the war, the memories, the former enemy and ahead were the friendly people of England, safe camps on the Salisbury Plain and, soon, repatriation home.

# NINETEEN

# A Dinner
# to the Troops

When the war finished, as well as joy and celebration, there was a sense of surprise among the Allies. Only eight months before, the German army had driven them back, Paris had been under threat and the Channel ports in jeopardy. Now, not only had the Germans been stopped, they had surrendered and were in total turmoil. The Allied planners had been focused on the 1919 summer offensive, when suddenly their thoughts had to turn towards how their troops should be utilised until a peace treaty was signed, and then how to get them home. Well before the armistice, in fact as early as January 1917, the AIF had been giving thought to the logistics for bringing troops home, but their efforts to make preparations had been hampered by the government in Australia, which had been slow in its decision-making and was not ready for such a profound turn of events.

The mammoth task of getting the troops home needed a special person, and who better for the job than General Sir

John Monash, the Commander of the Australian Corps. There were three stages that needed to be planned and organised. First, repatriation: the return of the troops to Australia; second, demobilisation: standing the army down from its war footing; and third, rehabilitation: returning the troops to civilian life. On 21 November 1918, Monash was appointed Director General of Repatriation and Demobilisation. His task was enormous: getting nearly 180,000 men, the wounded and convalescing, plus his estimate of 7,000 dependants, back to Australia. Apart from the men in France, Belgium and the United Kingdom, men also had to be returned home from the Middle East, Mesopotamia and Russia. In addition, a significant number of men had married local women and fathered children, so places also needed to be found on ships for these dependants.

A great challenge was finding enough ships to transport these men and their families home. Australia was competing for a limited number of suitable ships with troops from Canada, New Zealand, South Africa, India and a host of small colonies and protectorates. The massive army of the United States was also eager to return home. The Shipping Controller's job was made difficult by the great demand for ships, coupled with the Australian government's high standards, which specified the men should have ample space and good amenities. Given the challenges of procuring enough ships that met requirements, the return of the Australian troops would have to take place in increments. It might be up to a year before the last man was home.

So, how to determine the order in which the men should be sent back? The principle of fairness prevailed and a policy of 'first to come, first to go' was introduced, meaning that those who had served the longest were first in the queue to go home. Two other criteria were also taken into consideration: whether a man had heavy family responsibilities or a job waiting for him.

Monash devised a system of sorting the men into shiploads, or 'quotas', of 1,000, according to their priority for returning to Australia. As ships became available, quotas were assigned to them, in order of priority. But sorting the men into quotas based on their length of duty, and family and work, meant that long-standing battalions were torn apart and returned to Australia piecemeal. The Australian government had sought to bring each division home as one unit so that victory parades could march proudly through the cities and towns of Australia, but Monash was far more practical about who should get a berth on the next ship.

Initially, it was planned that wives and children of Australian soldiers would be sent home first, but it would mean these young English wives would have to wait months, maybe up to a year, in a strange new country until their husbands arrived. It was decided that 'family ships' would be dispatched at intervals to allow soldiers, their wives and children to sail together. By May 1919, dependants were a sizeable logistical problem, as on average 150 Australian soldiers were getting married each week. By the end of the year, 15,386 dependants had been shipped to Australia.

The approximately 40,000 wounded men and convalescents from hospitals across Britain had special transport needs, such as medical services and personnel, which further complicated how the limited number of ships was allocated. Right from the beginning, repatriation was slow. Nearly 20,000 men embarked from Britain during December 1918 and January 1919, but a shipping strike in February saw only 5,400 head home.

We know little of Private Lynch's time in England. His personal file shows that he went from the Australian base depot at Le Havre and arrived in England on 15 April 1919. As Nulla puts it, 'We're over in England thawing out a bit and waiting, ever waiting.' The following month, May 1919, the majority of Australians left France and arrived in England, swelling the population of the camps on the Salisbury Plain to 80,000 men and placing severe pressure on the Shipping Controller to find berths.

During this time, Monash kept a close eye on the men's welfare, ensuring where possible they had sporting events and concerts to keep them occupied. Well understanding the Australians' make-up, he knew that now their primary task – winning the war – had passed, the men needed a fresh purpose, otherwise boredom, desertion and unrest would mount. Monash exhorted the officers to give their men a different focus for their energies, to take them from their 'fighting morale' to a new 'reconstruction morale'.[1] What the men needed was a sense of the future; they needed training, education and what we today would perhaps call work experience. Most of all, they must be given a clear and optimistic vision of their place in the nation.

Canada had long before the armistice established an education programme for soldiers and it had inspired General Sir Brudenell White, the AIF Chief of Staff who presided over the Demobilisation and Repatriation Branch for a time. White recruited George Merrick Long, the Anglican Bishop of Bathurst, to run the AIF's education programme. Since May 1918, Long had been reviewing other armies' education schemes, researching the future Australian labour market and talking to troops about what type of training they wanted. Together with an academic staff, he formulated a wide-ranging programme offering the men educational and work experience options in the UK, other parts of Europe and America. There were three main strands of training: professional, for those seeking university degrees and a professional career; technical, for those wishing to learn a trade; and general, for improving basic literacy and numeracy skills. To do this, he needed the co-operation of the British education system, trade unions, leaders of industry and the people of Britain. And such help was not always forthcoming.

In any case, only one in three men took up the offer of education and training. Many had never had a job, had little idea about preparing themselves for one and believed that they should wait until they were home and had a sense of the career options available in Australia before they underwent training.

Some spent their time in boredom in the camps, forgoing a splendid opportunity. Perhaps being young and never having had a job except in the army, they had no idea of their future needs, their responsibilities or a possible career path. Certainly there was a deep concern for the future among the troops in England, who universally shared a deep longing for home. They realised how different Australia was, not only from continental Europe but also from the mother country. They had experienced the class system and privilege and felt uncomfortable with them. They had also seen the squalor of life, the pallid faces and the weak and underdeveloped manhood of both English and German troops. They yearned for space, clean air, the scent of eucalypts and the bush chorus, but most of all their families and girlfriends. A poem by P. Vance, published in a troop-ship paper, sums this up:

> Oh, London girls are sporty girls, and Cardiff girls are sweet,
> And the dark eyed girls of Charleroi are dainty and petite,
> But now I'm on the track for home the only girl for me
> Is the homespun, all-wool dinkum girl who's waiting on the Quay.
>
> I've had my fun, I must admit, and made the money go,
> For the sheelahs [sic] know the Aussie hat, from France to Scapa Flow.
> There was Maisie down at Margate, there was Maggie up at Frome,
> But I'm forgetting all the lot, now that I'm bound for home.[2]

They sat around in corrugated-iron camps and dreamt of home. Australia took on a new lustre and for some it became a nearly mystical place where everything was perfect and *fair dinkum*. Though the vast majority of the men came from the cities, they saw Australia and themselves as rural and the bush as somehow their home. This was reflected in the academic courses the men chose. Of those who did take up the offer of education and training, a great number attended agricultural courses such as animal husbandry, farm management and wool classing. Many of them found practical experience on British farms, particularly sheep farms.

For the authorities, keeping the men occupied and out of trouble was a major focus of their attention. Apart from the official distractions of education, sport and concerts, the men found time for letter writing, diary entries and painting. Men listed in a quota for embarkation were granted 14 days' leave. Those who still had close family connections in the UK journeyed to all corners of the island to see them. Some went to London to visit the Tower, Westminster Abbey, Buckingham Palace, Hampton Court and of course the West End. Some went to London and simply spent their savings and, when the money had run out, took the train back to their base camp on the Salisbury Plain.

Friendships began with English girls, many resulting in marriage, but many a heart was broken by an Australian Digger. Others found comfort in the ladies of the night, increasing the incidence of venereal diseases in the AIF, with many returning to Australia to spread their infections. Venereal disease was a problem in all armies but, according to Bean, the incidence in the Australian army was among the highest. Perhaps the disparity was due to the fact that the English and French soldiers weren't so far from their wives and lovers, while the Australians, better paid and further from home, might be more likely to visit prostitutes. Whatever the reason, all measures to curb STD cases failed, including designating the disease a 'crime' and noting it in a soldier's pay book.

Most of all, the men played their favourite game, two-up. It had become popular with Australian troops during the Boer War and had been revived in the earliest days of the AIF, at the beginning of the First World War. In the Australian War Memorial's collection there are many photographs and even early black-and-white movie film of men playing two-up. One photo of a game in progress, taken at Brown's Dip, Gallipoli, is especially poignant, for many of the men playing were dead minutes after the photograph was taken, when they were hit by a shell. Though technically illegal, the game was accepted by the officers, who turned a blind eye to it, much as they had to the men drinking while in the back areas, as it was seen as a harmless distraction and something to occupy them during their idle hours.

Even so, there were certain times when officers wanted their men to at least make a pretence of decorum. In *Somme Mud*, Nulla tells us:

> Our little crowd is mooching about the huts trying to fill in
> time somehow. A game of two-up is in progress and Longun
> and I are winning well. An officer drifts along to the game and

Dark, very friendly like, asks him, 'Goin' to have a spin, Sir?'

'No, you fellows want to take a bit of a pull. Playing two-up here today! Surely you know it's Sunday. Get round behind the huts if you must play.'

'What day is it behind the huts, Sir?' Dark asks, but the officer buzzes off so we get into an empty hut, fix a blanket on the floor and finish the game. [p. 413]

While in the Salisbury camps, the Australians were inoculated against the virulent and deadly Spanish influenza. Scientists were divided on the exact cause of Spanish influenza and the virus responsible for it would not be isolated until 1934, but men were inoculated against a more common strain of influenza plus bacteria that caused secondary infections such as pneumonia, which was often responsible for the rapid deaths of Spanish flu patients. During some periods of the repatriation process, hammocks were spaced further apart on the ships to prevent the spread of the illness. The fear was that shiploads of returning soldiers would be struck down on the nine-week voyage home and spread the disease far and wide upon their return. If even one case of influenza was detected on board, all the men were quarantined on their arrival in Australia, which must have been agony to the men, so tantalisingly close to their loved ones and homes. The pandemic had already hit Australia by then, but according to Bean, it was 'said that by *delaying* the epidemic the quarantine probably saved Australia a heavy toll of life'.[3] Spanish influenza took approximately 12,000 Australian lives and by the time the disease had petered out in 1919, globally it had caused more fatalities than the Great War.

In the chapter 'A Dinner to the Troops', Nulla and his mates find themselves being inoculated. By this point in the war they have undergone so many inoculations they don't know what this one is for and don't care all that much, but it was probably for influenza. Longun casually asks of the medical orderly administering the shots:

'What's this inoculation for, Dig?'
  The orderly gets a burst of wit and tells Longun, 'To guard against the prevailing epidemic of catching Pommy Brides.' We grin at Longun and wait. Longun gazes long and unlovingly in that orderly's face and screws his long neck to get a side view, too, and in a friendly sort of tone tells the orderly, 'You should be thankful that your face has saved you the necessity of being inoculated.' [p. 405]

On Anzac Day 1919, Nulla and his mates are dinner guests of the mayor of a town probably somewhere close to the 4th Division base camp at Codford, near Salisbury. It's unclear whether this dinner actually took place, but we do know that large dinners for Australian troops awaiting repatriation were common in the area around the bases. Nulla's attitude to this, the fourth Anzac Day, is an intriguing one. 'We're told, "Today's Anzac Day, don't you know?" We didn't know, or care much either.' [p. 406] The previous year, on the third Anzac Day, across the AIF there was much celebration. For the

45th Battalion a sports day had been planned as a celebration, cancelled only because of the German attack around Villers-Bretonneux and the Somme. Perhaps the difference now is that Nulla and his mates don't find much to celebrate about war.

With hostilities at an end, the opportunity arises for the men to look back on the conflict and their good fortune in living through it – and it is perhaps inevitable that thoughts turn to religious faith. Throughout *Somme Mud*, Lynch explores the place of religion in war, showing Nulla's attitude to be that the padres are not particularly relevant to the real concerns of fighting men. The characters' discussions become quite spirited when it comes to the hypocrisy of ministers of religion – but they never broach the topic of their own personal faiths. This is interesting given that Edward Lynch was a very religious man, came from a strong Roman Catholic family and attended mass regularly until his death. He even told his children that his rosary beads saved his life during the First World War, though we do not know how.

In 'A Dinner to the Troops', Lynch returns to the theme, having Nulla weigh the roles of God's grace and sheer luck in the survival of him and his mates, when so many others fell.

We've seen our fair share of the war . . . and come out alive, thanks to God's goodness and our own good luck.

We give our luck some credit and suppose there's something in what writers call the 'luck of life'. We joke and speak of our luck and attribute much of the daily good or evil to the fact that our luck was in, or out.

We don't openly speak of being preserved by the Grace of God, for somehow in the A.I.F. it doesn't seem the thing to dwell too much upon religious convictions. It isn't done, not openly at any rate. With luck it's far different. We can wax free about luck, shower it with praise, blame it for our own short-sighted madness or make it responsible for any bravery. When a man's modesty forbids him accepting the praise his actions have so well merited, he passes it off to his luck. Or, if he has been so careless over little things as to throw his hat down in Piccadilly Circus and defy six big military policemen to touch it, and gets landed in Warwick Square gaol for being drunk, disorderly and A.W.L., he's not to blame in the least . . . his luck was out, that's all. But religion, or luck, or both, we're going home to our own kith and kin. [pp. 404–5]

It would be another month, however, before Private Lynch and his mates of the 45th would begin their long journey home, a journey that for many was a mixture of excitement and anticipation, but also a time where old friendships and the bonds of the battalion would be broken forever. For them all, the time had come to return to Australia.

# TWENTY

# Till the
# Boys Come
# Home

On 3 June 1919, Private Lynch embarked from Devonport, Plymouth, on HMT *Beltana* as part of Quota 30. Like all the Australian troops prior to embarkation, he had taken 14 days' leave. He no doubt enjoyed, as did Nulla, 'various towns in the UK' and 'great times in London'. Then, after months of waiting, his quota took the train from Salisbury southwest to Exeter, and on to Plymouth. Along the way they were cheered and farewelled, and given tea, scones and souvenir cards by the pretty girls sent to meet them.

As the chugging, belching steamer went out past Drake's Island, down Cawsand Bay and on past Penlee Point, Lynch was leaving behind his fallen Australian mates and the post-war turmoil of Europe – a turmoil that even he had played a small role in. In the years to come, the fallout from the First World War would bring another terrible war, but that was in the future. For the moment, there was a new life and new hope, far across the endless horizon.

In a coda to the story running through *Somme Mud* of how war changes and matures Nulla and his mates, their ship docks at Cape Town, one of the places where they got drunk and disorderly on their journey to the war. How different they are now. They are no longer boys naively heading off on a great adventure; they are grown men who have experienced the absolute worst and the best of humanity and who have seen things they could barely have imagined previously.

> We enjoyed Cape Town, but in a calmer, maturer manner than when we bubbled over on our wild day there three years ago on our way to the war . . . Perhaps the thought that we're so near home . . . has blunted the edge off our wildness . . . Perhaps . . . the slackening of the usual discipline has given us the opportunity for indulging our wildness, and what's the use of mucking up when it's not against authority? Or perhaps we've just got more sense, or is it that the past three years have quietened us down more than we realise? [p. 417]

Following the armistice, the maelstrom of political change and social turmoil descended on Europe. Though the figures vary widely, an estimated eight million military personnel were killed; five million from Britain's allies and three million from Germany and her allies, plus an estimated 12 million civilians. Great tracts of France and Belgium were laid waste as were other countries where fighting had been waged. Industry and infrastructure were damaged, stockpiles of food were gone and crucial minerals and fuel sources depleted. Just beginning to approach the repair and restoration of whole countries, their infrastructure and society was beyond belief. And the human, physical and emotional damage of this war would take long into the future to repair and to heal; a residual pain remains even to this day.

Germany was in desperate straits. Disillusioned soldiers returning from the front found their families starving, cold and poor. There was political turmoil. In Berlin, the revolutionary communist Spartacist League, led by a former Reichstag deputy named Karl Liebknecht and 'Red Rosa' Luxemburg, took to the streets and occupied a number of government buildings. Having seen the success of the communist takeover in Russia, they demanded that the fragile German government establish a socialist republic. A struggle for control began between the Left and the Right; between the pro-communists demanding a socialist republic and disaffected war veterans and *Freikorps* paramilitary groups, who demanded a new nationalist Germany and the elimination of communism. The uprising in Berlin was quashed and the two communist leaders, Liebknecht and Luxemburg, served prison sentences and were murdered soon after. The disquiet and turmoil had just begun in Germany and would not finish for another 25 years, with the defeat of Hitler's Third Reich, in May 1945.

The armistice was only a temporary truce, so the conditions

of a lasting peace needed to be negotiated. On 18 January 1919, the first formal session of negotiations got under way in Paris and the French Prime Minister, Georges Clemenceau, was elected chairman. Twenty-six nations were assembled, including Australia, whose delegation was led by Prime Minister Billy Hughes. These nations had a wide variety of agendas and ideas on how to punish Germany and what the new post-war world should be like. The major players were Britain, France and America. France wanted Germany to suffer for starting the war and had a deep resentment of Germany and little sympathy for the idea of formulating a 'just peace', which America, at the other end of the spectrum, was arguing for. Even in Britain, there were calls to 'Hang the Kaiser' and 'Make Germany pay', but at the peace negotiations Britain took the middle ground between the two extremes of France and the United States. Pressure on President Georges Clemenceau and the British Prime Minister, David Lloyd George, was intense: they knew their political future could depend on how they responded to the public demand in their countries to bring Germany to its knees and never allow it to be strong enough to wage war again. Germany and her allies were excluded from the negotiations; Russia had already concluded a separate peace with Germany, in 1917.

Negotiations between what became known as the 'Council of Ten', continued from mid-January until mid-March. In late April, the German delegation arrived in Paris and in early May it was presented with the peace conditions that had been argued over and finally agreed upon by the victorious nations. The German delegation was appalled and immediately issued a protest about the unfair conditions and withdrew from further negotiations. Soon after, the leader of the German delegation, Ulrich Graf von Brockdorff-Rantzau, resigned, refusing to sign, but the Allied response was immediate: either sign within 24 hours or military operations would be resumed against Germany.

Hindenburg assured the newly elected German government that the army could not mount a defence against the Allies, so the Chancellor, Gustav Bauer, signed the treaty, four hours before the deadline was to expire. On 7 May 1919, the Treaty of Versailles was announced to the world.

There was one element of the treaty that all nations agreed upon: the introduction of the League of Nations, whose aim was to maintain international peace and security and prevent future wars. The 32 founding members agreed 'to respect and preserve [the] territorial integrity and existing political independence' of all other member nations. As a signatory to the peace treaty, Australia became a member of the League, a major step for the newly federated nation. Until then, Australia had barely been consulted about the signing of international treaties, which Britain had taken charge of.

On a summer afternoon on 28 June 1919, over 1,000 people crowded into the vast Hall of Mirrors at the Palace of Versailles and signed the treaty. The German representatives, Herman Muller and Johannes Bell, signed first. Once their signatures were on the paper, the great fountains in the palace gardens, which had been turned off since 1914, sprang back to life, to the cheers of the crowds.

As the HMT *Beltana* slowly ploughed her way south, Australia was coming to grips with the peace terms and a new future. The Treaty of Versailles had granted Australia a League of Nations mandate over the German possessions in New Guinea and the Pacific. These included German New Guinea (*Deutsch Neuguinea*), the Bismarck Archipelago (New Britain) and the scattered islands of Marianne, Caroline, Pelew (present-day Palau) and Nauru, with the joint administrative capital in Rabaul, in present-day Papua New Guinea.

On the domestic front, Australia was coming to grips with post-war needs such as the development of an efficient transport infrastructure across the vast continent. The linking of the major cities was noted as an urgent requirement and commercial aviation was seen as having a big future. In March 1919, while many Anzac soldiers still languished in holding camps in England, the Australian government offered a prize of £10,000 to the first Australian who succeeded in flying from the United Kingdom to Australia within a 30-day period. (In December 1919, the prize was won by Ross and Keith Smith, who made the journey in a Vickers Vimy.) Suburban railways were being constructed, with the first electric train running in Melbourne, from Flinders Street to Essendon.

Things were looking up in rural Australia. A massive one-hundred-million-pound sale of Australian wool to Britain was negotiated by Prime Minister Billy Hughes, followed by a one-million-ton wheat deal, again to Britain, worth £12 million over three years, and these buoyed the fortunes of hard-pressed farmers and graziers. The government encouraged returned men, some of whom had taken agricultural courses in England and visited farms to learn rural skills, to take up small land grants as 'soldier settlers'. It was hoped they would become part of a resurgent farm sector, but the scheme was to prove disastrous in most cases, particularly for those with limited farming skills who had been given small, uneconomic blocks of mallee scrub with limited water supplies.

The Australia to which Edward Lynch returned in July 1919 was very different from the country he had left nearly three years earlier. Jobs were hard to get. Many returned men, having been in the army virtually all their adult life, had no vocational training, no work experience and little to offer but their manual labour. Returned men took to the streets demanding jobs, and a number of riots and running brawls broke out as they clashed with police. In government offices, returned men demanded the jobs of those who had failed to volunteer for military service even though they were eligible. Given that one in ten employed Australians had state or federal government jobs, this was a potentially explosive situation.

Like Nulla, Edward Lynch returned to the family home in the Sydney suburb of Coogee, where they were mourning his beloved father, who had died only eight weeks before. Lynch was discharged from the army in August 1919 and early the following year began attending Sydney Teachers College. Here he met Yvonne Peters, another student teacher, and they married in June 1922. At the time, he was on his first posting, in the one-teacher school at Chatsbury, near Goulburn in New South Wales. These were the days when isolated one-teacher schools were common and when children would walk long distances to school, ride horses or come from their farms in sulkies or carts.

In 1923, the young couple moved to Kunama, halfway between Tumbarumba and Batlow on the northern edge of the Snowy Mountains. Two years after their marriage, Edward and Yvonne Lynch had their first child, whom they named Edward (Ned to his family). He was followed in August 1925 by Shirley, Richard (Dick) in February 1927, Gregory (Greg) in March 1931 and finally Moira in January 1938.

From Kunama, the family moved to Goulburn and, soon after, the Yass River, where Edward Lynch taught at the local school and at nearby Elizabeth Fields, travelling between his teaching posts in a horse and sulky.

Lynch's daughter Shirley remembers a frightening occasion when she and Ned were in the sulky with their father and he got out to close a gate. Something startled the horse and it bolted, racing off with the sulky and two small children. He took off after them and managed to stop the horse before the sulky tipped over.

Because of the travel required, Edward Lynch bought his first car, a Chevrolet, in 1929. In those days, you weren't required to have a licensed driver in the car with you when you learnt to drive. Shirley, who today lives in Coogee, remembers her father getting his driver's licence on her fourth birthday:

> The day we drove the 18 miles [29 kilometres] to Yass for Dad
> to apply for his licence, it was pouring with rain . . . Mum,
> Ned, Dick and I were in the car with him. We had hand-
> operated windscreen wipers and it was freezing cold and as
> Dad wiped, the rain froze on the windscreen and every little
> while Dad would get out with a bundle of newspapers and
> wipe the ice away. When we arrived in Yass and he went to
> the police station, they asked him how he had come in. 'I
> drove in, of course,' was the answer and the reply was, 'Well,
> anyone who can drive through this weather doesn't require a
> driving test.'

His daughter also remembers a more dramatic occasion involving the Chevrolet. In March 1931, while Yvonne was in Yass about to give birth to Greg, Edward Lynch stayed home to look after the children. Shirley takes up the story:

> Driving home in the late evening after heavy rain, we
> approached a creek crossing. A Merriman family lived nearby.
> Dad got out and walked into the water and gauged it safe to
> cross. He drove in only to find the culvert had been swept
> away and the car started to sink. He pulled out Ned and Dick
> and put them on the bank. By the time Dad got me out, the

water was up to my chest. As the only girl, I always considered I should have been taken out first. The Merriman family took us in and dried us off by the fire and fed us. Dad and the Merriman fellows went out to rescue the car with a rope and a horse and Dad had to dive under the water several times as he secured the rope.

It was sometime in the late 1920s that Edward Lynch first sat down to begin writing *Somme Mud*. His manuscript began with this simple dedication:

This narrative is dedicated to the sons of the Diggers of the First AIF in the hope that they will strive to recapture and perpetuate the Digger spirit of the older AIF.

The original draft of the book was written in pencil in 20 school exercise books, one chapter to a book, and it was from these tatty books that Lynch was later to type up the manuscript we have today. It was revealed by the family that these exercise books were stored in an outside shed in western New South Wales and, sadly, eaten by mice during a mice plague. Shirley was perhaps six or seven when he would sit her on a chair with her brothers and, with baby Greg on his knee, would read aloud the chapters as he finished writing them. It is not known how long he took to complete the book, but the original manuscript is 180,000 words, a sizeable novel and now a heavy tome in its fully hand-bound form. Shirley comments:

One of my dearest recollections is sitting around the open fire whilst he read us his latest chapter. I was so proud of him and of all the wonderful things he accomplished.

In 1930, the Lynch family moved to the small village of Jerrawa, between Yass and Goulburn. With the 1930s came the Depression, and for a young teacher on low pay with three young children life was very difficult. When Greg was born in 1931, teachers, like many in the public service, had their salaries reduced by one-third. As a lot of men did during these hard times, Edward Lynch shot rabbits, which Yvonne baked – stuffed and wrapped in bacon – to feed the family. Lynch also dressed in long-sleeved clothes and long gloves and put a net over his face to steal wild honey. Meat was sent from Gunning and collected from the station every Saturday by Ned. It was then put down one side of the well before being stored in a meat safe that hung in the shade of the verandah, ready for the evening meal. They had a cow and one of the chores for the boys was milking her twice daily; Yvonne made her own butter and clotted cream, something the children loved.

A keen sportsman, Edward Lynch enjoyed cricket and tennis. In the summer he played A-grade cricket and the family would travel with their father to ovals around the district, cheering his team along. Crowds followed their local teams and it was a great outing for the children, contained as they were by very small rural villages. In winter, he and Yvonne played competitive tennis, again visiting other towns for matches, one time even venturing as far as Canberra to play a game. Upon arriving at a new school posting, the first thing Edward Lynch would do was organise a working bee to build a tennis court. He even chipped out a small tennis court at home for his children, whom he encouraged to play after dinner and during school holidays.

Entertainment was very limited. The town was visited by the travelling picture show, which set up projectors and ran silent movies. Edward and Yvonne also encouraged the children to read, but due to the Depression they had few books. What the Lynch family did have was a radio – the only one in the town – and when the cricket was on the ABC, the locals would crowd into their kitchen and listen to the game. Shirley remembers:

> I used to be so excited when I heard the bat and ball connect, knowing the sound came from across the world. I have never really recovered from my disgust when, in my late teens, I discovered the sound was fabricated in the studio in Sydney.

(It was made by the cricket commentator Alan McGilvray tapping the head of his pencil on the table to simulate the sound of the ball hitting the bat.)

In 1937, just before Moira, the last baby, was born, the Lynch family moved to Numbaa, a small village south of the Shoalhaven River and east of Nowra, on the New South Wales south coast. Here Dick and Greg did some of their schooling and Edward Lynch taught in the single-teacher school. While in Numbaa, the Second World War began and, despite the fact that he still suffered from his war wounds, had pains in his foot and needed a metatarsal bar, Lynch joined the militia as an officer, no doubt passing on his own wartime experience to the young men who formed the unit.

In the final chapter of *Somme Mud*, while they are on board the *Beltana*, Nulla and his mates debate why they enlisted for the First World War. For many, it was partly out of 'love of country and pride and race' and partly because they were 'too flamin' frightened to face the things they were saying about coves who didn't enlist'. Nulla recounts:

> Of course we vow we'll never enlist again, yet we know that if ever the boys are on the job again, many vows will be swept aside by the thunder of marching feet, the marching feet of old mates. Mateship transcends reason. That has been proved on the battlefield time after time. Mateship is born or renewed when the country calls and that is how it should be and how it ever must be. Mateship. [p. 419]

Lynch heard the call of his country and of mateship, re-joining the Australian army in September 1941. On his re-enlistment papers, under 'Marks' the following are listed: 'Bayonet wound throat. Gunshot wound right foot and hand'. He was promoted to captain and posted to the 14th Australian Infantry Training Battalion in 1942, so the family moved to Sydney. He became the Commanding Officer of the Jungle Training School at Lowanna, inland from Coffs Harbour,

New South Wales, served for three years and two months in Australia and was discharged in October 1944. It was during this time that he typed up the manuscript of *Somme Mud*; double-spaced on foolscap paper, which was later photocopied and bound by his son Dick.

In the foreword of the typewritten manuscript, Edward Lynch wrote the following:

On many occasions we have been asked, 'How is it that you returned men never tell us what it was like at the war? What was it like?'

. . . Undoubtedly our people are justified in their demands to be told 'what it was like at war' and *Somme Mud* is just an attempt to answer the question from an infantryman's viewpoint.

No two men's experiences were alike in particular, though in general we experienced much the same.

*Somme Mud* is written around the war experiences of a young lad who was a wartime pal of mine . . . 'Nulla' of the 45th Battalion and his section . . .

If *Somme Mud* should happen to convey a typical picture of an infantryman's life at the war I shall feel that I have at least done something towards telling 'what it was like at the war'.

Even though Lynch expressly pointed to another man as the inspiration for Nulla, his daughter Shirley says of her father:

He was Nulla in the book and most of, if not all, the tales he told are about himself.

Lynch's surviving family members can unfortunately shed no light on the origin of the nickname 'Nulla' or the true identities of Nulla's six mates who appear in the story.

Though Edward Lynch tried to have the manuscript published during the 1930s, the pain of the war was then too recent for the general public and there would have been little interest from publishers. Though excerpts were published in the RSL magazine *Reveille*, to the end he remained disappointed about not having his book published. I understand from Lynch's family that his dying wish was for it to be published.

After the war, Edward Lynch returned to teaching, finally retiring in the late 1960s. He lived with his wife until her death in 1978, after which he moved in with one of his daughters and her husband. Slowly his mind went as dementia took hold and he died of kidney failure on 12 September 1980. Today he lies in the Roman Catholic section in the Northern Suburbs Cemetery in Sydney.

He is fondly remembered by his children as a kind and generous man, who was very supportive of their individual endeavours and a wonderful father. His focus was always on his family. He was a leader in his rural community and a well respected and loved teacher. Edward Lynch was a man typical of his generation and a proud Digger. And he was a great Australian.

# ACKNOWLEDGEMENTS

First and foremost I would like to acknowledge the late Edward Lynch, as without his wonderful story I would never have been inspired to follow in the footsteps of the 45th Battalion and write this book.

I would like to thank the Lynch family for their support, encouragement and endless patience. Edward Lynch's daughter Shirley provided the family photographs and answered my many queries, Ned Lynch checked that the facts pertaining to his father were correct, and Lynch's grandson Mike Lynch gave me support and friendship. Thanks again to Jane Harrison for granting me permission to publish *Somme Mud*.

At the Australian War Memorial I would like to thank Mal Booth, Head of the Research Centre, and Margaret Lewis, Manager of Information Services, for providing assistance with trench maps and, most importantly, putting the 45th Battalion War Diaries online. Peter Burness, Concept

305

Leader, kindly answered some rather odd queries and Craig Tibbitts, Curator of Official Records, checked the manuscript for historical inaccuracies. Also Pat Sabine, Head of Photos, Film and Sound, and Ian Affleck, Senior Curator of Photographs, provided advice on photographs and background information.

Thanks to Virginia Gordon for providing me with the full set of the *Official History of Australia in the War of 1914–1918*.

Thanks go to my publisher at Random House, Meredith Curnow, my editor Sophie Ambrose, and to Vanessa Mickan-Gramazio for her comprehensive edit of the original manuscript.

Thanks also to those many friends who offered encouragement and support and understood why I was never around.

Finally, I would like to thank my wife, Heather, and my boys for their patience in allowing me to work in peace and for keeping up the coffee, toasted sandwiches and soup.

# GLOSSARY

| | |
|---|---|
| A.I.F. | Australian Imperial Forces |
| A.W.L | Absent Without Leave |
| Blighty | Britain |
| block | defended barricade in a trench |
| Bull Ring | training area at Étaples, general training ground |
| bully beef | tinned meat common in Allied armies |
| chats | body lice |
| clink | gaol |
| C.O. | Commanding Officer |
| cobber | friend, mate |
| colour patches | distinctive shoulder badges indicating a division, brigade, battalion or unit within the A.I.F. |
| cove | man, bloke |
| dixie | metal container for eating food |
| duckboard | wooden decking |

| | |
|---|---|
| field dressing | bandage carried by all troops |
| Fritz | common name for a German |
| funk hole | hole in the side of a trench for sleeping and protection |
| furphy | horse-drawn cast iron water tank around which stories were told, hence the term 'furphy', a tall story, rumour or lie |
| gas | various poisonous gases used by both sides during the war |
| gas respirator | gas-mask used to prevent inhaling poisonous gas during a gas attack |
| 'get a Blighty' | getting wounded badly enough to be sent to England |
| hop-over | climbing out of the trench to attack the enemy line |
| H.Q. | headquarters |
| *Kamerad!* | German word meaning 'comrade', used when wishing to surrender |
| Lewis gun | American-designed lightweight machine-gun |
| lift | the artillery would 'lift' from one map reference to another at predetermined times so that following, attacking infantry, could assault the enemy trench |
| limber | two-wheeled cart used to carry stores or ammunition |
| Maconochie | a mixture of tinned meat and vegetables |
| Mills bomb | British-issue hand grenade |

| | |
|---|---|
| *Minenwerfer* | German trench mortar |
| mooching | hanging around, waiting, wasting time |
| mopping up | eliminating remaining enemy pockets of resistance after the main attack has gone through |
| no-man's-land | the dangerous land between two opposing trench lines |
| O.C. | Officer Commanding |
| O.R.s | other ranks |
| parados | the rear edge of a trench (the opposite of a parapet) |
| parapet | built-up front edge of a trench, which protected men |
| pill-box | concrete machine-gun emplacement |
| pioneers | infantry troops trained and equipped to perform light engineering tasks |
| platoon | army unit of thirty men under a lieutenant and sergeant |
| puttees | cloth strips wound around the legs from below the knee to the top of the boot |
| respirator | gas mask |
| reveille | dawn wake-up bugle call |
| route march | hard marching between two points |
| salient | prominent or projecting part of the line often protruding out from the main frontline |

| | |
|---|---|
| sap | trench dug towards the enemy from which more trenches radiate out each side |
| scabbard | metal sheath for a bayonet |
| screw picket | twisted metal post to hold up barbed wire |
| section | ten men usually under the command of a corporal |
| S.R.D. | Service Rum – Dilute.  This rum came in a concentrated form and needed to be watered down before drinking |
| stand to | stand ready for the enemy, usually at dawn and dusk |
| start line | the line from where an attack commences |
| Stokes mortar | British small trench mortar |
| strafe | fired upon by shells or machine-guns |
| stunt | action or attack on the enemy |
| tapes | cotton tapes laid down to designate the starting line for an attack |
| Taube | German fighter aircraft |
| Tommy | British soldier, deriving from 'Tommy Atkins' |
| wire | barbed wire |
| wiring party | group of men who put up barbed wire |

# NOTES

### One: Good-bye Sydney Town, Good-bye

1. Adam-Smith, Patsy, *The Anzacs*, Thomas Nelson, Melbourne, 1978, p. 9
2. Bean, C. E. W. (ed.), *Official History of Australia in the Great War of 1914–1918*, vol. III, Angus & Robertson, Sydney, 1942, p. 48

### Two: France and Fritz

1. Lee, Major J. E., *The Chronicle of the 45th Battalion AIF*, Australian Defence League, 1924, p. 36

### Three: Holding the Line

1. Bean, *Official History*, vol. III, p. 921
2. Bean, *Official History*, vol. III, p. 920
3. 45th Battalion War Diary for January 1917

**Seven: Straightening the Line**

1. Lee, *Chronicle of the 45th Battalion*, p. 37

**Nine: The Carrying Party**

1. Lee, *Chronicle of the 45th Battalion*, p. 40
2. Bean, *Official History*, vol. III, p. 956
3. Bean, *Official History*, vol. IV, p. 41
4. Lee, *Chronicle of the 45th Battalion*, p. 39
5. Bean, *Official History*, vol. IV, p. 69

**Ten: Mixing it at Messines**

1. Bean, *Official History*, vol. IV, p. 599
2. Ibid.
3. Bean, *Official History*, vol. IV, p. 595
4. Lee, *Chronicle of the 45th Battalion*, p. 48
5. Bean, *Official History*, vol. IV, p. 673
6. Red Cross Society Wounded and Missing Enquiry Bureau Records
7. Ibid.
8. Bean, *Official History*, vol. IV, p. 679

**Eleven: A Quiet Innings**

1. Lee, *Chronicle of the 45th Battalion*, p. 49
2. Letter in the AIF personal file of Lt. William Gocher, NAA Records
3. Lee, *Chronicle of the 45th Battalion*, p. 48
4. 45th Battalion War Diary for August 1917

## Twelve: Passing it on at Passchendaele

1. Lee, *Chronicle of the 45th Battalion*, p. 50
2. Lee, *Chronicle of the 45th Battalion*, p. 53

## Thirteen: Digging in at Dernancourt

1. Pedersen, Peter, *Villers Bretonneux: Somme*, Battleground Europe series, Pen and Sword, Barnsley UK, 2004, p. 67
2. Pedersen, *Villers Bretonneux*, from the diary of Private Robert Cude, p. 41
3. Pedersen, *Villers Bretonneux*, p. 22
4. Lee, *Chronicle of the 45th Battalion*, p. 59
5. *Beaucoup Australiens Ici: The Australian Corps in France 1918*, Department of Veterans Affairs, Canberra, 1999, p. 24
6. *Beaucoup Australiens Ici*, p. 25
7. Bean, *Official History*, vol. V, p. 360
8. Bean, *Official History*, vol. V, p. 416
9. Lee, *Chronicle of the 45th Battalion*, p. 62
10. Bean, *Official History*, vol. V, p. 404
11. AIF personal file of Lt J. S. Terras, NAA Records
12. AIF personal file of Private A. D. Wells, NAA Records

## Fourteen: Around Villers-Bret

1. Bean, *Official History*, vol. I, p. 16
2. Rule, E. J., *Jacka's Mob: A Narrative of the Great War*, Carl Johnson and Andrew Barnes (eds), Military Press, Melbourne, 1999, p. 127

3. Private John Hardie, 33rd Battalion, quoted in Pedersen, Peter, *Villers Bretonneux*, p. 34

4. Pedersen, Peter, *Villers Bretonneux*, p.113

5. Bean, *Official History*, vol. V, p. 603

6. Ibid.

7. Ibid.

8. Bean, *Official History*, vol. V, p. 604

9. 45th Battalion War Diary for 25 April 1918

10. Bean, *Official History*, vol. V, p. 674

11. McMullin, Ross, *Pompey Elliot*, Scribe, Melbourne, 2002, p. 409

**Fifteen: Hammering at Hamel**

1. Lee, *Chronicle of the 45th Battalion*, p. 65

2. Ibid.

3. Cooper, Duff, *Haig*, vol. II, p. 292, quoted in Bean's *Official History*, vol. VI, p. 157

4. Bean, *Official History*, vol. VI, p. 262

5. Lee, *Chronicle of the 45th Battalion*, p. 66

6. Bean, *Official History*, vol. VI, p. 270

7. Bean, *Official History*, vol. VI, p. 279

8. Bean, *Official History*, vol. VI, p. 285

9. Bean, *Official History*, vol. VI, p. 290

10. Bean, *Official History*, vol. VI, p. 291

11. Ibid.

12. Bean, *Official History*, vol. VI, p. 304

13. Rule, *Jacka's Mob*, p. 305, quoted in Bean's *Official History*, vol. VI, p. 304

14.  Bean, *Official History*, vol. VI, p. 306
15.  Bean, *Official History*, vol. VI, p. 309
16.  Bean, *Official History*, vol. VI, p. 328
17.  Bean, *Official History*, vol. VI, p. 335

**Sixteen: Leap-frogging to Victory**

1.  Rule, *Jacka's Mob*, p.128
2.  Rule, *Jacka's Mob*, p. 327
3.  Rule, *Jacka's Mob*, p. 339
4.  Rule, *Jacka's Mob*, p. 340
5.  Rule, *Jacka's Mob*, p. 345
6.  Rule, *Jacka's Mob*, p. 482
7.  Rule, *Jacka's Mob*, p. 518
8.  Ibid.
9.  Rule, *Jacka's Mob*, p. 525
10.  Rule, *Jacka's Mob*, p. 529
11.  Ibid.
12.  Rule, *Jacka's Mob*, p. 531
13.  Rule, *Jacka's Mob*, p. 534
14.  Lee, *Chronicle of the 45th Battalion*, p. 70
15.  Ibid.

**Seventeen: Following Fritz**

1.  Bean, *Official History*, vol. VI, p. 614
2.  Bean, *Official History*, vol. VI, p. 873
3.  Bean, *Official History*, vol. VI, p. 908
4.  Bean, *Official History*, vol. VI, p. 906

**Eighteen:** *Fini la Guerre*
1. Shirer, William L., *The Rise and Fall of the Third Reich*, Pan Books, London, 1975, p. 49
2. Lee, *Chronicle of the 45th Battalion*, p. 75
3. Bean, *Official History*, vol. VI, p.1053
4. 45th Battalion War Diary for March 1919

**Nineteen: A Dinner to the Troops**
1. Bean, *Official History*, vol. VI, p. 1057
2. Kent, David, *From Trench and Troopship: The Experience of the Australian Imperial Force 1914–1919*, Hale and Iremonger, Sydney, 1999, p. 196
3. Bean, *Official History*, vol. VI, p. 1073

# BIBLIOGRAPHY

Adam-Smith, Patsy, *The Anzacs*, Thomas Nelson, Melbourne, 1978

Bean, C. E. W. (ed.), *Official History of Australia in the War of 1914–1918*, Volumes I–VI, Angus & Robertson, Sydney, 1942

Davies, Will, *Villers-Bretonneux to Le Hamel: A Battlefield Driving Tour*, Department of Veterans Affairs, Canberra, 1998

Gammage, Bill, *The Broken Years*, Penguin Books, Melbourne, 1975

Johnson, J. H., *Stalemate: The Real Story of Trench Warfare*, Rigel, London, 1995

Jünger, Ernst, *The Storm of Steel: From the Diary of a German Stormtroop Officer on the Western Front*, Zimmerman and Zimmerman, New York, 1985

Kent, David, *From Trench and Troopship: The Experience of the Australian Imperial Force 1914–1919*, Hale and Iremonger, Sydney, 1999

Laffin, John, *Guide to Australian Battlefields of the Western Front 1916–1918*, 2nd edn, Kangaroo Press and the Australian War Memorial, Kenthurst, 1994

Lee, Major J. E., *The Chronicle of the 45th Battalion AIF*, Australian Defence League, 1924

Lynch, Edward, *Somme Mud*, Will Davies (ed.), Random House, Sydney, 2006

Manning, Frederic, *Her Privates We*, Serpent's Tail, London, 1999

McLachlan, Mat, *Walking with the Anzacs: A Guide to Australian Battlefields of the Western Front*, Hachette, Sydney, 2007

McKernan, Michael and Browne, M., *Australia: Two Centuries of War and Peace*, Australian War Memorial in association with Allen & Unwin, Canberra, 1988

McMullin, Ross, *Pompey Elliot*, Scribe Publications, Melbourne, 2002

O'Keefe, Daniel, *Hurley at War*, The Fairfax Library, 1986

Oldham, Peter, *Messines Ridge: Ypres*, Battleground Europe series, Pen and Sword, Barnsley, 2004

Pedersen, Peter, *Villers Bretonneux: Somme*, Battleground Europe series, Pen and Sword, Barnsley, 2004

Perry, Roland, *Monash: The Outsider Who Won the War*, Random House, Sydney, 2004

Prior, Robin and Wilson, Trevor, *The First World War*, John Keegan (ed.), Cassell, London, 2003

Reid, Richard, *Beaucoup Australiens Ici: The Australian Corps in France, 1918*, Department of Veterans' Affairs, Canberra, 1999

Remarque, Erich Maria, *All Quiet on the Western Front*, A. W. Wheen (trans.), Mayflower Books, London, 1972

Rule, E. J., *Jacka's Mob: A Narrative of the Great War*, Carl Johnson and Andrew Barnes (eds), Military Press, Melbourne, 1999

# Bibliography

Shirer, William L., *The Rise and Fall of the Third Reich*, Pan Books, London, 1975

Strachan, Hew, *The First World War: A New Illustrated History*, Simon & Schuster, London, 2003

*War Diaries of the 45th Battalion AIF*, Australian War Memorial, Canberra, 1916–1919

Westwell, Ian, *World War I: Day by Day*, MBI Publishing, Osceola, 2000

www.australiansatwar.gov.au

www.awm.gov.au

www.defence.gov.au

www.encarta.msn.com

www.firstworldwar.com

www.naa.gov.au

www.pbs.org

www.primeministers.naa.gov.au

www.ww1westernfront.gov.au

# Somme Mud

## The experiences of an infantryman in France, 1916–1919
## By E.P.F. Lynch
## Edited by Will Davies

'We live in a world of Somme mud. We sleep in it, work in it, fight in it, wade in it and many of us die in it . . .'

Private Edward Lynch enlisted in the army aged just eighteen. As his ship set sail for France, the band played and the crowd proudly waved off their young men. Men who had no real notion of the reality of the trenches of the Somme; of the pale-faced, traumatised soldiers they would encounter there; of the mud and blood and the innumerable contradictions of war.

Upon his return from France in 1919, Private Lynch wrote about his experiences in twenty school exercise books, perhaps in the hope of coming to terms with all that he had witnessed there. Now published here for the first time, his story vividly captures the horror and magnitude of the war on the Western Front as experienced by the ordinary infantryman.

Told with dignity, candour and surprising wit, *Somme Mud* is a testament to the power of the human spirit – for out of the mud that threatened to suck out a man's very soul rose this remarkable true story of humanity and friendship.

'This is a warrior's tale . . . a great read and a moving eye-witness account of a living hell from which few emerged unscathed'
*DAILY EXPRESS*

9780553819137